D1459550

COMPUTER
CONTRACTS

COMPUTER CONTRACTS

An International Guide to
Agreements and Software Protection

Hilary E Pearson MA, LLB

First published in Great Britain 1984 by Financial Training
Publications Limited, Avenue House, 131 Holland Park Avenue,
London W11 4UT

© 1984, Hilary E Pearson

ISBN: 0 906322 48 0

Typeset by Kerrypress Ltd, Luton
Printed in Great Britain by Unwin Brothers Ltd, The Gresham Press,
Old Woking, Surrey

Contents

Table of Cases

Table of Statutes

Preface

This book was born as the result of a software development project that went wrong. The developers, my clients, had written their own contract. That contract did not provide a means of resolving the problems that arose. The result was litigation, litigation my clients could not really afford.

My experience in dealing with other clients in computer-related businesses has shown me that this situation is regrettably common. I kept seeing home-made contracts for software development and licensing, many of which were clearly potential time bombs. The businesses which were using these contracts had generally been started by some bright, entrepreneurial engineer or programmer with a good idea but very little capital. There certainly did not seem to be money to spare to pay a lawyer to prepare contracts. Even if the businessman wished to use a lawyer, he might have difficulty finding one who knew anything about this new field.

This book is primarily designed to help the small computer business and the small business which has to use a computer, and the lawyer with such businesses as clients who does not specialise in the computer field and who may know very little about computers themselves. It is intended to be practical rather than theoretical, and for this reason case citations have been kept to a minimum.

The areas of law dealt with in this book are those which persons in the computer business are most likely to use; contract law, and the law relating to protection of ideas and products, often called intellectual property law. Because the computer-related business is often international in scope, the treatment of these two areas is wider than the law of a single country. The laws of England and of the United States of America are dealt with in more detail, the author having practised law in both countries.

My thanks are due, first of all, to the clients who gave me the idea for this book, and all the other clients in the computer business who have helped to teach me something about that business. My special thanks to the lawyers specialising in this area of law in other countries who provided me with information about the development of computer-related law in their countries; John Robinson of Marks & Clerk, London, Alan Lewis of Adams & Adams, Johannesburg, South Africa and John Singlehurst of Meredith & Finlayson, Ottawa, Canada. My thanks also to Robert Daunt of Monterey, California, with whom I have often discussed this area of law and some of whose contractual provisions I have borrowed shamelessly, and to Jackie Daunt, of Palo Alto, California, who supplied me with a lot of information, especially on European case law. I have also received assistance from colleagues in my firm, Arnold, White & Durkee of Houston, Texas, for which I thank them.

Finally and most importantly, my thanks are due to my husband, Peter Murphy. Himself an author, he encouraged me to begin this project, took over some household chores to give me more time to write, and kept my nose to the grindstone when the going was tough. I cannot thank him enough for his love and enthusiastic support.

Houston
April 1984

1   Introduction

The enormous growth of the computer industry in recent years has resulted in a similar growth in the need for legal services to this industry. However, by tradition, lawyers rarely have scientific or technical backgrounds, and most of them therefore are nervous of computers and of the people who produce and program them. Equally, most computer people are nervous about lawyers, and are not adept at explaining their technology to total laymen. This mutual suspicion and lack of understanding has tended to produce some very badly written contracts, which have later caused horrendous problems when things go wrong. Many a small, but promising, computer-related enterprise has been driven out of business by just one bad contract. Many non-computer businesses have similarly been put in an extremely serious financial position because vital computer equipment was purchased under an unnegotiated, inadequate contract. The purpose of this book is to alleviate some of this suspicion, and to assist the computer industry to use the law so as to protect and increase its business.

DEVELOPMENT OF THE COMPUTER

The first computing machine in modern history was a mechanical device, invented in 1642 by the famous French mathematician, Pascal. It could only add. In 1671 the equally famous German mathematician, Leibnitz, invented a machine that could add and multiply.

The first true computer, in that it was a machine that could perform any arithmetical manipulation, was the 'analytical machine' invented by the Englishman, Charles Babbage in 1833. Babbage was the first person to see how a general purpose computing machine could work, but he lived a century before the technology necessary to make such a machine practicable came into existence. The mechanical machines had many intrinsic problems, including the fact that they involved very complicated machinery, and were slow, cumbersome and had limited capacity.

The last of the big mechanical computers was the IBM Mark I, which came out in 1944 and was controlled electrically although it operated mechanically. However, hand-operated mechanical calculators to perform arithmetic operations continued in general use until the early 1970s.

The first important step in the development of the electronic computer came in 1939, when Professor Atanasoff at Iowa State College showed that vacuum tubes could be used to make a flip-flop circuit, one which switches between its two possible states each time a pulse of current is passed through. The flip-flop is the basic building block of all electronic computers. Using the binary system, these two states can represent numbers. Using sufficient flip-flop circuits, these numbers can be manipulated.

The first electronic computer came in 1943, its development spurred by wartime needs, in particular the development of the atomic bomb. It was called ENIAC, an acronym standing for Electronic Number Integrator And Calculator. It was wired to perform a particular function, and the wiring had to be physically changed in order for it to perform a different function.

The next step forward was the development of the concept of the program by von Neumann, who worked with the ENIAC group. The first programmable computers had stored programs built in in the form of alternative systems of hard wiring, which could be selected by setting a switch. The first such machine was built in Cambridge University, the first commercial machine was the Sperry Rand UNIVAC I. These machines used thermionic valves, and as a result took up huge amounts of room, required vast amounts of electricity, and required elaborate cooling systems as they generated enormous amounts of heat. Data were put into them in the form of punched cards. They were also enormously expensive.

The device which was to revolutionise the development of the computer and to make it potentially available to private individuals was the transistor. This was first developed at Bell Laboratories. This device, which used the properties of materials known as semiconductors, was capable of doing everything which a thermionic valve could do. However, it is very much smaller than the smallest valve, it uses very little power, and quickly totally replaced valves for all purposes.

The space programme of the 1960s provided the impetus to the development of the next step, the integrated circuit. The possibility of putting complex circuitry on a small piece of silicon, and of producing that silicon chip for a reasonable price, made possible first the inexpensive electronic calculator, and then the personal computer. It is this development which has made possible the 'computer revolution', of which we now hear so much. It has made it possible for the present generation of schoolchildren to become as much at home with the computer as the previous generation was with the television set.

THE COMPUTER INDUSTRY

The computer industry is at present in a stage of very rapid evolution and growth. The industry is also very young, as the first commercial computers only appeared in the 1950s, and the modern industry, based on the integrated circuit, only started in the 1970s.

In the early days, the only products of the industry were the big, extremely expensive mainframe computers, which were bought by government and major businesses only. These computers were produced by a few major companies, in particular IBM, Sperry Rand, Honeywell, Burroughs and Control Data Corporation. Software was included in the price of the hardware, and there was no independent software industry.

Increasing miniaturisation made possible the microcomputer in the early 1970s. Microcomputers were still too expensive for individuals, but were extensively used by smaller businesses. While the big manufacturers produced computers for this market, the greatly increased size of the market allowed other, smaller companies to develop and sell microcomputers successfully.

Personal computers, small enough to fit into homes and affordable by individuals, were made possible by the development of the integrated circuit industry in the early part of the 1970s. The first such computers were used by, and in general built by, computer enthusiasts. The first commercially produced computer which was not intended for such experts, but for the ordinary individual, was the Apple. Although a large number of such computers were introduced on to the market in the early 1980s, it is likely that the market will divide into two distinct segments, with only a few manufacturers in each. One segment will be the market for limited, inexpensive computers largely intended for home entertainment. The other will be for the more expensive, more sophisticated machine that will be used by individuals in business as well as in the home.

The software industry is even younger, and is experiencing even more rapid growth and development than the hardware industry. In the early days of the computer industry there was no such thing as software because programming was hard wired. Even after the independently programmable computer was developed, the software was usually supplied by the hardware manufacturer, thrown in free with the hardware. In the United States, anti-trust suits stopped the manufacturers from using this practice, known as 'bundling'. This permitted the development of a separate software business. This business was, however, almost exclusively concerned with the development of custom software for individual clients' business needs.

The development of mass publishing and marketing of software came with the growth of the personal computer. This market is still full of individual producers, although there are signs that the same shake-out which is occurring in the hardware side of the personal computer industry will also occur in the software industry.

HOW TO USE THIS BOOK

This book has been written with two distinct groups of people in mind: lawyers who do not have an extensive knowledge of computer law and technology, but who have clients involved in the computer field or who wish to develop some expertise in this area, and people involved in the computer field who are not lawyers but who cannot find a lawyer experienced in this field to help them, or cannot afford the services of such a lawyer, or who are simply interested in the law as it applies to their particular field.

To the lawyers: you should be aware that the term 'computer law' is a misnomer. There is no special branch of law devoted to computers, merely the adaptation of existing legal principles to fit new facts. This book does not cover all the areas where computers intrude into the field of law, for example, it does not deal with the problems of computer-related crime, or of the admission of computer-generated information into evidence. It deals only with the aspects of law which are mainly concerned in commercial transactions related to computers. Also, it is not a legal textbook; you will not find extensive citations of case law or theoretical discussions of legal principles. It is intended as a guide to the busy practitioner who needs answers to a client's pressing, real life questions. There is rather more theoretical discussion in the chapters on protection of hardware and software, but this is because the law is still so undeveloped in those areas. An understanding of the basic principles is necessary in order to try to predict, on your client's behalf, how the courts are likely to decide a particular question.

Although the emphasis of the book is practical, others may find useful material in the sections on protection through intellectual property concepts, as an attempt has been made to make the case law citations as complete as possible.

For the non-lawyers, the purpose of the book is to give them some understanding of what is involved when they make a business agreement, or when they put their brilliant new product on the market. There are certain transactions where informed self-help will see you through; there are others where you need professional help as a matter of self-preservation. An understanding of the contents of this book should help to provide you with both the information needed for the self-help, and with an appreciation of when you need a lawyer. It should also help you in your dealings with lawyers. First, you need to find a lawyer who has some expertise in this field, and they are still fairly rare. Secondly, a lawyer's task is made easier if clients have some appreciation of the problems that exist and so do not plunge ahead into transactions and then consult the lawyer when it is too late. However, you should also be aware that little else makes a lawyer's job more difficult than a client who fancies himself as an amateur lawyer — please be aware that this book does not qualify you as an expert on the law!

This book falls into two halves: the first deals with contracts related to various aspects of the computer business. This half itself is in two parts: the first deals with general background matters that need to be understood in order to produce a good contract, including an outline of computer technology for the lawyers, and an outline of contract law for the computer people. The second deals with the writing of specific types of contract. An attempt has been made to keep the approach as broad as possible, and to deal with the problems of both the vendor and the purchaser. Precedents are provided, but they should in general only be used for guidance. In particular, most of these precedents were prepared for use in the United States, because that is where the author now practises, and alterations may be needed to accommodate the differences in the laws of other countries.

The second half of the book deals with how to keep trespassers out of the territory of your ideas. The protection of the ideas and work that go into both hardware and software is the province of an area of law known as 'intellectual property' law. This covers things such as patents, copyright and trade marks. Unlike the law of contracts, which has had comparatively little difficulty adjusting to this new technology, intellectual property law is facing many problems, most of them as yet unsolved, in adapting concepts developed to protect earlier technologies for use with computer technology. Because the computer industry tends to be international in its outlook and dealings, brief discussions of the state of the law in the major industrial countries are included.

2 *Introduction to Computers for the Non-technical*

In order to write a contract of any type which deals properly with the needs of the contracting parties, it is necessary to have some understanding of the subject-matter of the contract. This understanding need not extend to technical details, in fact too detailed a knowledge can obscure the overall view that the draftsman needs to produce a comprehensive, comprehensible contract.

This general rule holds true in the field of computer contracts. It is therefore necessary for the non-technical reader to take a deep breath and plunge into the world of high technology and incomprehensible jargon that is computers. Technically expert readers are asked to skip this chapter for fear that they will become so upset with the oversimplifications it contains that they give up on the rest of the book.

HOW COMPUTERS WORK

There is no need to fear or stand in awe of computers; despite the amazing complexity of the electronics which make a modern computer work, it operates on a system of processing information which makes the abacus seem complex. A computer in essence is a very large number of switches which are either on or off. These two states can be represented by the numbers 1 and 0. All data fed into a computer must be translated into a series of combinations of these two numbers, which can then be manipulated. For example, the number two is represented in this two-character system, called a 'binary system', by 10, the number three by 11. When you type '2 + 3' into your computer, the figures and the command to add them together are translated into binary terms (there is no need to know how this is done for our purposes), 10 is added to 11, the answer 101 is then translated back to the figure 5 which appears on your screen. The reason why complicated manipulations can be achieved by such a simple system is because the computer performs each step at enormous speed.

In the very first electronic computers the circuits which performed these operations used thermionic valves, were very slow and took up huge amounts of space and power. Today virtually all computers use integrated circuits on silicon chips for this and most other tasks. Such chips contain huge numbers of tiny electrical circuits. The development of these chips, for which the space programme is largely responsible, has made possible the pocket calculator, upon which we all rely, and the personal computer, upon which more and more people are coming to rely. This book is being written using a word processing program running on an IBM Personal Computer.

HARDWARE

The heart of a computer is the central processing unit, usually called the CPU. Computer people are very fond of initials; we will come across a lot more of them before the end of this chapter. The CPU contains the devices needed to process information, including internal memory to hold the data to be processed and the program instructions needed to perform the processing, and a program controller which activates the circuits to perform these instructions.

Before going into more detail about the function of each of these devices, it is necessary to explain a little more about the various types of 'chips' which are used in the CPU and other parts of the computer. The heart of most modern computers, at least the smaller ones, is a large silicon chip known as a microprocessor. This is the 'brains' of the computer, controlling and coordinating the operations and performing calculations. Microprocessors currently commercially available are either 8, 16 or 32 bit devices. The word 'bit' is a good example of computer technical vocabulary which causes problems for the non-technical reader or listener because it is a new use of an ordinary English word. Other examples of such new meanings of everyday words can be found in the 'inescapable jargon' section at the end of this chapter. A 'bit' in computer talk is a single piece of computer information, one of the two binary digits, and is derived from the words BInary digiT. The numbers refer to the number of bits that the processor can process at once, the larger the number the more powerful the computer. Another problem you may have in following technical talk about micro-processors is the practice of the manufacturers of such chips to name their products by numbers or letters and numbers, and to distinguish between the various members of their family merely by changing the numbers. Unless your client is in the business of producing microprocessors or manufacturing hardware using these devices it is not necessary for you to learn what the numbers stand for.

The internal memory of the computer is also on chips. Memory chips are of various types, always referred to by their initials. The simplest of these is a ROM, which stands for 'read-only memory'. The information stored in a ROM has been programmed in during manufacture and it cannot be changed. ROMs are used in computers to store the information which is needed repeatedly, such as how to interpret commands and perform routine tasks. Such chips also supply the programs for arcade games and home video game machines. The next type is a PROM, 'programmable read-only memory'. When this type is manufactured it is 'blank', and the program is added later by special apparatus which sets the individual cells to the required pattern of ones and zeros. Once this has been done the program cannot be changed. ROMs are easier to make than PROMs, but, because they require a custom design for their manufacture, which is very expensive, they are only used when large numbers of identically programmed chips are required. A further refinement is the EPROM, 'erasable programmable read-only memory'. As the name indicates, the program in these chips can be erased, usually by exposure to ultraviolet light, and the chip can be reprogrammed. The major part of the internal memory, in smaller computers also on chips, is called dynamic memory or RAM (random-access memory). This memory can be readily changed, and information can be stored and retrieved from it at will. However, unlike read only memory, turning off the power supply wipes out the contents.

Internal memory is normally a relatively expensive form of data storage, and therefore most computers have some kind of external memory in a peripheral device. The term 'peripheral device' or 'peripheral' refers to the various pieces of hardware other than the CPU required to make up an operating computer. The least expensive form of external memory is magnetic tape, either on reels or in cassette form. The disadvantage of tape is that it is necessary to run through the tape in order to find the required piece of information, and this slows down the retrieval process. This disadvantage can be overcome by using a magnetic storage medium in the form of a disc. Using a principle somewhat similar to a gramophone record, the read/write mechanism can go directly to the area of the disc where the information is to be stored or retrieved. Discs are of two kinds, hard and floppy. Hard discs are capable of much higher storage capacity than the same size floppy disc, but are more expensive and harder to handle. Information is stored and retrieved by means of a peripheral called a disc drive, and a computer system may have several such drives.

In order for the CPU to be of any use, the user must be able to communicate with it. Input is usually by means of a keyboard, although there are a number of other input devices for special purposes. Many video games for computers are played using joysticks or similar devices to control images on the screen, and there are devices for use with computers that produce graphics which enable designs to be reproduced on the screen from the user's drawings.

It is also necessary for the computer to communicate with the user. This is most commonly done through a cathode ray display, either a special unit usually referred to as a CRT (standing for cathode-ray tube) or, in some home computers, an ordinary television set. If a permanent record is required, this is obtained using a printer connected to the computer. There are various kinds of printer which produce characters in different ways. One of the least expensive, which produces what is generally thought of as 'computer printing', is the dot matrix printer. The printing head in this printer consists of a large number of wires arranged in a regular array, which are pushed forward to strike the paper in a pattern of dots to produce the desired character. If print-quality characters are required, the most commonly used printer is a 'daisy wheel', in which the characters are on the ends of the spokes of a rimless wheel.

SOFTWARE

Hardware, complicated as it may be, is of no use without the instructions which make it work, which are called 'software'. The actual instructions must be in a form which the computer can 'understand', a series of ones and zeros. This is called 'machine code' or 'object code'. It is possible to write programs directly in machine code, and this is how programming was done in the early days of computers, but it is very complicated, tedious for the programmer, and any mistake can be fatal to the running of the program. Most of the work required to ensure that the machine code is accurate can be done much better by a computer program than by a human programmer. A program can be written to accept instructions for a computer in a code more or less resembling English, and to convert those instructions into machine code. The code used to operate such programs is called a 'language', and there are now a considerable number of such languages, usually designed for a particular type of use. Some common and widely used languages are Basic, often used by beginners because its instructions closely resemble English, COBOL, used for business purposes such as payroll and accounting programs, and ALGOL and FORTRAN, which are used for scientific purposes. A program written in such a language is said to be in 'source code'. The programs which translate the source code into machine code are of three types: assemblers, compilers and interpreters. There are technical differences between the three types in the way that they produce machine code, but it is not necessary to go into these differences here.

Although work is now being done on 'smart' computers which can to some extent reason and learn from experience, commercially available computers at the present time do not have such capabilities. This means that they can only carry out the task desired if they have been given a set of instructions which specifies correctly every step that must be taken to achieve the required result. This means that to write a successful program, the programmer must first fully understand the result required and the means of achieving such a result. This is the most difficult part of writing a program and the one that causes the most problems. All possible conditions must be catered for; the much repeated story about the computer that issued a bill for £0.00, followed by demands for payment which could only be stopped by sending a cheque for £0.00, is an example of failure by the programmer to anticipate a possible, if unlikely, situation.

The programmer prepares a flow chart, which is a means of symbolically representing a succession of events in graphic form. This flow chart will show the relationship between the steps needed to carry out the program, and is used to assist in the preparation of the logical sequence of instructions, and to check that no input or output records are overlooked and that the program will produce the required result. If the program will be lengthy, it is normally divided up into a number of subsystems or segments, each of which is individually flow-charted and coded. In this case an overall outline flow chart is used to ensure that each segment properly interacts with the others, and that nothing 'slips between the cracks' as a result of segmentation and is omitted from the whole system. Once the flow charts are completed the program is then coded in a suitable language. This coding is then tested with suitable data to ensure its accuracy. It is very unusual for a program to be right first time, and errors, known as 'bugs' in the computer world, must be detected and corrected. The cycle of testing and 'debugging' goes on until the program processes test data correctly in all normal operating conditions.

Unless the program is to be used exclusively by the person who programmed it, it is necessary for documentation to be prepared. This documentation is to enable the user to operate the program correctly, and will include such things as how to start and stop the program running, how to input data and how to operate commands within the program. If someone other than the programmer is to maintain the program (by correcting errors discovered in operation and by providing modifications and improvements), it is also necessary for program documentation to be provided, sufficient to allow another programmer to understand how the program works. Such documentation would typically include the program specifications, flow charts and source code.

Software is normally supplied on a suitable form of magnetic medium for the particular computer, tape reels or cassettes, floppy or hard discs. However, it can also be supplied in the form of programmed ROM, PROM or EPROM chips. These chips are often referred to as 'firmware', as they are a sort of cross between hardware and software.

Various units of information are used in the preparation and use of software. The smallest unit is the bit, which contains only the information conveyed by choosing between two possibilities, represented by one and zero. The smallest usable unit is the byte, which is a set of related bits; for example, each alphanumeric character can be expressed by one byte. The next unit is the word, which is a set of related bytes, such as a word in a human language or a telephone number. Words are organised into fields, which are a set of words containing related information such as a person's name or address. A record is a set of related fields, such as a person's name, address and telephone number. Finally, a file is an organised set of records, such as a collection of names, addresses and telephone numbers arranged alphabetically by surname.

COMPUTERS ARE NOT INFALLIBLE

It is sometimes hard to remember that computers are only machines, and that, like every other machine, they can go wrong. Not only can they go wrong, but they do go wrong in accordance with a fundamental law of the universe, commonly known as 'Murphy's law': if anything can go wrong, it will, and at the worst possible time. A good contract anticipates what is likely to go wrong during the performance of that contract and provides for what is to happen in such eventualities. While the various chapters dealing with the different types of computer contracts deal in detail with the things that are likely to go wrong with the subject-matter of that type of contract, this section is intended as a general overview of common computer problems.

First, it is always possible that faults will develop in the hardware. In that complex mass of microcircuitry that makes up most of a modern computer, a single loose connection may be enough to prevent the computer from working at all or, what is harder to diagnose, to make the computer act erratically in a certain respect. The performance of the hardware may also be affected by external factors such as the supply of current or the environment. Hardware faults, while they may not be easy to correct, are usually easy to provide for contractually, as they are equivalent to faults in any other type of goods which affect contractual performance. The mercantile law of all developed legal systems has an established, well defined set of rules for dealing with such a common event.

Faults in software may be much harder to diagnose and to deal with contractually. To begin with, it is necessary to determine that an error is due to the software rather than the hardware, and this is not always easy to do. Once the software has been pinpointed as the cause of the problem, the programmer who wrote the program may not be available, so another person must try to understand what the author of the program did in writing it. Writing software can be as individualistic as writing prose, but unless the structure of the whole program is understood, a correction in one place may itself cause an error in another. To make the analysis and correct the fault, the new programmer will require a source-code listing of the program, but the original supplier of the program may be reluctant to reveal the source code and thereby its secrets. When writing contracts for software, it is important to remember that there is no such thing as 'error-free' software, and therefore there must be a contractual provision for the correction of errors by the vendor or for the provision of source code to the purchaser.

Finally, it must be remembered that the data produced by a computer is only as good as the data and instructions put into it. When contracting for provision of computer services, such as those provided by a data processing bureau, there should be provisions governing responsibility for the accuracy of the supply and input of data.

INESCAPABLE JARGON

One of the main problems experienced by the lay person when dealing with people in the computer field is that they appear to speak a different language. It seems to have the same grammar as English, many of the words appear to be the same and have the same meaning as English, but there are other words which seem to be English but do not have the usual meaning and there are still other words which are not part of the usual English vocabulary. Some of these ordinary words with a different meaning have already been used in this chapter, such as 'bit', 'field' and 'file'; new words, such as 'byte', have also been used. The lexicon of computer jargon given below is far from complete; it includes only jargon you are likely to encounter as an outsider, and only new, technical words or ordinary English words used with a different meaning which cannot readily be discerned by the layman. There are a number of computer dictionaries in print to which the reader is referred for a comprehensive list and for fuller explanations.

access: the process of transferring data from a peripheral device to the CPU.

address: noun: the identification of the location of data; verb: to indicate a specific position.

algorithm: a series of steps or instructions for solving a particular problem.

applications software: software designed to solve a problem or perform a particular type of process.

architecture: the design of the computer, including the interaction of its hardware and software, which accomplishes design objectives such as speed of operation or ease of use.

ASCII: an acronym for American Standard Code for Information Interchange. This consists of a standard set of bytes representing each alphanumeric character and other commonly used characters.

batch processing: a method of data processing in which the data representing a number of records are stored and later processed as a group (cf. real-time processing).

baud: the unit measuring speed of transmission of data along a cable or telephone line, or the speed at which a peripheral (e.g., a printer) can accept data from the CPU.

benchmark: used in custom software development for a point of measurable progress in the development, such as completion of flow-charting or successful completion of testing.

boot: to go through the procedures required to load a program into the computer. (An abbreviation of bootstrap, a sort of computer joke; as some instructions must be given to get the program working the computer does not 'pick itself up by its bootstraps'.)

breadboard: the various electronic components which make up a particular device such as internal memory or a disc-drive controller are usually connected together and fixed on a board known as a 'breadboard'.

buffer: a temporary means of storing data, used when information is being transferred from one unit to another and the latter cannot handle the data at the rate it is being transferred. In cases where the overlap is small, such as from keyboard to CPU, buffering is usually done in internal memory; where it is large, such as from CPU to printer, it is usually done through a peripheral device.

bus: a major route for the transfer of data, usually from various sources to various destinations.

downtime: periods when a computer is unable to process data, due either to a fault or to routine maintenance.

dump: writing data from internal to peripheral memory, usually done to protect the data from loss due to machine failure.

entry: (1) the first instruction in a program or a subroutine, (2) a unit of information or an item of data.

gigo: 'Garbage In, Garbage Out', see the section on common problems above.

handshaking: descriptive of two devices which are able to communicate with each other.

hard copy: output in documentary form which humans can read.

identifier: a label used to identify a particular file or location in a memory store.

instruction: a command to the computer forming part of a program.

interface: noun: the connection between two units: verb: to form such a connection.

I/O: stands for input/output, and is used in connection with devices and software concerned with input to and output from a computer.

JCL: job control language, a language which enables the user to input, through an operating system, the instructions for the control of the job the computer is to perform.

listing: a print-out of a series of commands in a program, or of a series of records in a file.

key punch: a machine used to encode punched cards or paper tape, which provides one method of inputting data to a computer.

macro: a set of instructions in an operating system which can be activated by a single command.

menu: a list of options, usually displayed on the CRT, which can be selected by the user of a particular program.

modem: a device used to convert digital data into a form suitable for transmission along a telephone line, and to reconvert such data back into digital form, thereby enabling computers to communicate directly by means of a telephone line.

multiplex: to transmit several streams of data (such as telephone conversations) concurrently over the same communications channel. This is achieved by a device called a multiplexer.

number cruncher: a computing device capable of dealing with large numbers of numerical operations, rather than other types of data.

operating system: software used to control the system and to supervise the running of other programs.

patch: a set of instructions added to the coding of a program to correct an error.

real-time processing: a system of processing data simultaneously with its input to the system, cf. batch processing.

report: a printed output of data processed by a computer.

scrolling: the process of successively displaying data from internal memory to the CRT when the data require more than the area of the screen for display, so that the data can be read by the operator.

sector: part of the surface of a magnetic disc, which is recognised by the disc controller as one coordinate used to identify the location of stored information.

source code: program instructions written in a computer language other than machine code.

tractor: the device used to feed continuous form stationery through a printer.

3   Introduction to the Law of Contract for Non-Lawyers

WHAT IS A CONTRACT?

A contract is an agreement which gives rise to legally enforceable obligations. Not all agreements are enforceable in this way; only those which satisfy the requirements laid down by the law for enforceability. There are other kinds of legally enforceable obligations which do not arise from agreement, such as the obligations not to steal or to pay taxes.

Not only must the agreement be of the kind that is enforceable, its provisions must also be enforceable. A hundred years ago the predominant legal theory with regard to contracts was the theory of 'freedom of contract'. Parties of full age and capacity were assumed to reach agreement acting in 'enlightened self-interest', and the courts would enforce whatever they agreed. The only exceptions were contracts for purposes that were illegal or immoral, or contracts in which one party occupied a position of influence over the other and used that influence unfairly.

That position has changed. In our increasingly complex society, the courts and the legislature have come to realise that, in many cases, there is no true freedom of contract on the part of one of the parties to a contract because the other party has much greater economic power. The individual who purchases a car, however rational and concerned for his own interests, is totally unable to negotiate terms with Ford or BL. In order to protect the weak party in such cases, the law will imply certain terms into a contract, will prevent the strong party from trying to escape from certain obligations, and will refuse to enforce oppressive provisions.

FORMATION OF A CONTRACT

The basis of the common law of contract is the concept of a bargain. There must be an offer from one party, which is accepted by the other, and there must be some value given in exchange for the obligation entered into — this value is known as 'consideration'. These three elements will be considered in turn.

Offer

An offer is made when the person making the offer (the offeror) shows a willingness to enter a binding agreement on certain terms if and as soon as that offer is accepted by the person to whom it is addressed (the offeree).

An offer should be distinguished from a communication which may lead up to a contract, but which does not show an intent to be immediately bound. Such a communication is known to lawyers as an 'invitation to treat'. For example, 'I will sell you my car for £500 cash' is an offer. 'I am thinking about selling my car; would you be interested in it for about £500?' is an invitation to treat. In some common circumstances, it is not always easy to distinguish between an offer, which can be made by conduct, and an invitation to treat. The law has developed certain rules to deal with these situations. For example, when you go into a self-service shop, the display of goods is merely an invitation to treat. The shopper makes an offer to buy when he or she takes the item to the cash register, and the shopkeeper is free to accept or reject that offer. This means that the shopkeeper is not obliged to charge the price marked on the item. If a mistake was made in labelling the price, the shopkeeper can refuse to sell.

Clearly, an offer cannot be effective unless it is received by the offeree. However, in the case of offers made other than by direct contact, the offer is made at the place where it was dispatched, at the time at which it was dispatched to the offeree.

Acceptance

An acceptance may be made verbally, or (where appropriate) by conduct. However, the acceptance must be unconditional; an 'acceptance' which stipulates different terms from the offer is, at common law, not an acceptance but a counter-offer. It will be seen later that this common-law rule is not applied rigorously to certain commercial contracts, but otherwise it applies. The original offeror is at liberty to decide whether or not to accept the counter-offer.

In general, acceptance must be communicated to the offeror before a contract comes into existence. This is because it would clearly be unfair to hold the offeror to a contract which the offeror did not know had come into existence. On this basis, there are certain circumstances where fairness does not require direct communication. For instance, where it is the offeror's own fault that he did not receive the communication — he failed to read his mail or to check the input of his telex machine. Or, the terms of the offer may be such that no communication of acceptance is required, for example, an offer to buy goods can be accepted simply by sending the goods without separately communicating an acceptance. In the case of an acceptance sent by post, the acceptance is effective at the time of posting, providing that the use of the post was an authorised or a reasonable method of communication. If the offer specifies that only a particular method of communicating acceptance can be used, then that method must be used for acceptance to be effective. In general, the offeror cannot treat silence as acceptance.

Unless the offer indicates to the contrary, in general an offer can be withdrawn any time before acceptance. However, this withdrawal should be brought to the offeree's attention.

An offer is terminated by rejection, and 'rejection' includes the making of a counter-offer. An offer which is stated to be for a fixed time terminates on expiry of that time; in all other cases the offer remains open for a period which is reasonable in the circumstances. An offer may also lapse upon the occurrence of some specified condition, or upon the occurrence of some event which makes the offer impossible to perform. Once an offer is terminated, it cannot be accepted.

Consideration

In certain legal systems any serious promise is enforceable. However, the common-law rule is that a promise not made under seal is enforceable only if it is supported by consideration. The enforcement of promises made with the formality of a sealed writing is a historical remnant, which still applies in Britain, but which has largely been abolished in the USA.

What is meant by 'consideration'? The traditional definition is that it is some benefit to the promisor, or some detriment to the promisee. The word 'detriment' has nothing to do with whether there is a bad bargain, and is not used exactly in its normal sense. Perhaps a better definition of consideration is that it is the price paid for the promise. This fits in well with the common-law concept of contract as being a bargain. The common law does not enforce gratuitous promises. An exchange of mutual promises can be consideration for each other.

Although there must be some consideration of an economic value to make the agreement enforceable, the law is not in general concerned with the adequacy of the consideration. A nominal consideration, in the sense that it is clearly worth much less than the value of the performance promised in return, may be used to make enforceable what would otherwise be a mere gratuitous promise. The exception to this is where the inadequacy of the consideration is the result of oppressive conduct, of a type legally recognised as such, on the part of the party benefiting from the inadequacy. A promise to do something that the promisor was already legally obliged to do is not valid consideration.

Formalities

In general no formalities are required to make a legally binding agreement. The most important exceptions to this rule are:

(a) As stated above, in English law, a gratuitous promise can be enforced provided it is in writing which bears a seal and has been signed in accordance with certain formalities.

(b) Certain contracts by individuals must be under seal, although these are all connected with transactions in land and therefore do not come within the scope of this book.

(c) The laws governing the activities of corporations, which are entities created by law, may require a corporation to put its seal on all or certain kinds of contracts. The modern tendency is away from such requirements.

(d) Certain types of commercial contracts must, by statute, be in writing. In general, these include bills of sale, bills of exchange and agreements involving consumer credit transactions.

(e) Some contracts need not be in writing, but will only be enforced by the courts if their essential contents are proved by one or more written documents, which can be connected together, and at least one of which is signed by the person against whom the contract is to be enforced. The origin of this rule derives from the Statute of Frauds 1677. In its English home, the scope of the Statute of Frauds has been considerably reduced by later legislation, and it only applies to a guarantee by a third party to pay the debt of another if that person does not pay and to contracts for the sale of land. The Statute of Frauds was also transplanted to the USA, and it retains more of its original breadth in its new home. In most states in the USA (and contract is governed by state law), in addition to the two categories of contracts covered in England, contracts for the sale of goods worth more than $500 and contracts which cannot possibly be performed within one year of their making must also be evidenced in writing. The same is true of prenuptial agreements and marriage settlement agreements, but they are somewhat outside the scope of this book!

UNENFORCEABLE CONTRACTS

In addition to contracts which are unenforceable because of lack of consideration, or for failure to comply with a formality, there are certain contracts which the law refuses to enforce as a matter of public policy. Examples are:

(a) *Illegal contracts.* If the purpose of the contract is illegal, or if performing it involves an illegal act, the law refuses to deal in any way with the agreement, leaving the parties in whatever position they have got themselves into.

(b) *Contracts contrary to public policy.* An example of such an unenforceable contract is one which encourages the break-up of marriage. In jurisdictions where gambling is illegal, gambling debts are not enforceable.

(c) *Penalties.* While parties may agree that, if one of them breaches his obligations to the other under the contract, he will pay the other a sum which represents a good faith estimate of the actual loss suffered as a result of that breach, a provision that an unreasonably large sum is to be paid is regarded as a penalty, and is unenforceable.

(d) *Restraint of trade.* The law will not enforce a contract which prevents a person from earning a living. Employees can be prevented to a reasonable extent from competition with their former employer, provided they are able to continue to earn a living. These common-law rules have been modified by statute in many jurisdictions. Other agreements may be unlawful under antitrust or competition laws of the jurisdiction.

VARYING A CONTRACT

After a binding contract has been entered into, the parties may wish to change one or more of its provisions. In order for these changes to be legally binding, they must be supported by some consideration. If the change potentially benefits both parties, then that is in itself sufficient consideration. However, when only one party can benefit from the change, there must be consideration given by the benefited party.

As the varied contract is still a contract, the variation must be made in such a way as to conform with any formalities required for the original contract.

A question which comes up frequently in real life, which involves variation of a contract, is whether a debt can be satisfied by a part payment. The common-law rule is that a creditor is not bound by his acceptance of part of a debt in full settlement — he can change his mind and demand the full sum due. This does not apply to an unliquidated claim (i.e., one where the amount is not fixed), or where there is a genuine dispute over the claim. It also does not apply where there is some consideration for the reduced payment, such as payment at an earlier time than the due date, or payment in a different form at the creditor's request. The creditor may, in certain limited circumstances, not be allowed to go back on his promise to take less, where the debtor has relied to his detriment on the promise and it would be inequitable to allow the creditor to change his mind.

WHATEVER DID THEY MEAN? CONSTRUING THE CONTRACT

In order for there to be an agreement, there must be some common intent on the part of the parties to the agreement. This intent must be communicated through words. Unfortunately, words are not a precise instrument to convey what is in the mind. To quote from T.S. Eliot: 'Words strain, / Crack and sometimes break, under the burden, / Under the tension, slip, slide, perish, / Decay with imprecision, will not stay in place, / Will not stay still' (*Four Quartets*, 'Burnt Norton', V). The courts, faced with the impossibility of determining directly what was in the parties' minds, have laid down the rule that their intention is to be determined by the reasonable interpretation of the words they have used to express that agreement, and have laid down rules to guide that interpretation. The advantage of having such rules is that the parties can put their agreement into words with some certainty about how a court will interpret them if they end up in a legal dispute over the contract.

If the language used by the parties is so vague or incomplete that the court is unable to determine anything more than an agreement to agree, then the entire contract is unenforceable. The courts will, however, do their best to make an enforceable agreement out of what they have before them if the parties clearly intended to enter a binding contract. Thus, the courts will imply terms that are common in the type of contract before them, or terms that seem to be reasonable in the circumstances, rather than invalidate the whole agreement. They will not do this, however, with terms that are vital to the agreement, such as the price of unique goods, or the description of land.

Rules of Interpretation

The first and overriding rule is that if the words impart a clear meaning, then that is the meaning they must be given. The court-developed rules of interpretation given below only apply if the language used by the parties is ambiguous in meaning:

(a) The words used should be given their usual meaning unless they were clearly used in a technical sense. If the parties wish to ensure that a particular meaning will be given to a word, they should set out a clear definition of the word in their agreement.

(b) The words used should be interpreted in the context of the whole agreement and the circumstances in which it was made.

(c) If, out of two possible interpretations, one makes the agreement clearly unworkable or unenforceable, the court should choose the other.

(d) An ambiguity is construed against the party who was the cause of the ambiguity.

(e) Wherever possible, inconsistent clauses must be reconciled, although a provision which is totally inconsistent with the rest of the contract may be rejected.

(f) When a contract is printed, typewritten provisions prevail over printed provisions, and handwritten provisions prevail over both printed and typewritten provisions.

If a contract is in writing, the court will try to interpret it solely from the words used. In general, the court will not consider evidence of intention outside the words of the agreement — this rule is known to lawyers as the 'parol evidence rule'. However, if the ambiguity cannot be resolved by study of the actual words used, the court will look at evidence outside the 'four corners of the contract' to determine intention. This may include evidence of negotiations leading up to the contract, and of the practical interpretation put on the contract by the parties themselves by the way they perform their obligations, if performance has commenced.

Mistake

Even though the words used are clear and unambiguous, one or both parties may not have intended to have agreed to the meaning conveyed by the words because of a mistake. In general, the law's attitude to mistake is 'tough luck — you are bound by what you reasonably appeared to have agreed to'. There are, however, exceptions to this.

If both parties made a mistake which goes to the heart of their bargain, such as making an agreement which is physically or legally impossible to perform, then the contract is a nullity and both parties are released from their obligations under it. The law is, however, reluctant to find that there is such a mistake.

If only one party is mistaken, the contract will be enforced unless that mistake is of such a fundamental nature that there is, in effect, no agreement. The mistaken person must show that he would not have entered into the contract if he had known of the mistake. Further, there must be something that makes it just to allow that person to get out of the bargain: either the mistake must have been known to the other party, or the circumstances were such that he should have realised that the other party was making a mistake if he had thought about it.

These legal rules can operate harshly, so the courts, applying the principles of equity, developed other remedies for dealing with mistake. These include rescission, which means treating the contract as if it never existed but which is only available if the parties can be put back in their starting positions, and rectification (correction) of the agreement where it fails to set out the intention of both parties.

IMPLIED TERMS

In addition to the terms which the parties expressly spell out in their agreement, other terms may be included by implication. Implied terms may be categorised as those implied as a matter of fact, those implied as a matter of law, and those implied by custom.

Terms Implied in Fact

These are terms which a court will include to fill some obvious gap and which are needed to make a particular agreement workable. The court will only imply a term if it is obvious that the parties would have included it if they had thought about it. This is sometimes called the 'officious bystander' test, derived from the words of MacKinnon LJ in *Shirlaw* v *Southern Foundries (1926) Ltd* [1939] 2 KB 206, 277:

> Prima facie that which in any contract is left to be implied and need not be expressed is something so obvious that it goes without saying; so that, if, while the parties were making their bargain, an officious bystander were to suggest some express provision for it in their agreement, they would testily suppress him with a common 'Oh, of course!'

The term must not only be obvious, it must also be necessary to give the contract business efficacy. The court must not imply a term simply because it would improve the contract.

For a term to be implied in fact, it must not only have been obvious to both parties, but it must be clear that both parties would have agreed to it. Any term which is in the interest of only one of the parties will therefore not be implied.

Terms Implied in Law

Terms are implied in fact when a fictional intent of the parties is discerned. Terms are implied in law regardless of the actual intent of the parties. There are a very large number of such terms, many of them relating to particular types of contracts. Many are the result of the development of the common law, others are imposed by statute. They are generally imposed in the furtherance of some public policy, for example, to ensure that the parties to a contract treat each other with fairness and honesty, or to protect the economically weaker party.

These terms are too numerous to be dealt with individually here. Some of the more important implied terms, of which you should be aware, are the implied obligation of good faith and fair dealing between parties to a contract, and the provision that a person with ostensible authority to enter into that contract in fact has that authority. The latter provision is of particular importance to corporations; anyone whose official title would indicate that he is an officer of the corporation can bind the corporation, even if he in fact has no authority to do so. A number of terms are implied by the common law into employment contracts: the employee impliedly undertakes that he will serve his employer faithfully, that he is reasonably skilled, and that he will not act against his employer's interests, while the employer impliedly undertakes that he will provide safe premises and will not require the employee to do any unlawful act. There are also numerous terms implied by statute into employment contracts, so much so that in some jurisdictions, including the UK, freedom of contract between employer and employee has become illusory. Important terms are implied by statute into contracts for the sale of goods; these are dealt with below in the section dealing with such contracts.

Terms Implied by Custom

This particularly applies to commercial contracts. In particular trades and businesses there are often customary provisions which are common to everyone in the business. This can range from whole contracts, to single provisions. When it can be shown that both parties knew of these terms at the time of contracting, such customary terms are implied unless they are unreasonable, are expressly excluded or are inconsistent with the parties' own terms.

Even if terms are not common to the trade, they may be implied if the parties have dealt with each other on a number of occasions, and on each previous occasion a particular term had been expressly included in the agreement.

'THE SALESMAN TOLD ME, BUT IT WASN'T PUT IN WRITING'

We have all had the experience of buying something after hearing a salesman's glowing description of what the item will do, or after reading a glossy sales brochure, only to find on using the item concerned that it does not live up to those promises. This experience is regrettably common in the computer field, particularly with software. What is the legal position if you do not have those glowing promises in writing?

If no part of the agreement was put into writing, then in general those promises are enforceable, provided you can get the court to believe that they were made. In the case of oral contracts, it usually comes down to one person's word against the other. You may not be able to have them enforced if the court finds that they could not reasonably have been taken seriously, and were mere advertising 'puffs'. The modern tendency is to restrict more closely what can be said in advertising, and to treat representations by advertisements and salesmen as actionable representations.

If the agreement was in writing, then it may, by its terms, exclude liability for things said during negotiations leading up to the contract. It can do this expressly, by a disclaimer of all warranties and representations. It can also do this by the inclusion of an 'integration' clause, which provides that the written document constitutes the entire agreement between the parties, and that all prior negotiations, discussions, representations and understandings are of no effect unless expressly set out in the written agreement.

Even if the written agreement does not include a disclaimer or an integration clause, the parol evidence rule can make it difficult to have a verbal promise enforced. The general effect of this rule is that the court will not go outside the writing to determine what the parties intended to agree, unless a written term is ambiguous as written so that other evidence of the parties' intention is needed. Therefore, when this rule applies, evidence of the oral promises will not be accepted. While the modern tendency is to apply this rule less strictly than it had been applied in the past, it can still present a serious obstacle to the enforcement of an oral promise not included in the written agreement.

If the oral misrepresentation was serious enough, you may not be without a remedy. You will not be able to enforce the promise, but you may be entitled to damages, or you may be able to get out of the whole agreement. In order to get relief, you must first demonstrate that there was a misrepresentation of some relevant fact, upon which you reasonably relied, and which was a material cause of your decision to enter the contract. Where the person who makes the misrepresentation is someone with special knowledge, then a statement of opinion which is false may also be actionable.

Further, to get damages at common law, the statement either has to be a deliberate lie, or the person who made it has to be reckless as to whether it was true or not. However, in the case of someone who is in a special relationship to the person to whom the statement is made, that relationship being one where there would normally be an expectation that care would be taken on making the representation, then mere negligence giving rise to the falsity is sufficient. An example of such a special relationship, from the leading English case which established this principle, *Hedley Byrne & Co. Ltd* v *Heller & Partners Ltd* [1964] AC 465, is that of a bank which gave a credit reference regarding one of its customers. Other examples, from decided cases, are the relationships of accountants, surveyors and valuers to those who rely on their advice. In some jurisdictions, including England and Wales, there are statutes which provide that damages may be awarded in all cases of negligent misrepresentation, not just those involving a special relationship. The English statute is the Misrepresentation Act 1967, which provides that damages can be awarded 'unless [the person making the representation] proves that he had reasonable ground to believe and did believe up to the time the contract was made that the facts represented were true'.

As an alternative to damages, the innocent party may have the option to have the contract set aside. This is called 'rescission'. This remedy is available for all types of misrepresentation, even innocent (i.e., not deliberate or negligent) misrepresentations. There are, however, some limits to this right; the most important one is that it must be possible to put both parties back to the position they were in before the contract was entered into. You cannot rescind a contract for the sale of goods if you have either consumed or disposed of them. On the other hand, deterioration of the goods due to no fault of yours will not prevent rescission. To give a computer example, you cannot rescind a contract for the purchase of diskettes on the ground of misrepresentation after you have spilled coffee all over them, but you could do it with a disc drive which had become somewhat worn after normal use. The court does, however, have powers to make a fair adjustment when circumstances require it. Another important limitation is that you cannot rescind if you have affirmed the contract, either by word or by an act such as using the goods, after discovering the misrepresentation. You may also be barred if you wait too long.

You may also be without a remedy if the written contract excludes liability for misrepresentations. Under the Misrepresentation Act 1967, such a provision is ineffective unless it satisfies the requirement of reasonableness specified in the Unfair Contract Terms Act 1977. Other jurisdictions have similar provisions, and there is a modern tendency for the courts to refuse to enforce such a term if it is oppressive or unconscionable. Such a term in a standard form contract may very well be unenforceable, the same term in a contract negotiated at arm's length would be enforced.

While in general you cannot get an unwritten promise enforced when you have a written contract, in some cases the only real way to do justice is to enforce the promise — damages or rescission are not adequate. An example of such a situation was found in the leading English case of *City & Westminster Properties (1934) Ltd* v *Mudd* [1959] Ch 129. A tenant had for some time, to the landlord's knowledge, been living in a room in the premises from which he conducted his business. The landlord induced him to sign a new lease, which restricted use of the premises to business purposes only, by an oral promise that this restriction would not be enforced and that he could continue residing on the premises. When the landlord later tried to enforce the terms of the lease, the court prevented it from doing so by finding that the oral promise was a separate contract, collateral to the lease, and enforcing that collateral contract.

In conclusion, while you may not be totally without remedy if an oral promise is broken, you will be in a much stronger position if you insist on having all such promises which are important to you included in the written contract.

JUST SIGN HERE: STANDARD FORM CONTRACTS

We are all familiar with standard form contracts. When we buy a car, buy furniture on credit, sign up for a package holiday or take out a bank loan, we are faced with a standard form contract. If we want the goods or services, we have to sign and accept all the terms. Other transactions may involve a standard form contract which we don't even sign; the ticket you get when you drive into a parking garage or leave clothes at the cleaners' may include contractual terms. It is obvious that, with such contracts, the concept of freedom of contract on the consumer's part is illusory. The courts and the legislature in almost all jurisdictions have come to realise this, and have intervened to prevent the abuse of economic power which such forms can represent.

One of the most serious abuses of economic power is the use of such standard contracts to exclude or severely limit the liability of the stronger party under the contract. Fully negotiated contracts often include some limitation of the full contractual liability of one or both of the parties, but this is an acceptable mutual shifting of risks, often risks that can be insured against. In the case of such exemption clauses in standard form contracts, such a clause may be wholly or partially invalid, either by statute or under judge-made rules.

Firstly, an exemption clause will not form part of a contract which was not signed by the consumer unless it was clearly brought to his or her attention, or at least all reasonable steps were taken to do so. It cannot be hidden in small print, or on a notice posted in a place where the customer would not normally expect to find contractual terms. In certain types of contracts, such as consumer credit contracts, there may be statutory requirements about how any exclusion clause must be presented, for example requiring larger type or a distinctive colour.

Secondly, an exclusion clause in a standard contract will be very narrowly interpreted, and the slightest uncertainty construed against the party who imposes the standard form on the other. The courts are particularly reluctant to exempt such a party from the results of his own negligence, and only the clearest words will be interpreted as having this result.

In the United Kingdom, there has been extensive legislation in recent years controlling abuses of economic power, in particular limiting the use of exclusion clauses in standard form contracts. The most important piece of legislation in this respect is the Unfair Contract Terms Act 1977. This prevents exclusion of liability under certain terms implied into contracts for the sale of goods, at least in the case of buyers who are individual consumers. It also applies to certain obligations implied by law in hire-purchase agreements, and in contracts for the carriage or bailment of goods. 'Bailment of goods' means the situation where a person other than the owner of the goods is in possession of the goods with the owner's consent, for example, where goods are stored in a warehouse, or where they are on the premises of a repairer. Similar provisions have been applied to the supply of services by the Supply of Goods and Services Act 1982 (which does not extend to Scotland). Other statutory provisions limiting the use of exemption clauses are to be found in the Misrepresentation Act 1967, which prevents the use of clauses limiting liability for misrepresentation unless they are shown to be reasonable, the Public Passenger Vehicles Act 1981, s. 29, which deals with contracts for the conveyance of passengers, and a number of other Acts relating to particular kinds of contracts such as leases and employment contracts.

There is less legislation of this type in the United States, although some states such as California have been active in legislation designed to protect the consumer. However, the US courts have gone somewhat further than their UK counterparts in refusing to enforce grossly unfair provisions in one-sided contracts, or to delete the offensive provisions and enforce the remainder.

Provisions other than exclusion of liability may also be oppressive. The standard form may purport to strip the weaker party of certain rights he would otherwise have, or to give certain extra rights to the stronger party. An example of the former can often be found in bank guarantee forms, of the latter in estate agents' contracts which provide for the payment of commission to the agent whether or not the sale is to a buyer whom he found. A number of specific abuses have been dealt with by legislation, in particular those connected with consumer credit.

The above makes it clear that anyone proposing to use a standard form contract in business should have it carefully checked for enforceability by a lawyer knowledgeable in this area of the law. Similarly, anyone who has signed one of these contracts who now finds that the other party has defaulted but is claiming exemption for liability for such default because of a clause in the contract may not be without a remedy.

OUTSIDERS TO THE CONTRACT: PRIVITY AND ASSIGNMENT

A contract confers rights and obligations because of the agreement of the parties. Can rights and obligations be conferred on persons other than parties to the agreement? This could be done directly by the terms of the agreement, or by transfer of the original agreement to a third party.

Can rights and obligations be conferred on a third party directly by the terms of the agreement?

The answer to this question is in an area where there is great difference between the English and the American common law. In English common law, no one except a party can acquire rights under a contract, and no one except a party can be subjected to liabilities under it. It is possible for the parties to agree that their contract should confer a benefit on a third party, but that third party cannot enforce the contract.

There are a few, limited exceptions to this rule; certain covenants relating to land are enforceable by third parties who later acquire an interest in the land benefited by the covenant, a number of kinds of insurance contract are by statute enforceable by third-party beneficiaries. There is also an equitable exception, in that a trust of a promise to pay money may be created, and may be enforced by the person benefiting from the trust.

In the United States, on the other hand, when a contract provides for performance directly to a third person and shows an intention to benefit that person on the part of the promisee (the provider of the consideration for the promisor's performance), the third person can enforce the contract.

Can the rights and obligations be transferred?

The common law, which was accustomed to dealing only with tangible things, refused to consider that the benefit of a promise was a transferable piece of property, so in general a contract was not assignable to a third party. Assignment is the transfer of rights under an agreement without the consent of the other party. If the other party consented, the same effect could be achieved at common law by novation, which is the substitution of a new contract with the original promisor and the third party as parties, for the original contract. Equity allowed the assignment of purely equitable rights, and would protect other assignees by making the assignor enforce the contract. However, statute now allows the assignment of contractual promises, provided the assignment is in writing, is absolute, i.e., not subject to some condition before it becomes effective, and provided written notice is given to the promisor. In general no consideration is required to make the assignment effective against the promisor, although this is a complicated subject. If the contract expressly provided that it cannot be assigned, then this provision controls.

In the USA no formalities or consideration are generally required for assignment, but the absence of writing or consideration makes the assignment more easily revocable by the assignor before the agreement has been performed.

It is also possible in the USA, but not in England, to transfer duties under a contract, known as 'delegation', but the courts are generally more reluctant to permit delegation unless the new party is as able to perform as the original party was.

BROKEN PROMISES: WHAT HAPPENS IF THINGS GO WRONG

Various things can go wrong with an agreement. One party may not perform his promises at all, or may perform in such a way that the intended benefit was not received. The goods may not live up to the promises made about them. A change of circumstances may make it impossible to perform the contract, or may make performance worthless to one of the parties. What can be done about this?

First, it must be determined whether or not the other party has, in fact, done what he promised to do. This may involve interpreting the terms of the contract. Because the complaint that the other party has failed to perform in a timely fashion is such a common one, the law has evolved rules dealing with time of performance. In general, performance in a reasonable time is sufficient, what is reasonable being determined by the court in the light of all the circumstances. A plumber called to deal with a broken pipe which is flooding the premises would be expected to turn up and repair the pipe much more quickly than a painter called to paint a doorway. The parties can provide a date for performance, but even then the rule is that late performance will not be a breach sufficient to entitle the other party to get out of the contract unless it is clear that the time of performance is regarded as essential. Technically this is called 'making time of the essence'.

Failure to perform an obligation is called 'breach of contract' if the failure is caused by the fault of the non-performing party. The other party may then have one or more possible remedies for this breach.

Damages

Damages are always available, as of right, whenever there is a breach of contract. The purpose of damages is to compensate the injured party for any losses incurred as a result of the breach, although nominal damages may be awarded even though there has been no loss. The amount of damages awarded therefore depends on the loss to the injured party, not on any profit made by the defendant as a result of the breach.

Part of the loss arises directly from the breach. If a seller fails to deliver goods which are readily available on the market, the loss to the buyer is the difference between the contract price and what it would cost him to go out now and buy those same goods. If the goods are delivered but are defective, the loss is the cost of repair. However, the injured party may also have lost money as an indirect result of the breach. For example, the buyer of non-delivered goods may have already contracted to resell them at a profit, and will be liable to his own customer for breach of contract because of the defendant's non-performance; or a plaintiff's business may depend upon a computer and may have to close down if the computer fails. These indirect losses can often be much greater than the direct losses. The general rule is that the defendant is also liable for indirect losses, but only if they were of a kind which he could have foreseen as likely to occur from his breach, or if at the time of making the contract the possibility of these losses was drawn to his attention. However, it is very common in commercial contracts for a vendor to try to exclude or limit his liability for indirect damages. The validity of such attempts contained in standard form contracts is discussed above.

It is often difficult to quantify accurately the loss suffered as a result of a breach of contract. The defendant cannot be allowed to profit from the uncertainty caused by his own conduct, however, so the courts will award a 'best guess' provided the plaintiff puts forward proof that he actually did suffer loss, and the best evidence he can muster as to its amount.

The injured party cannot, however, simply sit back and let the damages mount up. He is under a duty to do what he reasonably can to lessen or 'mitigate' the amount of his loss. If non-delivered goods are available in the market-place, he should get replacements. He should find alternative sources of services. Failure to mitigate will result in the defendant only being ordered to pay the damages that would have been incurred if there had been mitigation, the plaintiff will be left to bear the rest of the loss himself. On the other hand, if his good faith efforts to reduce his losses in fact result in those losses being increased, the defendant is liable for the increased amount.

Specific Performance

In certain circumstances, monetary compensation is totally inadequate. If I agree to sell you the *Mona Lisa*, you cannot go out and get a replacement if I breach the contract. If there is no adequate substitute, and the breaching party still has it in his power to perform, then the court can order him to perform by a decree of specific performance. Failure to comply with this decree is contempt of court, which can result if necessary in imprisonment until the decree is complied with. Specific performance may also be ordered where it is impossible or extremely difficult to estimate the amount of damages, for instance breach of a contract to provide an annuity where the amount lost depends on how long the annuitant lives after the date of breach.

Unlike damages, this remedy is not available as of right, but lies within the discretion of the court. The courts may refuse to grant it if to do so would be unfair, or if it would work severe hardship on the defendant, or if the plaintiff has himself behaved inequitably, for example, by refusing to perform his part of the bargain.

Certain types of contracts will never be specifically enforced, in particular those calling for the provision of personal services, and those which would require constant supervision by the court. Gratuitous promises will not be enforced, and uncertainty in the terms will also prevent specific performance.

Injunction

The opposite side of the coin to specific performance, where someone is ordered to do something, is an injunction, which orders someone not to do something. In appropriate cases it may be possible to prevent a breach of contract by an injunction, where the contract is negative in nature, such as a contract not to sue.

Injunctions are also a discretionary remedy, and may be refused for the same reasons for which specific performance may be refused. Also, an injunction may not be used to enforce indirectly a contract of the type for which specific performance is not available.

Rescission

If a breach of contract is sufficiently serious, the injured party may have the right to escape from his own obligations under the contract. Unfortunately, this right is often referred to as 'rescission', although it differs in several ways from the right of rescission for misrepresentation discussed above. This imprecision of terms has also led, unfortunately, to some judicial confusion. The most important difference is that, in rescission for breach, there is no requirement that it must be possible to put both parties back in the position they were in before they entered into the contract.

This right to terminate for breach does not arise in the case of every breach. If the party in breach has failed to comply with a condition which had to be complied with before the other party became liable to perform his side of the bargain, then performance by the other party is excused. An example of such a condition would be that a purchaser should obtain letters of credit before the vendor becomes liable to deliver the goods, in circumstances where the vendor would be unable to obtain supplies unless he could show that the purchaser had a letter of credit.

Otherwise, in general the right to terminate only arises if the broken promise is fundamental to the contract, in the sense that it goes to the heart of the parties' bargain. There are certain exceptions to this statement; for example, in the UK, the Sale of Goods Act 1979 provides a right to terminate for failure to comply with certain requirements, regardless of the seriousness of the breach. In other cases, rescission has been allowed when damages would be inadequate but specific performance was inappropriate or unavailable. A rather grotesque example of such a situation occurred in the case of *Vigers* v *Cook* [1919] 2 KB 475, CA, where an undertaker performed his duties so negligently that it was not possible to get the coffin into the church for the funeral service. He was denied recovery of any part of his fees, as the breach was one which could not be compensated by money, but it was too late for specific performance.

The right to rescind for breach may be lost. The most common reason for this is that the injured party has waived his right to rescind, usually by insisting on continued performance by the other party after he learns of the breach. It should be pointed out that waiver of the right to rescind does not necessarily mean that the right to damages for breach has also been waived.

Different rules apply when the failure to perform is not the fault of the party concerned. Something unforeseen may have happened between the time of making the agreement and the time for it to be performed which makes performance impossible, and destroys the whole basis for the agreement. This is called 'frustration'. Two events which have between them supplied most of the case law on frustration were the cancellation of the coronation of Edward VII, at short notice, because the king was stricken with appendicitis, and the closing of the Suez Canal as a result of the wars between Egypt and Israel.

The effect of frustration is that both parties are discharged from their contractual obligations. However, the doctrine of discharge for frustration is very cautiously applied. The supervening event must have been genuinely unforeseeable, and as a result of its occurrence the whole commercial basis for the contract must have been destroyed. Mere inconvenience, or added expense, is not sufficient. If the contract can be construed as providing expressly what is to happen in such an event, even if that particular event was not foreseen, then the contractual provisions apply. If the parties should have foreseen the event, even if they did not in fact do so, there is no frustration.

Even if a breach has occurred, the innocent party may be barred by his own acts from action against the breaching party. There are two important bars, waiver and estoppel.

Waiver

This has already been mentioned in connection with the right to rescind for breach. The term means forbearance to enforce rights. It is not a permanent bar to enforcement, but will prevent taking action in respect of the particular breach which was waived. In order for there to be an effective waiver there must have been a clear representation by the injured party that he would not enforce his rights in respect of the breach, and it must, in some way, be inequitable for him to go back on that promise.

Estoppel

Classic estoppel applies when there has been a representation of fact upon which the other party relies to his detriment. The person making the representation is not then allowed to go back on it. While the classic doctrine can apply to breaches of contract, the more recent doctrine of equitable estoppel is more commonly relied upon as a defence to an action for breach of contract. This type of estoppel applies to representations of intention, rather than of fact, and is derived from, and closely related to the doctrine of waiver described above.

CONTRACTS FOR THE SALE OF GOODS

Every common-law system has, to some extent at least, codified its laws relating to contracts for the sale of goods. In the United Kingdom the relevant statute is the Sale of Goods Act 1979, which consolidated the Sale of Goods Act 1893 with some more recent legislation dealing with the subject. In the United States all states except Louisiana (which is not a common-law jurisdiction) have adopted all or almost all of the Uniform Commercial Code (UCC), and even Louisiana has adopted the section of the UCC relating to sales. There are also international conventions, dealing with international transactions, to which most of the major trading countries adhere.

This legislation applies whenever there is a contract for the sale of goods. By 'sale' is meant a transfer of title to the goods, as opposed to a loan or hire-purchase, for valuable consideration. 'Goods' are tangible items of property other than land. In the computer world, hardware is clearly goods, while the services of a data processing bureau are clearly not. With software the line becomes harder to draw: a diskette containing a piece of standard software such as a word processing program is probably goods, but what about a piece of custom software? The law has always had problems drawing the line between a contract for the sale of goods and a contract for work and materials. For example, if you agree with an artist that he will paint your portrait, the materials for the picture to be supplied by him, is that a contract for the sale of goods, the portrait, or for the artist's work and materials? Most authorities would seem to favour the latter, as the important thing contracted for was the skilled work of the artist. On the other hand, the little case law that there yet is on the subject, and all of the cases known to the author are from the United States, indicates that the courts would be inclined to treat custom software as goods. However, these cases all involved turnkey systems of bundled hardware and software. Further, the state of California, and some other states, tax the sale of software, whether custom or off-the-shelf, as if it were goods, unless nothing tangible changes hands.

The provisions of sale-of-goods legislation are detailed, and it is not possible to deal with them fully here. Instead, some of the aspects where the law relating to contracts for the sale of goods differs from the general law of contracts in the UK and the USA will be pointed out.

Formation of the Contract

UK
Ordinarily the failure to fix a price, which is an essential term, would make the contract too uncertain to enforce. Under the Sale of Goods Act 1979, provided the parties did intend to enter a binding contract, the buyer must pay a 'reasonable' price if no price is specified, what is reasonable being determined in the circumstances of the case.

USA
If the parties evince an intention to contract, silence on any essential term is treated as assent to a reasonable term filling the gap. The only essential term which will not be filled in if there is silence is the subject-matter — there must be sufficient certainty about what it is the parties are agreeing to buy and sell.

Secondly, the common-law rule that any attempt to vary the terms of the offer in the acceptance acts as a counter-offer is not applied. If the transaction is between merchants (so it does not apply to ordinary consumer sales) then the addition of further terms to the acceptance does not make it a rejection. If these new terms are consistent with the original offer, they form part of the contract unless specifically rejected by the offeror, otherwise they only form part of the contract if specifically accepted by the offeror.

Implied Terms

UK

An important feature of contracts for the sale of goods is that a number of terms are implied by the Sale of Goods Act 1979. The most important of these implied terms are:

(a)   A condition that the seller has the right to sell the goods and that there are no undisclosed third-party rights which will interfere with the buyer's possession of the goods.

(b)   A condition that, in the case of the sale of goods by description and/or sample, the goods will correspond to the description and/or sample.

(c)   A condition that, when the goods are sold in the normal course of the seller's business, they are of merchantable quality. 'Merchantable quality' is defined as meaning that the goods are 'as fit for the purpose or purposes for which goods of that kind are commonly bought as it is reasonable to expect having regard to any description applied to them, the price (if relevant) and all the other relevant circumstances'. This does not apply to any defects which were pointed out by the seller before the sale was made, or to defects which should have been discovered by the buyer in cases where he examines the goods before buying them.

(d)   A condition that, when the goods are sold in the normal course of the seller's business and the buyer makes known to the seller the purpose for which he wants the goods, the goods will be reasonably fit for that purpose.

Condition (a) cannot be excluded or restricted by the contract. The other conditions cannot be excluded or restricted in the case of consumer sales, but in all other cases such exclusions or restrictions are enforceable, provided they are reasonable in the circumstances.

USA

The UCC provides for implied terms similar to those implied by the UK's Sale of Goods Act 1979. These are:

(a)   A warranty that the title transferred is good and that the goods are free of any third-party interest. In the case where the seller is a merchant who regularly deals in that type of goods, there is a further warranty against infringement of a third party's rights by the goods.

(b)   A warranty that the goods conform to any representation or promise which is part of the basis of the bargain.

(c)   A warranty that the goods conform to any description which is part of the basis of the bargain.

(d)   A warranty that goods sold by sample correspond to the sample.

(e)   A warranty that the goods are merchantable — this means the same as it does under UK law.

(f)   A warranty of fitness for particular purpose — again the same as the UK law.

Any of the warranties can be limited or excluded by express provisions, provided these provisions are reasonable. The warranty of merchantability can only be excluded if it is mentioned by name, in conspicuous writing. Implied warranties may also be excluded by examination of the goods by the buyer before contracting, so far as perceivable defects are concerned, or because they have been regularly excluded in the prior course of dealings between the parties.

Transfer of Property

UK

For specific goods, or for generic goods once the specific items to be sold under the contract have been picked out (the technical term for this is 'ascertained'), the Sale of Goods Act 1979 provides that 'property', which equals ownership, of the goods passes from seller to buyer at the time at which the parties intend it to pass. However, the Act lays down rules which are presumptions about the parties' intentions when they make no express provision for the passing of property. These rules are:

(a)   Where there is an unconditional contract for the sale of specific goods in a deliverable state, the property in the goods passes to the buyer when the contract is made, and it is immaterial whether the time of payment or the time of delivery, or both, be postponed.

(b)   Where there is a contract for the sale of specific goods and the seller is bound to do something to the goods, for the purpose of putting them into a deliverable state, the property does not pass until the thing is done, and the buyer has notice that it is done.

(c)   Where there is a contract for the sale of specific goods in a deliverable state but the seller is bound to weigh, measure, test, or do some other act or thing with reference to the goods for the purpose of ascertaining the price, the property does not pass until the act or thing is done and the buyer has notice that it has been done.

(d)   When goods are delivered to the buyer on approval or sale or return, the property passes to the buyer when he either signifies his acceptance of the goods to the seller, or if he fails to return them by the time fixed for return, or, if no time is fixed, within a reasonable time.

(e)   In the case of unascertained goods, property passes when the specific goods which are to be transferred are earmarked for the buyer, with the consent of both parties.

The main importance of the passing of the property in the goods is that the risk of accidental loss falls on the party with the property. Thus, if the property has passed to the buyer before delivery, and the goods are destroyed through no fault of the seller before delivery takes place, the buyer remains obligated to pay for them.

USA
Under the UCC, title to the goods does not pass until the goods are delivered, but the buyer obtains a 'special property' and an insurable interest in the goods as soon as they are identified. The term 'identified' has the same meaning as 'ascertained' under the UK Sale of Goods Act 1979.

Performance of the Contract

UK
The Sale of Goods Act 1979 provides that the breach of certain terms on the part of the seller gives the buyer an automatic right to terminate the contract by rejecting the goods, regardless of the seriousness of the breach. These are delivery of the wrong quantity, either too much or too little, and delivery of the contract goods mixed with other goods. The buyer in each case has the choice of rejecting the whole delivery, or keeping the contract goods and rejecting the rest, or, in the case of an insufficient delivery, keeping the goods and recovering the difference in price and any damages resulting from the breach.

In order to protect these rights of the buyer, he is not deemed to have accepted the goods until he has had a reasonable chance to inspect them. However, if he retains the goods beyond a reasonable time required to make such an inspection, he will then be deemed to have accepted them.

USA

The buyer is given the right to reject the whole delivery, accept the whole delivery, or accept any commercial unit of the goods and reject the rest in the case of any failure of the goods to conform to the contract. However, if the time for performing the contract has not expired, the seller has the right, in the case of rejection, to try to cure his breach by making a delivery of goods conforming to the contract. Further, if the seller had reason to believe that the first delivery would be acceptable, he may in any case have a second try to deliver in conformance with the contract within a reasonable time if he promptly notifies the buyer of this intention.

The same rules as apply in the UK also apply in the USA regarding the buyer's right to inspect the goods and what constitutes acceptance.

Seller's Remedies

UK

The unpaid seller who has delivered conforming goods has remedies other than the normal contractual remedy of an action for damages. If he has not actually parted with possession of the goods, he is entitled to retain possession until he is paid. If the buyer becomes insolvent while the goods are still in transit, the seller has the right to stop them in transit and resume possession until he is paid. In the case of perishable goods, or when the seller gives the buyer notice of his intention to resell, if the buyer does not pay within a reasonable time the seller may resell the goods.

USA

The unpaid seller is given the same rights, although the provisions relating to resale are rather more complicated. The seller also has the right to demand cash payment if he discovers the buyer to be insolvent.

Buyer's Remedies

UK

Besides the right to reject, discussed above, the buyer has the normal contractual remedies of damages for breach of condition or for nondelivery, recovery of the price paid if there is total failure of consideration, and specific performance if that is available. The Sale of Goods Act 1979 has provisions relating to the calculation of damages.

USA
The buyer has the same rights as he has under the UK law.

CONTRACT IN CIVIL-LAW SYSTEMS

With the exception of some Muslim countries which use Islamic law, based on the Koran, all non-Communist countries of commercial significance have legal systems based on either the common law, or on civil law, which traces its origins to Roman law. All European countries, other than the UK and Ireland, are civil-law countries.

The theoretical basis behind the law of contracts in civil-law systems is different from that which underlies the common-law approach to contracts. The basis for enforcement of contracts in common-law jurisdictions is the concept of a bargain, which brings in the essential requirement of consideration. The civil law regards the fact of agreement itself as being the basis for enforcement, that one should be both morally and legally obliged to keep a promise. The definition of a contract in French law, which is the basis for many other legal systems, is that 'a contract is an agreement, by which one or more persons undertake, with respect to one or more other persons, to give, to do or not to do something'.

The main difference between these approaches is that there is no requirement of consideration in the civil law of contracts. A purely gratuitous promise, known as a *'contrat de bienfaisance'*, will be enforced under the same rules as a commercial contract.

However, in practice, the details of the civil law of contract are very similar to those of the common law. There must be a valid consent, and consent is not valid if obtained by duress, fraud or mistake; the parties must have legal capacity to contract; there must be certainty of subject-matter; and the contract must not be for an illegal purpose, or a purpose contrary to public morality. The substantive rules governing each of these requirements are very similar to the common-law rules discussed above. Certain types of contract, in particular, contracts for the sale of goods and employment contracts, are generally the subject of further legislation in each jurisdiction.

In general, no particular formalities are required, but again, this may differ from country to country for particular types of contracts.

In general, the same remedies as are given by the common law are available in the case of breach of contract, with the exception of specific performance.

This outline of the civil law of contract has of necessity been of the broadest and most generalised nature. Anyone entering a contract which is to be governed by the law of any civil-law country should always consult a lawyer qualified to practise in that country at an early stage in the negotiations.

LAWYERS CAN BE USEFUL

As this chapter is addressed to non-lawyers, who presumably have some thought of preparing their own contracts if they have bothered to get this far through this chapter, a warning about the limitations of what has been set out here on the law of contract is in order. The discussion has been, of necessity, drastically simplified, and many topics which could be involved in a particular contract have been omitted. This is particularly true of contracts which have a fair degree of statutory regulation, such as sale of goods, consumer credit and employment.

Further, the law described is a very generalised version of the common law, with some of the differences between the laws of the UK and the USA pointed out. The law in each common-law country will differ in some details from that described here, as a result of the case-law development in that particular country, and of that country's statutory provisions governing contracts.

In many cases the use of a lawyer to assist in the negotiation of an agreement and to prepare the written contract results in overall savings, however outrageous his fee may seem at the time. Most lawyers who practise in the field of commercial contracts make much more money out of the home-made contracts that go wrong than they do out of working on the formation of a contract. Obviously, you do not need a lawyer when you buy a box of diskettes or an inexpensive piece of software. However, whenever the contract involves major expenditure, or where the results of a breach of the contract could seriously damage your business or cause you substantial monetary loss, then you should at least have a lawyer who specialises in commercial contracts look at your proposed agreement before it is finalised or signed. If the contract in any way involves an agreement with a potential competitor, or is a distributorship agreement, and it is to be performed in the EEC or the

USA, or any other country with a system of laws governing competition, then you should always consult a lawyer with knowledge of such laws at an early stage. Otherwise you may not only have an unenforceable agreement, but also the possibility of a large fine or the imposition of treble damages.

4   Problems and Pitfalls of International Contracts

The business person who has business relationships with individuals or organisations located outside his or her own country, and the lawyer or other person who has to draw up a contract governing those business relationships, must be aware that there are matters which must be taken into consideration which do not arise in a purely domestic contract. For example, the fact that this is an international contract may mean that certain laws of your own jurisdiction apply to it which do not apply to purely internal contracts, such as the competition rules of the EEC or currency exchange control laws, and it may have to comply with certain laws or regulations of the other country, such as the US antitrust laws or government regulations in Third World countries controlling contracts which transfer technology to that country.

It is not possible in this book to give detailed guidance to those involved in international contracts, as the particular matters which must be taken into consideration will depend on the nature and terms of the contract and the particular countries concerned. Anyone contemplating international business dealings would be well advised to obtain professional help, legal and other, from people with experience of dealing with the country concerned. The purpose of this chapter is to alert you to some of the major potential problems so you will know when you need help to avoid them.

ANTITRUST: A SKETCH MAP OF THE MINEFIELD

First, a word of explanation concerning the rather strange term 'antitrust'. This is the American term for what the Europeans often call, more descriptively, competition law. It derives from the early history of the original American legislation regulating business competition, the Sherman Act of 1890. This was passed as a result of pressure from farmers and other small businessmen who found that they were being squeezed by the economic power of the big businesses, for this was the age of the so-called 'robber barons', men such as J.P. Morgan and Rockefeller who had built huge fortunes and extensive business empires with no restrictions on their business activities. The corporation law of those days did not allow subsidiary corporations, the modern method of putting together a number of businesses under the same control. Instead, the device of a trust was used; shares were surrendered to trustees in return for trust certificates. The trustees then exercised the voting power of the various companies' shares in the trust, thereby effectively constituting a central management for them all. This device was first used by Standard Oil, resulting in the trustees having virtual monopoly power over the oil industry, and this was soon followed in other industries. The Sherman Act was used by Theodore Roosevelt to attack the huge economic power of these trusts, hence 'antitrust'.

The USA was the first nation to regulate business behaviour in this way. The Sherman Act, which is discussed in more detail below, prohibits collusion between potential competitors which results in higher prices, more restrictive terms of trade, or other things which adversely affect the public and which would not exist if there were free competition, and also prohibits the acquisition of monopoly power. This Act remains the basis of US antitrust law, although there are other pieces of legislation which govern particular matters such as pricing and certain types of potentially anticompetitive behaviour. All other systems of law which regulate business behaviour in favour of freedom of competition, such as the EEC rules, owe a great deal to the American model, although they may differ in detail.

This chapter will deal in more detail with the two major systems of competition law, those of the USA and the EEC, as they are likely to affect contracts concerned with computers. The reader is warned, however, that this is a very complex field in which expert legal advice is necessary. The purpose of this section is to alert you to potential problems in this area, so that, if you see such a problem looming on the horizon, you can seek proper advice before it is too late. The consequences of antitrust violations can be very serious indeed.

US ANTITRUST

The basis for all US antitrust law is the Sherman Act (15 USC ss. 1–7). The main provisions of this piece of legislation are to be found in the first two sections, and are majestic in the simplicity and breadth of their language:

1.   Every contract, combination in the form of trust or otherwise, or conspiracy, in restraint of trade or commerce among the several states, or with foreign nations, is declared to be illegal . . ..
2.   Every person who shall monopolize, or attempt to monopolize, or combine or conspire with any other person or persons, to monopolize any part of the trade or commerce among the several states, or with foreign nations, shall be deemed guilty of a felony . . ..

The Sherman Act only provides for criminal penalties for its breach; the right of private action for damage caused by antitrust violation, and the provision for treble damages, were added by s. 4 of the Clayton Act of 1914, (15 USC s. 15).

In the tradition of the common law, the American courts have used this broad language to construct a detailed, yet flexible, system of rules governing business behaviour. The most important concept which was developed by the Supreme Court in interpreting these provisions is that of *per se*/rule of reason analysis of the legality of a particular business practice. This approach derives from the English common-law approach to contracts in restraint of trade, and may be expressed in the following way:

(a)   Certain business practices are so clearly anticompetitive that they are *per se* illegal, that is, they are held to be illegal without any analysis of their actual effect on competition. An example of a *per se* illegal practice is a conspiracy by merchants to fix prices, so that the public has no option but to pay whatever price is demanded.

(b)   All other practices are examined under the 'rule of reason'. The English judges, who had pronounced restraints of trade to be illegal in the late middle ages, acknowledged that certain restraints were necessary in certain types of transactions, and would be allowed, provided they were reasonable in the circumstances. One of the earliest examples of this was a case involving the sale of a business: if the buyer cannot prevent the seller from immediately setting up a competing business, then the seller is being allowed to collect the purchase price for his business and then take back some or all of what he sold. The English law is that the seller can be restrained, in a reasonable manner, from acting in such a way as to take back the benefit of his bargain. The same concept was introduced into American antitrust law by the decision of the Supreme Court in the *Standard Oil* case of 1911 (*Standard Oil Co.* v *United States*, 221 US 1 (1911)). The court held that the Sherman Act was only intended by Congress to restrain 'undue limitation on competitive conditions'. In applying the rule of reason the court is called upon to make an economic, rather than a legal, analysis of the effects of the act complained of. The first step in this analysis is to define the 'relevant market' concerned. This is not always an easy task — if the acts complained of affect the price of bananas, is the relevant market only that for bananas, or is it all fruit? The most common test for this is called 'cross-elasticity of demand': if bananas are unavailable, will the consumer perceive an apple or orange to be an acceptable substitute? For those of you anxious to know the answer, the Commission of the European Communities has held that he or she will not (*Re The United Brands Co.* [1976] 1 CMLR D28). Having defined the relevant market, the court must then consider whether the defendant's conduct has unduly restrained trade in that market.

Although the rule-of-reason analysis depends upon the facts of the particular case, and also ultimately upon the court's perception of what is 'reasonable', the operation of the principle of judicial precedent makes it possible to give some guidance about the likely decision in respect of certain types of agreements which have common characteristics. Some of the developed rules which apply to certain types of computer contracts are given below.

One word about the geographical scope of US antitrust. Because of the constitutional considerations of a federation of states, which is what the USA is, federal antitrust law only applies to acts which have an effect on trade between states, or between a state and a foreign nation. However the word 'effect' is widely interpreted, so it may be possible for an agreement between two entities in a single state to have effects beyond the boundaries of that state, making federal law apply. Similarly, it has been held by American courts that acts taking place outside the United States are subject to US antitrust law if they were intended to, and did, have an effect on trade in the USA.

The following types of computer contract may possibly contain provisions which are prohibited or of dubious validity under US antitrust law, and any foreigner considering entering such a contract with an individual or organisation in the USA should obtain expert advice on the potential antitrust consequences before any contract is signed:

(a)   Sales of goods covered by US patents or copyrights. No post-sale restrictions, whether about resale price or any other matter, are enforceable. Once title to the goods has passed to the buyer, the patentee or copyright holder cannot control what happens to the goods, although they can still prevent infringement of their rights, e.g., by the buyer using the goods to produce infringing copies.

(b)   Licences under US patents. This is most likely to apply to licences to an American company to manufacture and/or sell in the United States hardware covered by a US patent, or which contains a patented component. The nature of the patent monopoly means that certain types of restrictions which would normally be illegal, such as limitations on the territory of the licence, or the field in which the licensed goods can be used, are permissible. However, restrictions which do not directly arise from the nature of the patent monopoly are judged under the same rules as ordinary contracts. Thus, any attempt to fix the licensee's retail prices is *per se* illegal, a requirement that the licensee must purchase certain unpatented supplies needed to operate the licence from the licensor will be judged under the rule of reason (and is usually only reasonable if it is necessary to ensure the proper working of the patent).

(c)   Licences of trade secrets. This could apply to both hardware and software. A trade secret, sometimes referred to as 'know-how', is information which is commercially valuable which is preserved by its owner by keeping it secret. This can be information which is patentable but which has not been published by being contained in an issued patent, or information which is inherently unpatentable, such as the best method of running a particular plant. Such information may be shared with others through a licence to use the information, and such licences are increasingly being treated by the courts as having many characteristics in common with patent licences. While trade-secret protection depends exclusively on contract and the tort of unfair competition, as opposed to the government grant of a monopoly, as in patents, trade secrets may have considerable commercial value and importance and this is now recognised by the courts in most industrialised countries. Because there is no statutory monopoly, restrictions tend to be more carefully scrutinised, and even when reasonable should only operate for the period during which the trade secret can reasonably be expected to remain a secret, sometimes called the 'reverse engineering' period.

(d)   Copyright licences. This is most likely to apply to software.

There is much less case law on copyright licences than there is on patent licences. As copyright is not a monopoly in the way that a patent is, there are fewer special considerations that apply to restrictions in copyright licences.

(e) Distributorship agreements. The restrictions which most frequently occur in distributorship agreements which have potential antitrust problems are those giving the distributor exclusivity of either territory or type of customer. At one time the courts held that all territorial restrictions were *per se* illegal as they prevented competition in the sale of those particular goods, but this position has relaxed in recent years, and the rule of reason is now applied. Territorial restrictions are generally held to be reasonable where the distributor needs protection while building up a market for a new product, or where restricting intrabrand competition leads to increased interbrand competition — the situation where, without the protection, the weaker manufacturers will go to the wall, leaving a virtual monopoly for the survivors. Any type of pricing control is, however, *per se* illegal. While a manufacturer is free to choose who he will deal with, and this includes terminating an existing distributorship, he cannot use threats of termination to impose illegal restrictions indirectly, nor can he do so at the request of his other distributors who may wish to get rid of a discounter.

(f) Joint venture agreements. Unlike distributorship agreements, which are 'vertical' in that they involve parties on two different levels in the chain of distribution, joint venture agreements are normally between two parties at the same level who are therefore potential, if not actual, direct competitors. Such agreements are said to be 'horizontal', and the more relaxed attitude referred to above does not apply to them. Anyone contemplating a joint venture, either for research or production, with an American organisation, should ensure that they have expert legal advice at all stages of the negotiations.

COMPETITION LAW OF THE EUROPEAN ECONOMIC COMMUNITY

The main competition law provisions for the EEC are to be found in arts 85 and 86 of the EEC Treaty. These to some extent mirror ss. 1 and 2 of the Sherman Act, and their main provisions are as follows:

Article 85
1. The following shall be prohibited as incompatible with the

common market: all agreements between undertakings, decisions by associations of undertakings and concerted practices which may affect trade between member states and which have as their object or effect the prevention, restriction or distortion of competition within the common market . . .

2. Any agreements or decisions prohibited pursuant to this Article shall be automatically void.

Article 86

Any abuse by one or more undertakings of a dominant position within the common market or in a substantial part of it shall be prohibited as incompatible with the common market in so far as it may affect trade between member states.

Despite the many similarities between these provisions and those of the Sherman Act, it must always be remembered that the ultimate purpose of the two is different: the EEC provisions are designed to ensure a truly common market between sovereign nations, the American provisions are designed to ensure a truly competitive economy within one nation.

There are other differences: Art. 85(3) provides for an exemption from the provisions of the rest of the article for agreements, etc., which are for the public benefit. While this encompasses the American rule of reason it goes somewhat further than most American courts are prepared to go in considering overall public benefit as a factor in the rule-of-reason analysis. Article 86 deals only with an abuse of a dominant position, while the Sherman Act, s. 2 is addressed to the acquisition of a dominant position.

European competition law rules with respect to patent, copyright and other intellectual property rights are more complex than the equivalent American rules, because these rights are national, and may vary from country to country. Article 36 of the EEC Treaty expressly provides that prohibitions or restrictions on imports are permissible for the protection of 'industrial and commercial property', which term includes patent and similar rights. Article 36 has a proviso, however: 'Such prohibitions or restrictions shall not, however, constitute a means of arbitrary discrimination or a disguised restriction on trade between member states.' Through case law, the European Court of Justice and the European Commission are in the process of developing rules which are an attempt to balance the need to protect national intellectual property rights with the need to ensure free trade between the member states. The most important of these rules is the doctrine of 'the exhaustion of rights', which is that once the patentee or copyright or trade secret owner has put the goods protected by his rights on the market in any of the member states, he can no longer control what happens to those goods, in particular he cannot prevent their importation into another of the member states. Individual cases have led to refinements of this doctrine, which cannot be gone into here, but it remains a keystone in the European Commission's thinking on the subject.

As noted above, art. 85(3) provides for exemption from the provisions of the rest of the article. The European Commission is the only body empowered to grant such exemption. Exemption is applied for by a procedure called 'notification'. The Commission has also established a procedure for getting advice that a particular agreement does not fall within arts 85 and 86, called 'negative clearance'. The main advantage of notification is that, until an exemption is either granted or refused, the parties cannot be fined under the enforcement provisions enacted under art. 87. Its main disadvantage is that the procedure usually takes a considerable period, sometimes years, during which the legality of the agreement is in doubt. In order to relieve the considerable burden placed on the Commission by the notification procedure, certain common types of restrictive provisions in certain common types of contracts have been granted a block exemption without the need for notification. Currently the Commission is in the final stages of preparing a Regulation relating to patent licences which will provide for block exemptions for licences which contain only certain provisions. This is a complicated area in which expert legal advice should be sought.

An outline of the EEC provisions affecting the six types of computer contract considered in respect to American law is as follows:

(a)   Sale of patented or copyrighted goods. The doctrine of exhaustion of rights prevents any post-sale restrictions.

(b)   Patent licences. Virtually all patent licences are currently notifiable, as the block exemption Regulation is not yet in effect. However, it is advisable to make such licences conform to the provisions of the latest draft of the Regulation.

(c)   Trade-secret licences. The European Court and the Commission have so far taken a much less positive attitude to trade secrets than the current American judicial attitude. The draft patent licence Regulation contains some provisions relating to trade secrets — in practice the two are often licensed together.

(d) Copyright licences. There are no special regulations in existence or proposed for copyright licences. The doctrine of exhaustion of rights applies to copyright (*Deutsche Grammophon Gesellschaft mbH* v *Metro-SB-Grossmärkte GmbH & Co. KG* [1971] CMLR 631).

(e) Distributorship agreements. While exclusive distributorships for one country are permissible, there can be no provisions preventing the distributor exporting to another member state or indirectly attempting to prevent parallel imports into that distributor's territory. Regulation 67/67/EEC provides for a block exemption for certain provisions commonly found in distributorship agreements provided the provisions of the Regulation are complied with.

(f) Joint venture agreements. European jurisprudence has not so far developed the horizontal/vertical distinction of American antitrust, and joint ventures which do not involve an actual merger are treated in the same way as other agreements under art. 85. There is not at present any Regulation covering joint ventures, so agreements must be individually notified for exemption.

In conclusion, antitrust and competition law is a minefield, and the consequences of charging through it ignoring the hazards can be almost as dangerous as doing the same thing through a real minefield. In the United States, antitrust violations can result in the criminal prosecution of officers of the corporation as well as the corporation itself, with the possibility of severe fines and imprisonment, and they can also result in lengthy and expensive civil litigation with the prospect of the award of large damages, which are then trebled, and having to pay the plaintiff's attorney's fees. It has not yet been established whether an individual has a civil right of action under the EEC competition rules, although the House of Lords accepted for the purposes of interlocutory injunction proceedings that there is such a right in the UK; *Garden Cottage Foods Ltd* v *Milk Marketing Board* [1984] AC 130, HL. However, the European Commission has power to enforce those rules by imposing stiff fines on offenders.

WHICH LAW GOVERNS?

When parties to a contract fall out and find that they are unable to resolve their differences amicably, they normally seek some outsider to resolve their dispute. This outsider can be a court, invoked through litigation, or an arbitrator chosen in some way by the parties. In deciding this dispute, it may be necessary for the judge or arbitrator to apply the general law of contract. Even before getting to this stage, it will also be necessary to decide which tribunal should hear the case and decide the dispute. When both parties are located in the same legal jurisdiction, these matters are easy to decide; the applicable law will be that of that particular jurisdiction, and that law will determine which court in that jurisdiction should try the case (this is called 'venue' by lawyers). The governing jurisdiction is often called the 'forum'.

For the non-lawyers reading this, it should be pointed out that a 'legal jurisdiction' is not necessarily the same thing as a country. For example, the United Kingdom is made up of three jurisdictions, England and Wales, Scotland and Northern Ireland. Scotland is not even a common-law jurisdiction, as the other two are; its law is based on Roman law, although certain statutory law is the same for all the United Kingdom. In countries with federal constitutions, such as the United States, Canada and the Federal Republic of Germany, each constituent state is a separate legal jurisdiction.

When the parties are not located in the same jurisdiction, obvious problems arise in the event of a dispute. Who is to decide the dispute, where, and applying which general law? Each established legal system has developed its own set of rules for deciding such matters, known as 'conflict of laws'. However, there are considerable disadvantages to relying solely upon the operation of these rules. Firstly, the parties may dispute which is the proper forum to decide which law shall apply, because the rules relating to conflicts of laws differ depending on the jurisdiction applying the rules. Once the case has been brought before a court, that court must conduct a judicial inquiry to determine which law should apply, which can be expensive and time-consuming. Even then, it is possible that that court may, under the conflict of laws rules of the jurisdiction it is in, decide that venue is properly elsewhere, so that the case must be restarted in a different jurisdiction, which may then proceed to apply its own conflict of laws rules . . . and so on.

Many of these problems can be avoided by the parties agreeing on which law should apply to their contract, and which tribunal should resolve the dispute. However, human nature being what it is, if the parties wait until a dispute has actually arisen before attempting to decide these matters, the chance of their reaching an agreement is reduced, and indeed agreement may be impossible. Obviously, it is better if agreement is reached at the outset, and made part of any written contract.

The laws of most industrialised countries allow the parties to a contract to stipulate in that contract which law should govern the terms of the agreement, known as the 'proper law of the agreement'. There are a few general exceptions to this freedom; the most common exceptions are as follows:

(a) Parties to a truly domestic contract, that is, parties located in the same jurisdiction, cannot avoid their own law by stipulating that their contract should be governed by some other law, unless there is some compelling reason why that other law should apply. For example, two English companies would not normally be allowed to choose to have their contract governed by the law of Malaysia, but this might be a valid provision if the contract is to be wholly performed in Malaysia.

(b) The forum court in which they bring the dispute may refuse to apply the chosen law unless it has some reasonable connection with the parties or their contract. British courts apply this rule, as do United States courts under the Uniform Commercial Code, or when the law of the state concerned follows the *Restatement* rules (Restatement (Second) of Conflict of Laws).

(c) The forum court may refuse to honour the parties' choice of law on the grounds of public policy.

(d) The law of the country of one of the parties may vitiate a choice of law in certain circumstances; for example, Belgian law provides that any Belgian distributor whose distributorship is wrongly terminated may sue the manufacturer in Belgian courts under Belgian law, regardless of any choice of venue or choice of law contained in the distribution agreement.

How to choose a law to govern the contract? First of all, it should be a choice which is likely to be upheld by the courts of any likely forum. This means that, at least, the law chosen should have some reasonable connection with the parties or the contract. Normally the law chosen is that of one of the parties to the contract. In the case where one party is also a party to a number of other contracts almost identical in form, such as a licensor, or the manufacturer in a distribution agreement, it is reasonable for that party to insist that all such contracts be governed by the same law, its own. This means that, if one of these contracts is litigated and a particular provision found to be invalid, it will be easy for all the other contracts to be amended accordingly. Normally the stronger of the parties insists on its own law, but there are circumstances where this may not be a wise choice. If the forum is to be a different country from that whose law governs, there is a danger that the foreign forum will misunderstand or misapply the governing law, particularly if different languages are involved. In many countries, including England and the United States, foreign law is a question of fact, to be decided by evidence. If there is no evidence about what the foreign law provides, it is assumed to be the same as the law of the forum. Also, where a party from a major industrialised country is dealing with a party from a Third World country, insistence on the law of the industrialised country may be regarded as a slight on the legal system of the Third World country. This could sour relationships with the government of that country as well as with the party, and there is a chance that the courts of that country may disregard the provision as being unconscionable or contrary to public policy.

In conclusion, in most cases it is highly desirable that the contract specify which law it is to be governed by, but it is not possible to lay down hard and fast rules about the choice of that law. Each party should carefully consider, before discussing the matter in negotiations, which law would best serve its interests as a whole, and how flexible it can afford to be in negotiating this subject.

WHO SHOULD DECIDE DISPUTES?

The best answer to this question is: if possible, the parties themselves. Unfortunately, this is often impossible, and it becomes necessary for the dispute to be referred to a third party for decision.

The traditional third party, provided for by all legal systems, is a court of law, and litigation is in general the only method of resolving the dispute unless the parties agree otherwise. A particular jurisdiction may provide that some other method must be tried first, for example, in the United Kingdom, disputes relating to employment contracts must first be heard by an industrial tribunal; in California, all lawsuits in which the primary relief sought is damages of less than $15,000 must go to arbitration. Such provisions do not in general remove the right to a hearing by a court of law, but merely delay it in the hope that the earlier proceedings will satisfy the parties.

The main alternative to litigation is arbitration. In order for arbitration to be the exclusive method of dispute resolution, and for it to be binding, it must be agreed to by both parties. This agreement can occur at the time the dispute arises, but for the same reasons that choice of law should be made at the outset, so a provision for arbitration, if desired, should be included in the written contract.

Before inserting an arbitration clause into a contract it is necessary to find out whether the governing law permits and enforces such a provision. Most nations with significant commercial interests do provide for the validity of arbitration clauses because arbitration is a common method of settling disputes in trading and shipping contracts. It is also necessary to investigate whether an arbitral award obtained by either party would be enforceable against the other. If the arbitration is held in the jurisdiction of the losing party, then the laws of that jurisdiction will normally provide for a method of enforcement. If it is held elsewhere, the award will only be enforceable if the losing party is subject to a jurisdiction which will enforce foreign arbitration awards through some treaty provision. Most industrialised nations do have some provision for enforcement of foreign awards.

The major advantages of arbitration over litigation are as follows:

(a) Arbitration proceedings are held in private and the oral and documentary evidence produced by the parties is not open to public scrutiny — this is particularly useful if trade secrets or other confidential information is involved.

(b) Arbitration is by nature a conciliatory proceeding, as opposed to the adversarial nature of litigation — this can be important if the parties are to have a continuing relationship after the resolution of the dispute in question.

(c) It is possible to select as arbitrator a person who has knowledge of the particular commercial or technical issues involved. This can save a great deal of time and effort otherwise required to educate a non-specialised tribunal — and most judges are non-specialised. This is particularly useful in the computer industry. If the arbitration is to be heard by a panel of arbitrators, then it is usual to select at least one lawyer and one technical person.

(d) Arbitration is almost always quicker than litigation, and it may also be less expensive.

(e) The timing and location of the hearings can be arranged to suit the parties — this can result in a considerable saving of money both in the time of valuable employees and in lawyers' fees.

There are also some disadvantages to arbitration which should be kept in mind when deciding whether to insert an arbitration clause. The major disadvantages are as follows:

(a)   The law of the relevant jurisdiction may not permit certain issues to be arbitrated, which could effectively prevent the rest of the dispute from being resolved by arbitration; for example, United States courts have tended to hold that matters which could affect the public interest, such as antitrust or patent validity, cannot be decided privately by arbitration. (It should be noted that United States patent law was amended on 27 August 1982 to include a section, 35 USC s. 294, which provided for voluntary and binding arbitration of patent validity or infringement. It will be interesting to see what the courts will do with this when it comes before them.)

(b)   The law of the relevant jurisdiction, while permitting voluntary arbitration, may not allow such arbitration to be binding even if the parties agree to this. English courts have tended to resist any attempt to deprive them of the right to review decisions on points of law made by arbitrators.

(c)   The informality of the arbitration hearing means that the rules of evidence are rarely followed, which can result in the introduction of unreliable evidence. This could be particularly dangerous in the case of a single arbitrator who is not a lawyer.

(d)   The arbitrator is not bound to decide the case on strict legal principles, and there is a tendency for awards to be made on the grounds of what is 'fair', or on the basis of compromise, which may be a satisfactory method when the dispute is purely factual but is clearly unsatisfactory when a point of law or contract interpretation is at issue.

(e)   In small cases the cost of arbitration may be higher than the cost of litigation, because in arbitration the parties must bear the full cost of the hearing, including the arbitrator's fee, whereas the costs of a court hearing, such as provision of a room and the judge's salary, are largely borne by the state.

(f)   In a complicated case, arbitration need not be speedier than litigation, largely because arbitrators are usually unable to spend more than one or two days at a time hearing a case as they are people with a business or profession of their own to attend to. Because of difficulties in arranging hearing dates convenient to all concerned, a lengthy hearing may be spread out over several months, whereas a court trial is normally heard continuously until the hearing is completed.

(g)   There are usually no provisions for pre-hearing discovery of the other party's evidence — this may be an advantage or a disadvantage, depending on the circumstances!

Most jurisdictions require an arbitration clause to be mutual to be enforceable. It should also be possible that a party may be held to have waived a right to arbitration under an arbitration clause by its actions, such as filing a pleading in response to the commencement of litigation by the other party.

The clause should provide for the method of arbitration, and for the place where the arbitration is to take place. A common method for providing for the former is to specify that the arbitration is to take place under the rules of a recognised organisation providing arbitration facilities. In the case of international contracts, it may be best to specify the rules of the International Chamber of Commerce (ICC), which are widely accepted. As to place, in general it is best to select a major commercial centre (so that suitable arbitrators will be readily available) in the jurisdiction whose law governs the contract. In certain circumstances, however, it may be necessary to provide for the arbitration to take place in a neutral country — for example, when contracting with quasi-governmental entities in a totalitarian state.

In the event that no provision for binding arbitration is included, it is desirable to specify the forum for any litigation between the parties concerning the contract. This will normally be the courts of the jurisdiction whose law is the governing law, as such courts are best able to apply that law. It is desirable to make it clear that the parties' intention is that the chosen forum should apply the chosen law. Suitable clauses can be found in Chapter 6.

In conclusion, the decision whether to include a provision for binding arbitration of contract disputes is one which can only be made in the light of all the circumstances. It is probably desirable from the point of view of the supplier of hardware or software in any computer contract because it will make it possible to have the dispute decided by at least one person who is familiar with the technology and the industry concerned. This will be an important consideration until a new, computer-literate generation grows up when it will be as usual for judges, juries and lawyers to understand computers as it now is for them to understand cars.

TECHNOLOGY TRANSFER TO COMMUNIST COUNTRIES

Anyone contemplating entering a contract involving the transfer of any kind of high technology or technical information to an entity in a Communist country should be aware that there may be particular problems with such a contract which are not present in other cases.

The first possible problem may arise from the action of a Western government. Most of the countries in the industrialised, non-Communist world have some regulations governing transfer of technology to the Communist world. It is impossible to be more specific here, because such regulations vary from country to country, and are usually drafted in very detailed, technical language. Also, these regulations can vary from time to time for any one country, depending on changes in the political climate; for example, until the normalisation of relations between the USA and China it was not possible to export American goods or to give American technology to the People's Republic of China, but now such export of goods and information is possible, subject to certain limitations. Other regulations may be imposed to deal with a temporary crisis, such as the embargo placed by the American government in 1982 on the export of certain goods to Russia in response to the imposition of martial law in Poland. Before entering negotiations for the sale of computers and related goods, or the transfer of related information and technology, to an entity in a Communist country you should check the latest regulations put out by your government. If the goods or technology originated, even in part, from another country, you should also check the terms of the contract under which you acquired them. You may find that you are obliged to abide by the export regulations of the originating country if you re-export the goods or technical information. This is certainly true of goods and information originating from the USA.

It is important that you make these checks *before* you start negotiating with the other party, and, if the negotiations are prolonged, again before you sign the written contract, so that you are not placed in the position of finding that you are unable to deliver what you have promised because its export to that particular country is forbidden. You should also be sure to include in the contract a provision exempting you from liability if, at a later time, performance becomes impossible because of a new government regulation. Such a provision is often included in what is usually called a '*force majeure*' clause, see Chapter 6 for further discussion of such clauses.

The next problem may arise from the laws and regulations of the country with which you are dealing. While the governments of such countries are usually anxious to obtain computer goods and technology from the West, they are often reluctant to pay for it in the so-called 'hard' currencies. It may therefore be difficult to negotiate for payment in such currency, and, even if such payment is agreed to, it may be difficult to obtain payment. In a number of recent cases the Western company has agreed to take payment in kind from the Communist country in order to avoid some of these problems. Advice on this type of problem may be obtained from the department of your government concerned with trade and exports, or from national chambers of commerce and similar bodies.

If you are relying on patent, copyright or trade secret protection for the items you are proposing to export, you should be aware that the protection available under these intellectual property rights in Communist countries is usually limited and may be non-existent. This is something else that should be investigated before commencing negotiations, and its impact on your rights elsewhere discussed with a lawyer specialising in this area.

It is an essential part of the Communist system that the government controls most aspects of the structure of society. This means that, in any Communist country, the commercial entity you are dealing with is controlled to some extent by the government. It also means that the courts of that country are controlled by that same government. It is therefore important to try to get agreement that any dispute concerning the contract is decided somewhere other than in those courts. In the likely event that the other party will not agree to have the dispute resolved in your country, you should try to get agreement on some neutral, but commercially developed country. Switzerland is a common choice, although, as Swiss law varies from canton to canton, either Geneva or Zurich should be specified. This is a case where you may wish to insist on an arbitration provision, rather than being faced with litigation in a strange court system. The choice of governing law should also be carefully considered; the law of the Communist country is likely to be unfavourable to you. If you cannot insist on your own law you should try to have the law of a neutral, industrialised country instead. If you have provided for resolution of disputes in a particular country, it is obviously sensible to provide that the law of that country shall govern the contract.

TECHNOLOGY TRANSFER TO THIRD WORLD COUNTRIES

In this section, the term 'Third World countries' is used to denote those countries which are not presently highly industrialised. It is not possible, without making this book twice as long and twice as expensive, to go into details of the particular laws, regulations and trading outlook of each of the nations forming part of this group, so this section will give merely a general overview of things anyone seeking to deal with entities in such countries should be aware of. As with all generalisations, not all of what is said here is necessarily true of any particular country. Anyone considering dealings with foreign countries, and this is true for other industrialised nations as well, should first investigate as far as possible the laws, regulations and trading conditions in that country. This information can often be obtained from the department of your government concerned with trade, or from the trade mission of your country's embassy in the country in which you are interested.

Third World governments have increasingly realised that what they require from the developed countries is the technology and know-how needed to develop their own industries, rather than aid in the form of food or money. This realisation has led to the drafting of a proposed International Code of Conduct on the transfer of technology. This drafting was done through UNCTAD, the United Nations agency concerned with fostering international trade. Not all of the provisions of this code have yet been agreed upon, in particular many of the industrialised nations are objecting to provisions which could lead to the forfeiture of industrial property rights owned by their subjects, and to the characterisation of certain widely accepted business practices as restrictive and therefore invalid. The code is mainly aimed at the concerns of the developing countries to be free from economic colonialism, and their fear of the multinational corporations (some of which, it must be admitted, are wealthier than many nations). Its major provisions are as follows:

(a)   The code would cover a very wide range of transactions, even those between industrialised nations.

(b)   States would have the right to regulate and control the flow and effects of technology transactions between their nationals and nationals of other countries. This right to regulate would include regulations designed to ensure social and economic national goals.

(c)   Approximately 20 business practices would be prohibited as being restrictive. Most of these practices are already condemned by developed systems of competition law, such as that of the EEC and US antitrust law. Examples of such practices are price fixing, tying, post-contractual restrictions. Others are more controversial as they are generally permitted under established competition law. These provisions would prohibit requirements of quality control and use of the licensor's trade marks and quantity or field-of-use restrictions. The government of the recipient country has the power to accept an agreement containing one or more of these prohibited practices on political or economic grounds if it considers the agreement will have no overall adverse consequences.

(d) An international machinery would be set up to monitor and promote the transfer of technology to the Third World from the industrialised nations.

(e) Provisions aimed at controlling abuse of a dominant position are proposed. While these are mainly aimed at the multinational corporations, they would also apply to government cartels such as OPEC.

Another international body under the UN concerned with technology is WIPO, the World Intellectual Property Organisation. Most countries are members of an international union for the protection of intellectual property rights, established by a treaty called the Paris Convention. Under WIPO, amendments to this Convention have been proposed and are currently being discussed at various international meetings. These amendments are largely aimed at helping the developing countries by making it easier for their nationals to acquire and retain technology and its associated property rights. The proposal which is being most strongly resisted by the developed countries is one that a patent should be forfeit for failure to work the invention within four years from grant of the patent, or that a compulsory licence could be granted after 30 months of non-working after grant, or for 'abuse' of the patent. Many people feel that such draconian provisions will work to the disadvantage of the developing nations, because companies in fields where it takes a long time to get a patented product on the market, such as the pharmaceutical industry, will simply refrain from applying for patents in developing countries or from licensing the patented technology to such countries.

While neither the Code of Conduct nor the amendments to the Paris Convention has been agreed, you should be aware that many developing countries are setting up their own laws and regulations which have similar effects. There are also some regional agreements which control restrictive business practices and which may require agreements to be reviewed and approved by the relevant government body. An example of such an agreement is the ANCOM agreement, setting up the Andean Common Market, comprising Bolivia, Columbia, Ecuador, Venezuela and Peru. One practice prohibited by the ANCOM and some other South American nations is the payment of royalties by a national subsidiary to its foreign parent.

Many of the comments made in the section on dealing with Communist countries also apply to dealing with Third World countries. In particular, there are usually exchange controls, and government reluctance to allow royalties to be paid in hard currency. Many governments also limit the amount of royalties that can be paid to foreign licensors, so it may require considerable creativity for the foreign licensor to obtain a proper return on his investment. Beside the possibility of payment in kind, mentioned above, you may also be able to increase your return by the supply of components or services, or by acquiring equity in the licensee's business.

5   General Principles of Negotiation

It is possible to negotiate to some extent over the terms of almost any contract. The degree of negotiability naturally varies considerably, from clause-by-clause negotiation with the parties in roughly equal positions to negotiations over cash as opposed to credit price in a retail sale. In computer terms, the purchaser of a large mainframe system or an extensive custom-designed software system should have wide powers of negotiation, the purchaser of a piece of standard software or a box of diskettes is unlikely to be able to improve his position other than by shopping around for the best price. The purpose of this chapter is not to go into details of negotiating strategies and methods, those wishing to know more about this subject should read one or more of the many books on the market dealing with these topics. Rather, the purpose of this chapter is to point out how some of these general principles apply to the negotiation of computer contracts at home and abroad.

HOW TO PLAN FOR NEGOTIATIONS

It is assumed that you have done all the initial planning and investigation, and have decided what type of system, hardware and/or software, you require. It is also assumed that this is a sufficiently substantial transaction to make negotiations over contract terms possible. You are now investigating possible vendors who can supply your needs. Many people do not think about the negotiation process until after they have selected a vendor, but to achieve best results planning for negotiations should begin at this earlier stage.

When contacting potential vendors for quotations or tenders, you should also ask for a copy of that vendor's standard form of contract for the transaction. This should be carefully studied to identify terms and conditions which would be contrary to your interests. For example, are there limitations on the vendor's liability for the quality or performance of the items supplied? If there are such limitations, and it is almost certain that any standard form contract will seek to restrict the vendor's liability to the utmost extent allowed by the relevant law, the risk arising from such limitation should be assessed by calculating your loss in the worst possible case. The same type of risk analysis should be done in respect of each clause which is to your disadvantage. You should then investigate the attitude of each potential vendor to such clauses, and the likelihood that such clauses can be altered by negotiation, by sending each of them a 'contract specification', which sets out the terms you would like to see in the contract and asking the vendor's reaction to each of them. Your selection of a vendor should be based on its reaction to crucial contract provisions as well as the terms of its tender. Saving money by taking the lowest tender may prove to be very expensive if that vendor insists on a severe restriction of its liability and it then fails to perform.

Obviously, the more competition there is for your business, the easier it is to persuade a vendor to negotiate rather than insisting on its own contractual terms and conditions. In the case of custom software development, in particular, it is often not possible to obtain a large number of quotations before selecting a vendor. This is because in most cases it will be necessary for the potential vendor to do a lot of preliminary research into your requirements before it can give a meaningful quotation for the work to be done, and the vendor usually requires to be paid for this preliminary investigation, with the cost deducted from the contract price if it is awarded the contract. While it would seem that this problem can be avoided or minimised by having just one preliminary investigation done and asking all the vendors to quote on the basis of this investigation, this may cause problems later if the selected vendor is not the one who made the investigation. This is because there are many ways to produce the same result when writing software, and information relevant to the method of working of one software house may be meaningless or even misleading to another software producer.

Having selected a vendor who is prepared to negotiate, detailed preparations for negotiations should begin. The differences between each of the vendor's contract terms and its equivalent in your contract specifications should be analysed, and the maximum compromise between the two which is commercially acceptable to you should be determined. This compromise is your fall-back position, beyond which you should not go in the heat of a negotiating session. If the vendor will not come up to this position on any particular clause, your negotiators should leave the clause for further consideration, and a decision about whether further compromise is acceptable or whether negotiations should be started with another vendor who is likely to be more flexible in this respect should be taken after full consideration. It is of assistance to have analysed each clause beforehand for its relative potential risk, so that it may be possible to achieve your objective for major-risk clauses by using your agreement to accept the vendor's position on lesser-risk clauses as a trade-off.

You should also investigate, as far as possible, the background of the people who are to negotiate on behalf of the vendor. Are any of these people in a sufficiently senior position to be able to bind the vendor by their agreement, or will all positions reached during the negotiations have to be referred back to higher-level management for decision? This is an unsatisfactory position, but if it cannot be avoided you should be careful that no binding agreements are made on your side during the actual negotiations. Will a lawyer be present for the vendor? If so, you would be well advised to have your own lawyer present. Will a very senior member of the vendor's management be present? If so, you should ensure that a similarly senior member of your organisation is there. You should also try to determine who will be leading their team, if more than one person is involved. Similarly, if you use a team of negotiators you should ensure that the leader is designated in advance and that each member understands his relevant role. There have been too many examples of technicians giving away points which required a business rather than a technical analysis and which a manager or business person would not have conceded.

FOREIGN NEGOTIATIONS

Everything that has been said so far in this chapter applies to all negotiations, whether at home or abroad. There are further factors to take into consideration when negotiating contracts with a foreign organisation, and even better planning is required if the contract that results from the negotiations is to be the satisfactaory basis for a successful business relationship. These factors differ from country to country, and only some general guidelines can be given here.

The overseas negotiator will only be successful if he or she can realise how much each one of us is influenced by the culture in which we were brought up. We all have attitudes, values, assumptions and prejudices which, although we may not realise it, are the product of our cultural environment, shared by all or most people brought up in the same culture, but which are not shared by people from other cultures. Unless the negotiator is sensitive to cultural differences, serious misunderstandings can result, or even serious offence may be given unconsciously, souring the business relationship from the start or even causing a breakdown of the negotiations. Therefore an important part of planning for overseas negotiations is an investigation of the culture and customs of the people with whom you will be negotiating. There may, of course, be little or no difference; a British businessperson should have few problems of this sort dealing with an Australian, a New Zealander, an English-speaking Canadian or an American. On the other hand, a person from any of those countries will have many problems dealing with a Japanese, even a Japanese who speaks English very well, unless they are aware of the many differences between the two cultures. Because Japan is such an important economic power, further consideration is given below to factors which should be taken into account when negotiating with a Japanese organisation.

The negotiator must also have some understanding of the political and economic systems of the country concerned, particularly in the case of Third World and Communist countries. It is important to have good advice on these matters, and also to visit the country for yourself to understand the problems at first hand. It may be necessary, in order to do any business at all, to have an agent in the country who has influential contacts and who can act as a go-between to work with the individuals in government whose approval of business deals is required.

A common problem is that of bribery. This is another area where cultural differences may cause serious misunderstandings. Some payments to officials, which may appear to be bribery to someone from Britain or America, may be regarded in the country concerned as a normal part of that official's pay, and the payments are made at an accepted rate. This is morally no different from the custom of tipping a waiter or a taxi-driver at a rate set by custom such as 10%; in some countries, such as Singapore, such tipping, widely accepted in the West as a part of that person's normal emolument, is illegal. There is no doubt, however, that in many countries morally unacceptable bribery occurs, to the extent in some cases that business cannot be done without it. The foreigner must then make a moral as well as a business decision, being aware that indulging in such practices abroad may make him liable to prosecution or adverse publicity in his home country.

NEGOTIATING WITH THE JAPANESE

In Anglo-American culture, negotiation is seen as an adversarial process, with both sides manoeuvring for the best position. The development of an on-going business relationship occurs once the contract is completed and operating. This is not true in Japan. Japanese culture places great stress on compromise and the avoidance of conflict, and on the development and maintenance of harmonious relationships. One result of this is that Japanese are taught to conceal strong emotions (leading to their reputation as 'inscrutable'), and politeness demands that you say what you think your listener would like to hear. Those familiar with the conventions of the culture are able to understand the speaker's true meaning through subtle signals, but those raised in a culture which stresses open speaking, and this is particularly true of Americans, may completely misunderstand the speaker, who himself does not realise that the misunderstanding has occurred.

This emphasis on harmony means that, to the Japanese, the purpose of negotiations is to build a business relationship, rather than to stake out territory and establish positions as it is in adversarial negotiations. It also results in the traditional Japanese dislike for lawyers and for resolution of disputes by litigation. Therefore, if you are a lawyer negotiating with Japanese on behalf of a client, it is necessary to stress that your role is to facilitate the transaction and that you are not taking an adversarial position. This emphasis on harmony also explains the importance attached by the Japanese to social contacts between business associates, with extensive entertaining in restaurants and night-clubs. The Japanese regard these periods as an important part of the negotiating process, and you should do so too if you want the negotiations to succeed.

It is widely known that the Japanese have an elaborate system of social hierarchy and courtesies. It is important to know the position of the person or persons you are dealing with in the hierarchy of that organisation, and never to show more respect or favour to a person lower in that hierarchy than you do to his superior. One important business ritual is the exchange of business cards at the beginning of the first meeting. These business cards should be of very good quality, engraved on one side in Japanese and on the other in English or your own language.

Although most Japanese learn English at school, this teaching lays most stress on reading and writing, and many have problems with the spoken language. It is advisable, whenever possible, to conduct negotiations in Japanese using an interpreter, unless the person with whom you are dealing is really comfortable in English.

Virtually all contracts involving computer technology will require approval of some sort from the relevant government ministry. Ministry officials are often involved in negotiations at an advisory level. Usually this advice is given to the Japanese party, but you should get an independent check on the advice being given if you are being pressed to make major concessions on the grounds that the ministry has advised that this is necessary to get approval for the contract.

NEGOTIATING WITH DEVELOPING COUNTRIES

In dealing with one of the developing countries, sometimes referred to as the 'Third World', it is particularly important to be familiar with the political and economic system of that country, and also to have some knowledge of its recent history. It may be necessary to have very different contractual provisions in a country that has a relatively stable political system from those needed in a country which has a history of repeated political coups. The more distant past may also be important if that past included a colonial period. Most former colonies are very sensitive to anything that appears to be economic colonialism, and the Western businessperson must be careful not to rely too heavily on using a superior technological position as leverage to extract major concessions in the negotiating process. This could lead to government interference, refusal of approval, and will certainly sour business relations between the parties. It is also necessary to take into account the various exchange control and other problems outlined in Chapter 4 in deciding on desirable contractual provisions.

6 General Principles of Contract Preparation

Some people write contracts the way they write letters to their friends — they put things down as they think of them, repeat themselves once or twice, and assume that the reader will have the same background of knowledge that they have and will know what they mean. After all, the parties to the contract have been negotiating for some time, they know what they agreed and what the terms they are using mean, don't they? Unfortunately, people who write contracts in this way overlook one vital fact; contracts are not intended to be read by the parties who reached the agreement enshrined in the written contract, but by outsiders affected by the contract and by judges and arbitrators called in to decide disputes between the parties, and these people determine what the parties agreed by what they read in the document purporting to contain the terms of that agreement.

Therefore, a good contract should be written in such a way that a complete outsider can pick up the document and determine whether the parties had provided for the event that has taken place or whether they agreed to a particular thing, without undue effort, and without any reasonable possibility of coming to a conclusion which is not what the parties themselves intended when they made their agreement.

The main purpose of this chapter is to set out some of the ground rules of contract preparation. The existence of rules does not mean that you have to suppress your own natural style of writing, or that there is only one way to write contracts. Instead, think of the rules as a basic framework, which will give stability and structure, to be filled in in accordance with your own style and preferences.

The chapter will also consider how to use precedents to the best advantage, and will discuss some of the standard clauses, called 'boilerplate' in the USA, which are useful in almost any type of contract.

PLANNING THE CONTENTS

There are two stages to planning: the first is to ensure that the parties'
agreement is as complete as possible or as is practicable in the
circumstances, and the second is to ensure that what they have agreed is
set out logically and completely in the written contract.

How to make sure the agreement is complete

While optimists make the best deal makers, pessimists make the best
contract writers. To ensure that the agreement is as complete as possible,
you have to foresee what could go wrong, and make provision for it. Of
course, some disasters are unforeseeable but the law provides for such
catastrophes under the doctrine of frustration. In fact, this crystal-ball
gazing must go wider than things going wrong; you must also think
through each step of the things that the parties will have to do in
performing their obligations, and ensure that the mechanics of
performance have been provided for. If agreement is for a
manufacturing licence, how and when are the royalties to be paid, what
happens if a payment is late, what happens if the licensee goes bankrupt,
if he just loses interest and does not sell any licensed items?

This careful step-by-step analysis at the outset should preferably be
performed by someone other than the persons who have negotiated the
deal itself. This is particularly true where the negotiators are the people
who will carry it out. There is a natural tendency on the part of such
people to get on with this exciting new business opportunity and to leave
the details to be 'ironed out' as they go along. Unfortunately, while this
may work while the parties have a close working relationship, and none
of the things to be 'ironed out' has an adverse effect on only one of the
parties, sooner or later a wrinkle too convoluted to be smoothed in this
way will arise. The parties' enthusiasm to get started on the deal must be
restrained long enough to cope with anticipated problems at the outset.
This is where the lawyer, as not involved with the implementation of the
deal but familiar with his client's business and with the course of the
negotiations, can be very useful.

Of course, the degree of crystal-ball gazing that needs to be done
depends greatly upon the nature and importance of the contract. The
purchase of a computer system for a large amount of money, upon which
the running of your business will depend, requires extensive and careful
thought about possible problems, because those problems could be
catastrophic. The purchase of an additional terminal for an existing

system does not. Similarly, in the software field, a contract for the custom development of a software system which will tie up a significant proportion of the manpower of a software house for a considerable period, and which could cause serious economic loss to the customer if it fails to function properly demands much more thought and care than a licence for a piece of standard, well established software. There is nothing to stop you taking great care over the provisions of any contract, but such care would not be cost-effective for the less important contracts.

How to ensure that the contract is complete

The written contract should not only contain everything that the parties agreed, it should also be possible to locate any particular term of that agreement without the need to read the whole document through several times. The key to achieving both goals is organisation and planning. You should expect to spend at least as much time preparing to write a contract as you spend actually writing it, and as much time again checking what you have written.

Following the steps set out below should ensure that the contract is as complete and orderly as it can reasonably be:

(a) Prepare a framework before you start to write any provisions.
(b) Define your terms.
(c) Put provisions in their place in the framework in some logical order.
(d) Check for completeness.
(e) Check for consistency.
(f) Whenever possible, have it reviewed by someone else.

Preparing a framework

The terms of any agreement can be arranged into a number of groups. Preparing the framework for the written contract involves determining what those groups are, and then arranging them in some logical order. For example, a software licence would probably have the following types of provisions:

(a) Rights granted and reserved by the licensor.
(b) Payment by the licensee.
(c) Protection of the licensor's property rights.

(d)   Warranties and exclusions of liability.
(e)   Maintenance of the software.
(f)   Termination of the licence.
(g)   Resolution of disputes.
(h)   General provisions.

A contract for the purchase of hardware, to give another example, typically has the following types of provisions:

(a)   Description of the goods sold.
(b)   Associated services provided.
(c)   Price and method of payment.
(d)   Delivery.
(e)   Maintenance.
(f)   Warranties and exclusions of liability.
(g)   Resolution of disputes.
(h)   General provisions.

You will observe that both of these frameworks follow a similar order; they start with what the parties exchange at the outset (licence for royalties, goods for cash or on credit), continue with things that are to occur during the normal running of the agreement (protection of licensor's copyright or trade secrets, warranties, maintenance) and then go on to the end or possible end of the agreement (termination, disputes resolution). It is traditional to put the general 'boilerplate' provisions at the end. While this is by no means the only logical order in which to set up the framework, it is recommended as the most common one, and the one most people find easiest to follow.

Define your terms

All but the most simple contracts should contain a definition section, preferably at the beginning of the contract so that the reader is aware that there are defined terms as he starts to read. There are two reasons why a contract should have definitions; first, to ensure that technical words or words used in a non-dictionary sense are understood by an outside reader and to deal with any possible ambiguities of meaning, and second, to provide a form of shorthand to make the body of the contract more readable.

The 'shorthand' definitions are a particularly useful device. Suppose, for instance, that the parties had a prior agreement to which it is necessary to refer in the new contract. In order to prevent uncertainty over which of the two agreements is being referred to at any point, it is necessary to give sufficient details to distinguish them without any possibility of ambiguity. Suppose the prior agreement was between the same parties, and was made on 31 January 1982; you could say, every time that agreement is referred to, 'the licence agreement made between the parties hereto on 31 January 1982'. However, it is much simpler and clearer to choose a shorthand term such as 'the 1982 Agreement', and state in the definition section that 'the 1982 Agreement means the licence agreement made between the parties hereto on 31 January 1982.' Once defined, you can use the shorthand term for each reference to that agreement in the body of the contract.

When you use a defined term, there should be a standard 'key' which will tell the reader that he is looking at a defined term; this is usually done by using capital letters for the initial letter or the whole word, or by putting the word in quotation marks. Whichever key you choose, you must use it consistently throughout the whole document.

Although the definition section should preferably come right at the beginning of the contract, it will not be the first thing you write. Instead, as you write the body of the contract, every time you use a word which needs to be defined for certainty or clarity, or you use a phrase more than once which could be conveniently expressed by a shorthand term, write that word or term with its definition on a separate piece of paper. When you have finished writing the contract, then arrange your complete set of definitions in some logical order (e.g., alphabetical, or in the order in which they first appear in the contract) and insert the complete list as a labelled 'definition section' wherever you have decided to put it in the contract.

Fill in the framework in logical order

Just as putting the organisational framework into a logical order helps the outside reader, so putting the provisions which go into each section of the framework in logical order also helps to give clarity. For example, a logical order for the provisions relating to royalties in a licence would be:

(a)   Amount to be paid.
(b)   Method of calculating that amount (e.g., if the royalty is to be

paid based on the price of goods sold by the licensee manufactured under the licence, is this the retail or the wholesale price, can the licensee deduct overhead costs, packaging and shipping costs, what about sales taxes?)

(c)   Frequency of payment of royalties.
(d)   Method of payment.
(e)   Accounting to the licensor.
(f)   Allowing the licensor to verify the licensee's royalty accounts.
(g)   Interest on late payments.
(h)   Effect of failure by licensee to make payments.

Using such an orderly procession of concepts not only helps the reader to understand and to find readily if provision has been made for a particular situation, it also helps the writer to ensure that he has not omitted any important terms.

One useful technique for keeping the contract clear and readable is the use of appendices. This is particularly useful when you wish to incorporate long, technical descriptions, such as the specifications of a software system, into a contract. Instead of writing the whole specification out in the main contract under a clause dealing with 'description of the system', put that specification in a separate document called 'Appendix X', refer to Appendix X at the appropriate point in the contract ('the specifications of the System are set out in Appendix X to this agreement') and attach it to the main agreement. This technique is also useful when you are preparing a standard form contract. Instead of leaving lengthy gaps to be filled in with the details which differ from transaction to transaction, refer at the appropriate points to appendices, which can then be separately prepared and attached to the standard form contract.

Check for completeness

When you think you have finished writing, you should then read what you have written carefully to check that it is complete. This is a double check; you must ensure that you have included all the terms that the parties actually agreed to, you must also check that there are no terms which should be included which were overlooked by the parties when they reached their agreement. It is often easier to spot such lacunae once the written agreement has come into existence than at the time the parties were negotiating. It is even easier to spot them if you have followed a logical order in writing the contract as suggested above. These omissions should be drawn to the parties' attention and dealt with before the contract is signed.

Check for consistency

Once the contract is complete, it must then be very carefully checked to ensure that it is internally consistent. This should include checking the following factors:

(a)   Are any of the provisions in any way inconsistent with any of the other provisions? You should particularly watch for provisions which, although not clearly inconsistent, create doubt about their relative effect when read together. For example, the section on payment may set out a schedule of provisions for payment of interest in the event of late payments, including payments several months late, while the termination section provides for termination in the event of any payment being more than 30 days late. Any potential conflict between the two provisions should be defused by an express provision that the option to terminate or to allow the contract to remain in existence and to collect interest lies with the party to whom the money is owed, and that failure to terminate on any particular occasion does not waive the right to terminate for late payment on any subsequent occasion.

(b)   Have defined terms been used in a consistent manner throughout the contract?

(c)   Where one clause refers to another clause, are the numbers right? This is particularly important where, as usually happens, changes have been made to the original draft, inserting or deleting provisions.

Review by another

The old adage 'two heads are better than one' is certainly true of contract writing. In all but the simplest contracts, a second, experienced reader, will almost always find something that the original writer has omitted. Also, it is much easier for someone coming fresh to the document to spot inconsistencies, ambiguities and unclear phrasing or terminology.

THE USE AND ABUSE OF PRECEDENTS

Although no two business deals may be exactly alike, in general most contracts of the same type contain similar provisions. Why, therefore, reinvent the wheel when there are already numerous contracts in existence which contain wording which will cover what you want to say?

There are two main sources of precedents for contract preparation which are used by lawyers: they may refer to similar contracts which they or individual colleagues have prepared on an earlier occasion, or they may use one or more of the published books of precedents which are available. These books fall into two types. The first contains very little text and numerous precedents, from which the user is left to select as he thinks appropriate. The second type tries to explain the principles behind the drafting of particular clauses and types of contract, and generally contains fewer precedents. This book comes within the latter category.

One of the main values of a proper use of precedents is that it saves time, and therefore expense. In most cases a factory-produced chair does the same job as a hand-carved one. Another good reason for using established precedents, especially for standard clauses, is that they will be familiar to the judge who has to interpret them. If that clause has been given a particular interpretation in one case, the operation of the doctrine of judicial precedent results in the same clause being given the same meaning in subsequent cases, wherever possible. This means that the parties can include that clause in their agreement with considerable certainty about how a court will subsequently interpret its meaning.

On the other hand, improperly used precedents can cause enormous problems. It is important to remember that a precedent can never be slavishly copied, it must always be carefully examined to ensure that it does provide exactly what the parties to this agreement intended. The use of precedents can save time, it can never save thought. It is also important to ensure that the precedent was prepared with the same law in mind as the law governing the agreement you are preparing, and that that law has not changed since the precedent was prepared. In the case of clauses which have already received judicial interpretation, it is important to know what that interpretation was.

GENERAL-PURPOSE PROVISIONS

There are a number of general-purpose provisions which apply to almost every type of contract. Most lawyers who regularly prepare contracts develop their own standard set. It is still important, however, to understand the effect of each of these provisions before incorporating them into a contract, as they may not all be appropriate. Therefore, the meaning and effect of the most commonly used general provisions are discussed below, then precedents for these provisions are given.

Term of the contract

Whenever a contract has continuing obligations, thought should be given to the length of time those obligations are to last, that is, the term of the contract. In some cases the length of the term is governed by law; for example, a patent licence cannot provide for payment for royalties for use of the patent after the patent has expired. Similarly, some types of agreement such as distribution or joint venture agreements may be invalid under antitrust or competition laws if they are for too long a period. This is a very tricky area, and anyone entering a contract with a potential competitor should seek advice from a lawyer specialising in this area of the law.

In some cases, it is desirable to make the contract for a relatively short term, which is renewable. The provisions for renewal should be clearly spelled out in the contract. It is usually desirable to have some sort of notice provision, for the sake of certainty. The period of such notice, particularly if it is of an intent not to renew, should be sufficient for the other party to have a reasonable opportunity to make alternative business arrangements.

Termination

Termination of a contract obviously occurs automatically on expiry of the term. However, in most cases it is desirable to give one or both parties the option to terminate the contract before expiry of the term upon the happening of certain events. Chapter 3 described how a sufficiently serious breach of contract by one party gives the other party a right to terminate the contract. However, because of the uncertainty of the application of this law to any particular facts, the contract should give an express right of termination if specified breaches occur.

(a) The licensor or the vendor should insist upon a right of termination in the event of non-payment of sums due under the contract after the expiry of a specified period after the due date for payment. There should also be a provision that failure to exercise this right in respect of any particular payment ('waiver') should not prevent its exercise in the event of a subsequent non-payment. The other party should make sure that this right of termination can only be exercised upon notice, to allow for the possibility of a payment being lost in transit.

(b)   There should also be a provision for termination upon breach of other obligations. This should provide that reasonable notice of the breach complained of must be given to the defaulting party, with termination only if the default is not cured before the expiry of the notice period. What is 'reasonable' will depend upon the particular circumstances. Where both parties have obligations under the contract, this right of termination should be mutual. It is also prudent to provide that this right of termination does not exclude any other remedy given to the injured party by the relevant law.

(c)   It is also advisable to have a provision for termination upon the insolvency or bankruptcy of either party. Such a provision needs to be carefully drafted to ensure that it is in accord with the bankruptcy laws of the relevant jurisdiction. In particular, the present US bankruptcy law severely limits the right to terminate an executory contract upon bankruptcy.

A termination provision should also spell out what is to happen upon termination. For example, in the case of a software licence, provision for the return or destruction of all copies of source or object code in the licensee's possession or control should be made. It is also necessary to provide that certain obligations, especially the obligation to keep confidential information secret, survive the termination of the contract.

Recovery of property upon bankruptcy

In the UK a seller can provide that he retains property in the goods until they are paid for, even though the buyer has possession of them. This retention of title has been held to give the seller the right to recover the goods or the moneys received from their resale by the buyer, as against a receiver appointed when the buyer became insolvent. Such a clause, known as a 'Romalpa' clause from the name of the case in which this holding was made, *Aluminium Industrie Vaassen BV* v *Romalpa Aluminium Ltd* [1976] 1 WLR 676, should include an express provision that the buyer holds the goods as bailee for the seller. Even with such a provision, problems may arise from the doctrine of 'reputed ownership', which vests in the trustee in bankruptcy all goods which are apparently owned by the bankrupt in his trade or business. To get around these problems as far as possible, the contract should provide that any goods covered by the Romalpa clause should be stored and marked so as to indicate the seller's ownership, and that the proceeds of their sale should be put into a separate, earmarked account.

In the USA there is a possibility of providing for the impounding of goods not paid for until the provisions of the Bankruptcy Act, which provide protection for the seller, are complied with. There have not yet been any court decisions on the validity of such provisions.

Governing law

The question of the choice of law to govern a contract has been fully considered in Chapter 4.

Resolution of disputes

If there is no express provision, disputes between the parties will be resolved by the legal process of the governing jurisdiction. The full process of litigation is not a good way of solving disputes between the parties which are not so serious as to terminate the contract, nor is it well suited to resolving highly technical issues. The parties to a computer-related contract should always seriously consider providing for arbitration, which is fully discussed in Chapter 4.

Attorney's fees

In the United Kingdom the general rule is that the winner of litigation is paid a substantial proportion of his expenses of litigation, including what he has paid his lawyers, by the loser. In jurisdictions where there is no such rule, as in the United States, provision should be made for payment of attorney's fees in the event of litigation. It should be noted that, in a number of states, a provision that only one party will get attorney's fees if it wins is extended by statute to be mutual.

Force majeure

This clause covers what is to happen if events beyond the control of either party, such as government regulation, war or natural disasters, prevent performance of the contract. The most usual provision suspends the operation of the contract until the obstacle is removed, with a provision for optional termination if the suspension exceeds a specified period, or if the obstacle to performance is clearly permanent.

Notices

Whenever there is any provision in the contract which involves one party giving notice to the other, specific provision for the manner of giving the notice, and the address to which it should be sent, should be provided. As the general law provides that a notice takes effect upon mailing, unless non-receipt is proved, the parties for their own protection should provide in the contract for some form of notice which will come to the attention of the other party. This can be done by providing for service by a form of mail which provides for certificate of receipt, the notice not to be effective unless the sender receives such a certificate. In view of postal delays, especially in the case of international mail, the clause should also provide that the notice only becomes effective upon receipt, or after a specified number of days from the date of mailing in the approved manner.

Amendments

It is important to provide that the contract can only be amended in writing, signed by both parties. Otherwise, a considerable opportunity for misunderstanding can arise, as many written contracts can be validly amended orally.

Waiver

In view of the fact that rights arising from breach by one party can be waived by conduct as well as by words, there should be a provision that a waiver can only be relied upon by the breaching party if it is in writing. There should also be a provision that a waiver of one breach does not act as a waiver of any subsequent breach.

Assignment

The acceptability to one party of a right of assignment of the contract by the other party will depend upon the nature of the obligations of the assigning party. If they cannot be adequately undertaken by anyone else, there should be an express prohibition on assignment. Otherwise, assignment should only be allowed upon written notice and the prior consent of the party, such assent not to be unreasonably withheld. The governing law may provide for certain types of involuntary assignment, such as to a trustee in bankruptcy, which cannot be controlled by such clauses.

Integration

This clause provides that the written agreement is to be treated as the entire agreement between the parties, superseding all previous representations and negotiations. This clause is beneficial, particularly to vendors and licensors, as avoiding problems that may arise from a subsequent assertion by the other party that oral representations were made by salesmen or in brochures and have not been complied with. However, the presence of such a clause makes it particularly important that the written contract does, in fact, include the complete agreement between the parties.

Severability

Sometimes a provision of a contract may later be found to be illegal, or may have become illegal because of a subsequent change in the law. Because the law gives the courts a discretion whether to refuse to enforce the entire contract or the whole of a particular provision because part of the contract or provision is illegal, or merely to delete the invalid portion and enforce the rest, it is desirable to have an express provision that any provision or part of a provision found to be invalid is severable, and the rest remains enforceable.

Headings not controlling

Often, for the sake of clarity and ease of reading , a contract is drafted with brief descriptive headings to each clause or group of clauses. As these descriptions are necessarily brief, and therefore can be inaccurate, it is preferable to ensure that they cannot be used in interpreting the contract by an express provision to that effect.

PRECEDENTS

Term of the contract

Licence agreement
This Licence is effective from the date on which it is executed by the
parties, and shall remain in force until terminated by the Licensee upon
_____ months' written notice, or under the provisions of clause _____
[termination provisions] below.

Services agreement
This Agreement shall be for a term of _____, and either party shall have
the right to renew for a similar term by giving _____ months' written
notice to the other party prior to the expiry of the term.

[This provision has the disadvantage that it can tie an unwilling party
to the contract simply because the other party goes on renewing. If there
is a likelihood of this happening, the provision below would be better.
For further comments on renewal of service contracts, see Chapter 10].

This Contract shall be for a term of _____, and shall be automatically
renewed at the end of this term for a further term of _____ unless [the
supplier of services] gives at least _____ months' notice prior to the expiry
of the term of its intention to terminate to the [customer], or [the
customer] gives at least _____ days' notice prior to the expiry of the terms
of its intention not to renew to [the supplier].

Termination

Non-payment
This Agreement may be terminated by the Licensor [or Vendor] upon
_____ days' notice in the event of non-payment of all or any part of any
sum due under this Agreement unless full payment thereof is made
within the said notice period.

Other breaches
This Agreement may be terminated by either party upon _____ days'
notice in the event of a material breach by the other party of any of the
terms of this Agreement unless the breach is fully cured within the said
notice period.

Insolvency

UK, company   This Agreement may be terminated by either party upon 24 hours' notice if the other party has a receiver appointed of the whole or any substantial part of its assets, or if an order is made or a resolution is passed for the winding up of the other party, except where such winding up is for the purposes of amalgamation or reconstruction such that the company resulting (if a different legal entity) shall effectively agree to be bound by or assume the obligations of this Agreement and is a company to which the other party cannot reasonably object.

UK, individual   This Agreement may be terminated by either party upon 24 hours' notice if the other party has a receiver appointed of the whole or a substantial part of his assets or if he becomes bankrupt or has execution levied against him.

UK, partnership   This Agreement may be terminated by the Licensor upon 24 hours' notice if any of the partners of the Licensee partnership has a receiver appointed of the whole or a substantial part of his assets, becomes bankrupt, dissolves the partnership or has execution levied against him, except that in the case of dissolution of partnership the Licensor will not unreasonably withhold consent to the continuance of this Agreement with the remaining partners upon the same terms and conditions.

USA   This Agreement may be terminated by either party upon 24 hours' notice in the event that the other party shall be or become insolvent, cease doing business as a going concern, make an assignment for the benefit of its creditors, admit in writing its inability to pay its debts as they become due or if there are any proceedings instituted by or against it in bankruptcy or under the insolvency laws or for reorganisation, receivership or dissolution, except such proceedings as are mandatory on the part of the affected party and are terminated without prejudice to the other party within 60 days.

[Note that, under the present US Bankruptcy Act, the validity of this provision, at least once formal bankruptcy proceedings have commenced, is doubtful.]

Recovery of property upon bankruptcy

UK, Romalpa clause

The property in [the goods supplied under the Agreement] will not pass to the Buyer until the contract price has been paid in full. The Buyer will hold the Goods as a bailee for the Seller, and will store and mark the Goods so as to indicate clearly that they are the property of the Seller. Sums received by the Buyer from the sale [or lease] of the goods shall be placed in a separate account, clearly designated as being for this purpose.

USA, software lease or licence

This Agreement is executory in nature, and so long as Licensee has any continuing payment obligations hereunder, Licensor shall be entitled to protect its rights in the Software by impounding the same in the event of the bankruptcy or any similar event occurring to or involving Licensee. No trustee, receiver or debtor in possession shall have any right to retain copies of the Software nor to sell or license versions of it in any form, unless all of the provisions of 11 USC s. 365, part of the US Bankruptcy Act, have been complied with and Licensor adequately protected.

Governing law

The validity, construction and performance of this Agreement shall be governed by the law of ⎯⎯⎯.

Arbitration

Any controversy or claim arising out of, in connection with or relating to this Agreement or a breach of performance thereof, shall be resolved by binding arbitration in ⎯⎯⎯, subject to the commercial arbitration rules of ⎯⎯⎯. The full costs of the arbitration (including attorneys' fees) shall be shared equally by the parties [or, shall be borne by the losing party].

[It may be desirable to provide specifically that at least one of the arbitrators shall have technical knowledge about computers or experience in the computer industry.]

Attorneys' fees

In the event of arbitration, litigation or other legal proceeding between the parties arising from this Agreement, the prevailing party shall be entitled to recover, in addition to any other relief awarded or granted, its reasonable costs and attorneys' fees incurred in the proceeding.

Force majeure

Notwithstanding any other provision in this Agreement, no default, delay or failure to perform on the part of either party shall be considered a breach of this Agreement if such default, delay or failure to perform is shown to be due entirely to causes beyond the reasonable control of the party charged with such default, including, but not limited to, strikes, lock-outs, or other labour disputes, riots, civil disturbances, actions or inactions of governmental authorities or suppliers, epidemics, wars, embargoes, storms, floods, fire, earthquakes, acts of God or the public enemy, nuclear disasters or default of a common carrier. In the case of the happening of any such event, the time for performance required by either party under this Agreement shall be extended for any period during which performance is prevented by the event. However, the other party may terminate this Agreement by notice if such event preventing performance continues for more than 180 days.

Notices

Any notice required or permitted by this Agreement shall be in writing, and shall be deemed given to the intended party when copies are delivered personally to the party or to the president of a corporate party, or _____ days after a copy is sent by certified or registered mail, addressed to the party, or to the secretary [president in the USA] of a corporate party, at the address set forth below:
  [addresses of the parties]
  Either party may change its address as set forth above by a written notice to the other party given in the manner specified by this clause.

Amendments

No amendment or modification of this Agreement or any provision of this Agreement shall be effective unless in writing and signed by the party against whom such amendments or modification is sought to be enforced [or, signed by both parties].

Waiver

No waiver of any rights arising under this Agreement shall be effective unless in writing and signed by the party against whom the waiver is to be enforced. No failure or delay by either party in exercising any right, power or remedy under this Agreement, except as specifically provided in this clause, shall operate as a waiver of any such right, power or remedy.

Assignment

This Agreement shall not be assignable by either party without the prior written consent of the other, such consent not to be unreasonably withheld. This Agreement shall be binding upon and inure to the benefit of the heirs, successors and assigns of the parties hereto.

[This is a simple, mutual term. Particular conditions may make it desirable to limit further, or prevent, assignment by one or other of the parties. For example, when services are to be provided, the party providing the services should only be able to assign upon proof that the assignee is equally qualified to carry out the services.]

Integration

This Agreement constitutes the entire agreement between the parties concerning the subject-matter hereof, and supersedes all prior agreements, both oral and written, representations, statements, negotiations and undertakings.

Severability

If any term or provision of this Agreement shall be held to be invalid, illegal or unenforceable, the remaining terms and provisions of this Agreement shall remain in full force and effect and such invalid, illegal or unenforceable term or provision shall be deemed not to be part of this Agreement.

Headings not controlling

Headings used in this Agreement are for reference purposes only and shall not be deemed part of this Agreement.

7 Hardware Contracts

INTRODUCTION

'Hardware' is a term that covers a wide variety of items, and the considerations that should be taken into account when contracting for hardware will depend somewhat on what is being contracted for. Obviously, the purchase of a Cray supercomputer system costing in excess of $10 million is very different from the purchase of an Apple personal computer, or a new terminal to add to an existing business system.

This chapter is not concerned with the purchase of hardware which is commonly sold at retail, mainly personal computers and their peripherals. As with all retail sales, these are sold under standard form contracts, and the only negotiation of terms open to the purchaser is to try to get a better price, or to get something else included (usually software) as part of a package. This chapter is concerned with the type of transactions which are large enough that the purchaser can negotiate at least some of the contract terms with the seller.

The amount of negotiation possible will depend upon the size of the vendor. In the case of mainframe computer systems, the market has fairly well stabilised itself, leaving a handful of giants such as IBM, Hewlett-Packard and Burroughs as the only suppliers. It is difficult to get such suppliers to vary the terms of their standard contracts, in particular in the area of warranties and limitation of liability. It is different with the smaller business systems, such as the minis and the larger micros. There are at present a large number of smaller vendors of such machines, with whom it is possible for a purchaser to negotiate contract terms. However, the purchaser should be aware that many of such vendors are financially unstable, and there are at present too many similar but incompatible machines on the market. This means that there is a real risk that the vendor may not be around in the future when maintenance is needed, or would not be able to make good any loss incurred by the purchaser if the machine proves to be defective.

While this chapter is concerned with hardware, in practice many purchases of the type discussed in this chapter will include at least some software as part of the deal. The most common types of software sold bundled with hardware are operating systems and other software needed for the basic functioning of the system, such as communications software. Contractual provisions relating to bundled software are discussed in this chapter, but the reader is also referred to the discussion in Chapter 9 about standard software. If the hardware vendor is also to provide custom software for the system, Chapter 8 should be referred to.

The purchaser of a business computer system generally has one or more specific purposes for that system in mind. He should therefore negotiate both the purchase and the terms of the contract in terms of the results to be achieved, rather than the descriptions of the specific hardware required to achieve those results. In most cases, the purchaser will be relying on the expertise of the vendor for the selection of the hardware required.

CONTENTS OF THE HARDWARE CONTRACT

The following areas should be dealt with in the contract:

(a)   Specifications of the system.
(b)   Delivery, installation and acceptance.
(c)   Performance standards.
(d)   Cost and payment.
(e)   Documentation and user training.
(f)   Services and supplies.
(g)   Maintenance.
(h)   Remedies for foreseeable breaches.

Specifications of the system

The system should be specified both in terms of what it is to do and what it is to contain. In general, the manufacturer will have sheets showing the detailed technical specifications of each of the hardware components, and these should be attached to the contract as exhibits, or incorporated by reference. When individual components are to be combined, it is also desirable to have specifications for the configuration.

When the system also includes software, specifications for each piece of software, and for the whole configuration should also be included. It is harder to provide specifications for software than for hardware, because what is to be described is function rather than physical characteristics. This problem is discussed more fully in Chapters 8 and 9.

The performance of the system should also be specified and warranted by the vendor. With an existing system, the purchaser should have performed benchmark tests as part of the system selection process. These tests will have described the results, both in terms of output and time taken to achieve that output, expected by the user. This description should be incorporated into the contract and made the basis for the warranty of performance. Where the system is a new one, and was not available for benchmark testing, the parties must negotiate an equivalent description acceptable to both parties for inclusion in the contract.

It may be desirable, from the purchaser's point of view, to incorporate other system documentation such as hardware and software manuals into the contract. The vendor should be reluctant to have such detailed specifications included, particularly if it is giving a performance warranty based on such specifications.

Whenever the system is to be used in conjunction with an existing system, the specifications of that system necessary to ensure compatibility with the new system should be set out. This is to give a measurable standard for the warranty of compatibility which the purchaser should insist on from the vendor. Similarly, if the user has informed the vendor that the system is to be included in a future enlarged system, specifications for compatibility with the future system should be set out. Similarly, where the system is to be used with existing or proposed peripheral devices from other manufacturers, interface specifications are needed. The purchaser should similarly seek a warranty that the equipment will satisfy these interface specifications.

Delivery, installation and acceptance

The purchaser will normally need to have the system up and running within a defined time, and may suffer serious losses if there are delays in delivery and installation. This can be a serious problem in the case of new equipment, particularly in an industry where announcement of a product well before it is ready to be shipped is regrettably common.

The purchaser should ensure that the contract contains a defined schedule of delivery dates for each of the components of the system, both hardware and software. While these dates should be specific, a range of a week or so should be allowed for each date, to allow for transportation difficulties and the like. Whenever a particular configuration cannot function unless all its constituent components are present, the delivery schedule should make this clear, and specify that delivery of any of the components is ineffective until all components necessary for proper functioning are delivered.

The vendor should be required to give at least 30 days' notice of delivery so that the purchaser can prepare for delivery and installation. Ideally, the purchaser should also have a right to postpone delivery for a defined period if for some reason he is not ready for delivery on the specified date. This period should be reasonable in the circumstances: the longer the period between signing the contract and delivery, the longer the period of optional postponement should be.

If the purchaser is likely to suffer loss if delivery is delayed, he should ensure that he is given a right to cancel the contract if the delay extends beyond a specified time from the agreed delivery date, together with a right to recover damages caused by the delay. The period should be chosen so as to give the vendor a reasonable chance to perform, but to protect the purchaser against incurring excessive losses. For lesser delays, whenever possible there should be a liquidated damages provision for a fixed sum payable for each day after seven or ten days after the specified delivery date.

Usually the purchaser is responsible for preparing the site for the installation. The requirements should be defined by the vendor, and attached to the contract as an exhibit. The user should be aware of the details of these requirements before the contract is signed, and should ensure that he can meet them in time for the scheduled delivery. Preferably, a timetable for site preparation should be agreed. The user may also require advice from the vendor during the preparations, and this should be provided for.

Installation will normally be carried out by the vendor, although assistance may be required from the purchaser. The contract should specifically provide for insurance on the equipment after it has reached the purchaser's site, because the contract will normally provide that title to the equipment does not pass until it is paid for, and the purchaser would be foolish if he agreed to pay more than a down-payment before the equipment is installed and working. Preferably, the purchaser should agree to extend his insurance coverage until title passes, otherwise the purchaser should insist on an express provision that risk does not pass until title passes.

Once installation is complete, the vendor will certify to the purchaser that the equipment is functioning according to specification. The purchaser is now responsible for carrying out pre-acceptance testing to ensure that the equipment does indeed meet the contract specifications. The contract should spell out the tests to be performed, and the results which will be deemed satisfactory. The tests should be designed to show that:

(a)   The hardware components operate according to the contract specifications.

(b)   The software components operate according to the contract specifications and fulfil the listed functions.

(c)   The whole system performs as well as the system tested under the original benchmark tests, or, if a new, previously untested system, that it satisfactorily performs the agreed benchmark tests.

(d)   Where appropriate, the system is compatible with the previous system.

(e)   Where appropriate, the system interfaces with the third-party peripheral equipment listed in the contract.

(f)   The system performs according to the specified reliability standards.

A time-limit for completing the tests should be set, and the procedure for notifying the vendor of deficiencies laid down. The vendor should be given a defined time in which to correct any deficiencies, with a provision for retention of at least some of the payment until the system is in an acceptable state. In general, acceptance testing of hardware can be done relatively quickly, with well defined standards. The only exception is the reliability testing, which of necessity will take some time to ensure that no hidden glitches remain. As will be seen in Chapter 8, acceptance testing of software is a different matter, presenting serious problems.

Performance standards

There are two types of performance standards which should be provided in the contract. The first relates to the functions that the system is to perform; these have already been discussed under 'specifications'. The second relates to the reliability of the equipment. It is no good having equipment which performs perfectly while it is working if it spends more than half of the time down.

Reliability should be defined in measurable parameters, such as frequency and duration of failure. This should include both component and system failure. A reasonable time between each failure should be specified to give a standard of reliability in terms of frequency of occurrence. Because the user is concerned not only with how often a breakdown occurs, but how long his system is out of commission each time a breakdown occurs, a second reliability standard is required. This is usefully defined in terms of the maximum acceptable percentage downtime. The 'downtime' is the time between failure and repair. The percentage downtime is the proportion of downtime to the total expected working time of the system.

Enforcement of reliability standards is something that vendors and purchasers have difficulty agreeing upon. Ideally, the purchaser would like the vendor to guarantee performance absolutely. The vendor should be reluctant to be tied to a set of absolute standards when dealing with something as complex and temperamental as a computer system. Even if the purchaser has sufficient negotiating power to force the vendor to give an absolute guarantee, it is probably wise not to do so. A vendor tied in this way is more likely to seek to escape from responsibility by blaming breakdowns on factors due to the purchaser, such as the environment or misuse by the purchaser's personnel. It is often very difficult if not impossible to determine the exact cause for a system or component failure. In these circumstances, the purchaser is better off in the long run with a vendor who has voluntarily undertaken some responsibility for reliability. This could be a recognition that the standards set out in the contract are reasonable, and an undertaking to use best efforts to meet them, coupled with some remedies available to the purchaser in the event of serious failure to meet these standards. These remedies could include a right to withhold at least part of payments due, or a right to replace the defective part himself and deduct the cost from payments due. The purchaser should also try to include a 'lemon' clause, by which he can insist on having a hopelessly defective part or component replaced, rather than leaving the option of repair or replacement to the vendor, which is the type of clause usually favoured by vendors.

The contract should provide for the provision of a back-up system in the event of a serious system failure which cannot be repaired in a reasonable time. Back-up facilities should be available whatever the cause of the system failure, although if the failure is something the vendor is liable for, he should bear the cost of supplying the back-up. This back-up is normally at an installation owned by the vendor, or the vendor may be able to arrange such facilities with another of its customers with a compatible configuration. The back-up equipment should be available at reasonable notice, and should be reasonably accessible to the purchaser.

While the availability of back-up facilities will be sufficient to deal with most normal situations, it will probably not be enough in the event of a disaster which destroys the equipment or which disables it for a long time. The vendor should agree to provide a replacement system within a specified time if requested by the purchaser, and to give the purchaser reasonable assistance in overcoming the effects of the disaster. Of course, the purchaser should have insurance to cover such disasters.

Cost and payment

The equipment may be purchased outright, it may be purchased under some type of credit arrangement, or it may be leased. Obviously, the amount and method of payment for the equipment will depend upon which of these alternatives applies to the contract in question. These types of provisions are common to commercial contracts dealing with any types of goods, and are not considered here.

Before choosing a method of payment, the tax implications should be carefully investigated. If the equipment is new, there may be some type of investment tax credit if the equipment is purchased out of capital. As computer systems of the type dealt with here usually represent a significant outlay for the business concerned, tax savings could be considerable.

The purchase of a computer system usually involves the provision of more than just the equipment. The vendor will usually supply at least some services, and may also supply items such as magnetic storage media, printer ribbons and paper. Some of the services supplied occur at the beginning, such as installation, training of the personnel who are to use the system, and repairs under warranty (it is normal for an initial warranty period to be given for hardware, as is given on most electrical and mechanical equipment). In general, those services should be included with the cost of the equipment. The service most usually supplied on a continuing basis is after-warranty service and maintenance. This is discussed below. Other services supplied after the initial period, for which provision for payment must be made, could include the provision of back-up equipment, assistance in the event of a disaster, and further personnel training.

The contract may also provide for credits to be given against payments subsequently due in certain circumstances. For example, it has been suggested above, in the section dealing with performance standards, that the purchaser should have a right to replace a defective component himself if he is not receiving satisfactory service from the vendor, and the cost of this replacement should be offset against payments due from the purchaser to the vendor.

In the case where delivery is to be some time after the contract is signed, the purchaser should insist on a provision protecting him against any price increases before the date of delivery.

Where supplies are to be provided during the term of the contract, the purchaser should also insist that some price protection in respect of these supplies is built into the contract. If this is not done, and these supplies cannot be obtained readily on the open market or the purchaser has entered a firm commitment to obtain these supplies from the vendor, the purchaser can find himself at the mercy of a monopoly supplier, particularly if the relationship between the parties has deteriorated for some other reason. Usual methods of price protection are a limitation on the percentage increase in any one year, or tying increases to a recognised official price index.

Where it is anticipated at the time the contract is entered into that the system will be expanded in the future with further equipment from the vendor, the purchaser should get price protection for that expansion equipment. This is particularly necessary where the expansion equipment required can only be obtained from that vendor, putting the vendor into a monopoly situation. The purchaser should be very wary in these circumstances of purchasing in the first place from a vendor who will not agree to a reasonable price-protection clause.

Documentation and user training

Documentation, in the form of hardware and software manuals and technical data sheets, and user training materials, is vital to the successful utilisation of the system. The documentation to be supplied should be defined in the contract. Documentation is normally supplied free or at nominal charge. The purchaser should be given a right to use this documentation freely, subject only to confidentiality protection. The purchaser should also have the right to make as many copies as needed, or be given the right to purchase copies of the documentation at a cost approximating to the cost of photocopying the originals. It is to the vendor's advantage to restrict the right to copy, particularly where trade secrets are involved, but to discourage illicit copying by making it easy and cheap to obtain further copies.

It is usual for the documentation for a system to be revised and improved as experience with the system increases. The purchaser should therefore have the right to be supplied with all revisions of the documentation relating to his system. Again, this should be supplied free or at nominal cost under the same terms as the original documentation, as it is to the vendor's advantage to keep his customers informed of the latest developments which may help the purchaser to solve or even avoid problems which the vendor would otherwise be liable to fix.

It is also to the advantage of both parties for the vendor to provide thorough training to the purchaser's personnel who are to operate the system. The initial training to be provided should be specified in detail in the contract, including factors such as the length of the course, its location, and the maximum number of attenders. It is usual for the vendor to supply the initial training free, and in this case the amount of free training should be specified. It is preferable for the training to be, at least in part, on the purchaser's own system. The purchaser should also be able to request further training, at any time during the term of the contract, and provisions for reasonable charges for such training should be set out. Where the courses are supplemented by educational materials, provision should be made for the supply of such materials, and for reasonable restrictions on their use to protect the vendor's proprietary rights in these materials. The purchaser should have the right to conduct his own in-house training courses using the vendor's materials, particularly after the system has been in operation for some time when the vendor's interest is likely to be concentrated on his newer systems.

Services and supplies

Preferably, the supplies needed in the operation of the equipment should be specified in the contract, particularly if anything unusual, expensive or hard to obtain is required. Where these supplies can be obtained from sources other than the vendor, it is preferable to have specifications set out in the contract, so that a subsequent malfunction cannot be blamed on unsuitable supplies from third parties. If there is any danger that the vendor will object to the purchase of supplies from third parties, the matter should be resolved during negotiations, and a list of acceptable vendors of the supplies listed in the contract. Where the supplies can only be obtained from the vendor, then price protection for the purchaser must be included (see above). In jurisdictions with laws governing competition, it is usually unlawful for the equipment supplier to insist that the purchaser obtain supplies of standard items only from him.

In addition to training and maintenance, which are discussed elsewhere in this chapter, there are other services which may be supplied by the vendor. These include things such as systems design, software conversion, data conversion, site design and project management. Any such services to be provided should be specified in the contract, together with the method of payment for such services if not provided free. Frequently, such services will be provided under a separate contract, and suitable provisions may be found in the corresponding chapters of this book.

Maintenance

Maintenance after the expiry of the warranty period is usually supplied by the vendor. This may be provided for in the purchase contract, but most vendors prefer to have a separate maintenance contract.

It is traditional in the industry to provide for an annual fee for maintenance, regardless of the amount of work required. In the case of an established system, it may be advantageous for the purchaser to try to negotiate a time-and-materials basis for charging, as the equipment is unlikely to need large amounts of maintenance. Hardware is becoming increasingly reliable as the technology matures. On the other hand, with a newly marketed system, the chances of major repair and maintenance work being required are increased, and the fixed 'insurance' fee contract is probably preferable from the purchaser's point of view.

In the case of large systems, maintenance should be done on-site, except possibly for small peripherals such as terminals. The contract should provide that vendor personnel will be available full time as required for such on-site maintenance.

The contract should provide for notification by telephone to the vendor of problems, and there should be a target and a maximum response time specified. While the vendor can reasonably undertake to respond to a request within a specified period, it is harder to set standards for the time in which the repair should be completed, as this can vary widely depending upon what was wrong. However, it is important from the purchaser's point of view that some standard is set against which performance can be measured. The best compromise is probably for the vendor to promise best efforts to repair as quickly as possible, coupled with a financial penalty if the maximum percentage downtime is exceeded (see 'performance standards', above).

In order to carry out maintenance, the vendor will require access to the system, and may also require assistance from the purchaser's personnel. These should be provided for in the contract. The vendor may also require access for regular preventative maintenance, and the amount and frequency of such access should be specified. The intention to carry out preventative maintenance should be given well in advance to the user, so that a mutually convenient time can be agreed.

The maintenance contract should be renewable by the user for the life of the equipment, and should be assignable with the equipment if it is sold. While the vendor should be able to increase the price from year to year to reflect increased costs, the user must be protected against excessive increases by a price protection mechanism. As the purpose of the contract is to ensure that maintenance is provided by the most knowledgeable and experienced source, the vendor should not be entitled to subcontract the work, nor should the vendor be able to assign the contract except as part of the assignment of the whole of its business related to the user's system.

Remedies for foreseeable breaches

Cancellation by vendor prior to delivery
The purchaser will have incurred costs in selecting the system and negotiating the contract and in preparing to receive the system. The purchaser will also suffer damage because further delay will occur in obtaining a system because the purchaser must now go back to the selection and negotiation stages with another vendor. The costs prior to signing the contract should be known, and it should be possible to make a reasonable estimate of the other costs on a monthly average. The contract should therefore provide a liquidated damages clause, requiring the vendor to pay the precontract costs plus the estimated sum for each month that has elapsed between the signing of the contract and the cancellation.

Cancellation by the purchaser prior to delivery

The vendor will have similar precontract costs which can be specified. The other loss will be that from the lost sale, and will depend upon the circumstances. If the system is a standard one that can be sold to another purchaser, the most that the vendor has lost is his profits. In the case of a system in great demand for which the vendor cannot produce enough equipment, it is arguable whether the vendor is even entitled to lost profits. However, if the system is a special one which would require considerable modification to make it saleable to another, the purchaser would be liable to pay the price of the system, plus the cost of modification, less the price paid by the new purchaser. It is difficult to provide for damages of this type by a liquidated damages clause. The vendor would probably be better advised to seek the normal contractual damages, which are readily calculable.

Failure to deliver on schedule

As this type of damage is hard to quantify, a good faith attempt to estimate the cost to the purchaser of each day's delay should be made and incorporated in a liquidation damages clause. Delay beyond a certain period should give the purchaser a right to terminate.

Failure to provide an acceptable system

A date for completing the acceptance period should be set, with a timetable for the testing. For each day beyond this period in which the system has failed to meet all the specified acceptance tests, a fixed sum representing a good faith estimate of the cost to the purchaser of such delay may be payable. If the system cannot be made acceptable within a reasonable time, the purchaser should have the right to terminate.

PRECEDENTS

System specifications

Hardware components

The hardware components to be supplied by Vendor are listed in schedule _____ to this Agreement. Each such hardware component will conform to the detailed specifications respecting said component contained in said schedule. The hardware components shall, for the purposes of delivery, installation and performance under this Agreement, be grouped together in the configuration set out in schedule

_____ to this Agreement. Any such configuration shall be deemed incomplete and undelivered if any component comprised in that configuration has not been delivered, or is not operational, or fails to operate according to the acceptance criteria laid down in paragraph _____ of this Agreement.

Software components

The software components to be supplied by Vendor are listed in schedule _____ to this Agreement. Each such software component shall conform to the detailed specification respecting such component contained in said schedule. The software components shall be grouped together with associated hardware components in the configurations set out in schedule _____ to this Agreement. Any such configuration shall be deemed incomplete and undelivered if any component, whether hardware or software, within that configuration has not been delivered, or is not operational, or fails to operate according to the acceptance criteria laid down in paragraph _____ of this Agreement.

System performance

The Vendor warrants that the system delivered under this Agreement will meet the performance criteria set out in the Purchaser's benchmark tests, contained in schedule _____ to this Agreement.

Compatibility

The Vendor acknowledges that the Purchaser intends to use the system delivered under this Agreement in conjunction with the Purchaser's existing system [or, the Purchaser's existing peripheral equipment or, further equipment which the Purchaser intends to purchase during the life of this system], the specifications of which are set out in schedule _____ to this Agreement, and warrants that the system delivered under this Agreement is both data compatible and program compatible with the other equipment described in said schedule.

Interface requirements

The Vendor warrants that the equipment sold under this Agreement can be connected without modification and without damage to the equipment set out in schedule _____ to this Agreement.

Delivery, installation and acceptance

Delivery

The components to be delivered under this Agreement shall be delivered according to the delivery schedule set out in schedule ____, it being agreed that the delivery of any group of components listed therein shall not be complete until all the components in that group have been delivered. The Vendor shall give the Purchaser at least ____ days' notice of the commencement of delivery according to this schedule.

Postponement of delivery

The Purchaser may, by ____ days' notice to the Vendor, delay delivery by a period to be specified in the notice, of any or all of the components or groups of components beyond the delivery date set out in schedule ____ , provided that such delay shall not exceed ____ days.

Termination for failure to deliver

Any delay in delivery of the system, or of any component or group of components in excess of ____ days beyond the date set out in schedule ____ shall give the Purchaser the right to cancel this Agreement upon ____ days' written notice. The Purchaser may, at its option, in lieu of cancellation set a further date for delivery, time being of the essence, upon condition that the Vendor pay to the Purchaser the sum of ____ for each day of delay after the Purchaser gives notice of its intention to exercise this option, this sum being a good faith estimate of the damage to the Purchaser as the result of such delay. If delivery has not been made by this specified further date for delivery, the Purchaser may immediately cancel the Agreement and return any components which may have been delivered at the Vendor's expense.

Site preparation

The Purchaser shall, at its own expense, prepare the site for installation in accordance with the preparation specifications set out in schedule ____ to this Agreement. The Purchaser agrees to complete these preparations not later than ____ days before the scheduled date of delivery of the equipment, and shall give notice of such completion to the Vendor. The Vendor shall be entitled to inspect the site prior to delivery, and shall notify the Purchaser of its approval or disapproval. Notice of disapproval shall set forth in detail each deficiency discovered and the Purchaser shall promptly remedy each such deficiency. The Vendor may, at its discretion, delay delivery until all such deficiencies have been remedied. If the Vendor shall fail to inspect the site prior to delivery, the site shall be deemed to have been approved by the Vendor, and the Vendor shall be liable for remedying any deficiency later discovered.

Installation
The Vendor shall be responsible, at its own expense, for installation of the equipment, including installation of all connections with power, utilities and communications services. Upon completion of installation, the Vendor shall notify the Purchaser that installation is completed and shall certify that the equipment is fully operational and ready for use.

Risk of loss
It is agreed that title to the equipment shall not pass to the Purchaser until payment is made in accordance with paragraph ____ of this Agreement. Any risk of loss prior to receipt by the Purchaser of the Vendor's certification that the equipment is ready for use shall be borne by the Vendor. Thereafter, the risk of loss shall pass to the Purchaser, who agrees to maintain insurance covering all conventional risks in an amount equal to the replacement cost of the equipment with an insurer approved by the Vendor, which insurance shall waive rights of subrogation against the Vendor.

Acceptance testing
Immediately upon receipt of the Vendor's notice that installation is complete, as provided for in paragraph ____ above, the Purchaser shall commence acceptance testing according to the schedule set out below. The Vendor agrees to give the Purchaser all reasonable assistance in performing this testing.

(a) During the first business day following the receipt of such notice the Purchaser will determine whether the operating characteristics of the equipment meet the specifications set out in schedule ____ to this Agreement.

(b) During the ____ business days following receipt of such notice, the Purchaser will run the benchmark tests described in schedule ____ to this Agreement.

(c) During the ____ business days following receipt of such notice the Purchaser will operate the equipment in accordance with its normal operating practices to determine whether the standards of reliability set out in schedule ____ to this Agreement are met.

In the event that the performance of the system fails to meet any of the specifications, the Vendor shall, at its own expense, either (i) modify, adjust or repair the system so as to meet the specifications, or (ii) replace defective components or add such other components as may be necessary to meet the specifications or (iii) at the Purchaser's option, negotiate a reduction in the price of the system; however, if no agreement on the amount of such reduction can be reached within _____ days of the Purchaser's exercise of this option, the Vendor shall perform under (i) or (ii) above. After any such adjustment, etc., the tests shall all be run again and, if the system still fails to meet the specifications, the Purchaser shall have the right to terminate this Agreement. In no event shall payment be due for any part of the system [other than the downpayment provided for in paragraph _____] until the system meets the specifications set out in this Agreement.

Performance standards

Defining standards
For the purposes of this Agreement, 'system failure' shall be defined as meaning any of the following:

(a)   The system fails to operate at all.
(b)   The system fails to operate in accordance with the performance specifications set out in schedule _____ to this Agreement.
(c)   A hardware or software component is inoperative or defective, rendering the whole system useless to the Purchaser.

For the purposes of this Agreement, 'downtime' shall be defined to mean the following:

(a)   The time that any system failure continues.
(b)   The time during which the system is being repaired or maintained, unless such repair or maintenance shall not prevent the Purchaser from making its normal use of the system.
(c)   The time during which the system cannot be operated because of potential danger from such operation to the Purchaser's personnel.

For the purposes of this Agreement, the agreed reliability standards shall be the mean time between system failure and the downtime percentages set out in schedule _____ to this Agreement.

The Vendor recognises that the reliability standards defined in this paragraph and set out in schedule _____ are reasonable, and it will use its best efforts to meet these reliability standards, including replacement of unreliable components. In the event that either or both of the reliability standards are not met in any two or more consecutive months, the maintenance charges [or, in the case of a lease, the rental payments] for such months shall be reduced by a percentage equal to the amount by which the percentage downtime for that period exceeds the percentage downtime set out in schedule _____. In the event that the failure is caused by a defective component and the Vendor fails to remedy such failure within _____, the Purchaser shall be entitled to replace the defective component and charge the Vendor for the costs of such replacement.

Back-up availability
In the event that the system is unavailable for use due to a system failure for more than _____ hours, the Vendor will make available for the Purchaser's use the back-up facilities described in schedule _____ to this Agreement.

Disaster availability
In the event that the system is rendered permanently inoperative as the result of any natural or other disaster, the Vendor agrees to waive any delivery schedule priorities and to deliver a replacement system within _____ from the date of the Purchaser's request for such a system. The price for this system will be the lower of the list price then current, or the purchase price of the system delivered under this Agreement plus _____% per year for each year between the delivery date of the system which is the subject of this Agreement and the date of the request for replacement.

Cost and payments

Price protection prior to delivery
If the Vendor's established list price for any component to be delivered hereunder shall be less on the date of installation than the price for such equipment as specified herein, such lower price shall be payable; if it shall be greater, then the price set out in this Agreement shall be payable.

Price protection for supplies
The charges set out in schedule _____ to this Agreement for services and supplies shall not be increased for a period of _____ [at least 12 months] after the date of delivery of the system. Thereafter, such charges may be increased once every 12 months by an amount not to exceed _____% [or, a percentage equal to the percentage increase in the _____ price index for the preceding 12 months].

Price protection for expansion equipment
The Vendor agrees that it will supply upon request from the purchaser at any time within the _____ years following delivery, additional items similar to and compatible with the items listed in schedule _____ to this Agreement. The price of these items shall in no event be more than the price paid under this Agreement for such items, plus an increase of _____% per annum for each year from the date of this Agreement to the date of such order [or, a percentage equal to the percentage increase in the _____ price index for the preceding 12 months].

Documentation and user training

Documentation availability
The Vendor will provide the Purchaser with at least _____ copies, cost free, of the following manuals which the Vendor represents to be the entire documentation needed by the Purchaser for operation of the system. [List manuals.] The Purchaser may not reproduce these manuals in any form, and the Purchaser agrees to keep the contents of the manuals confidential. The Purchaser is entitled to purchase as many further copies of the manuals as it requires from the Vendor at the prices set out below. The Vendor agrees that, if at any time it is unable to supply manuals at the Purchaser's request, the Purchaser may make the requested number of copies of those manuals which the Vendor is unable to supply. Such copies may be made only for the Purchaser's own internal use.

Rights to future documentation
The Vendor agrees to furnish to the Purchaser all future documentation and revisions of documentation developed for the system or for similar systems and which would be useful to the Purchaser. Where such future or revised documentation is furnished free of charge to other customers of the Vendor, it shall be furnished free of charge to the Purchaser;

where charges are made to such other customers, it shall be furnished to the Purchaser at the Purchaser's request at the published prices.

User training

The Vendor will make available to the Purchaser up to _____ days of training in the use and operation of the system at no cost to the Purchaser except for travel and living expenses connected with the training which shall be borne by the Purchaser. The time and location of such training shall be mutually agreed between the parties. The Purchaser may request the Vendor to provide further training, at times and locations to be mutually agreed, at the cost per student day then charged by the Vendor to its other customers. In the event that the Vendor is unable to supply any such requested training, the Purchaser shall be entitled to conduct such training internally with the Purchaser's own personnel, and the Purchaser shall be entitled to use and reproduce the Vendor's training material for the purpose of conducting such training. The Vendor will also make available to the Purchaser, at the Vendor's list price, all materials used by the Vendor in connection with any and all training courses and related to the Purchaser's system.

Services and supplies

Supply specifications

The supplies needed for the satisfactory operation of the system are set out in schedule _____ to this Agreement, together with the specifications for such supplies.

Acceptable sources of supplies

The Vendor acknowledges that the following vendors are acceptable as suppliers of supplies which meet the specifications set out in schedule _____.

Protection for vendor–supplied supplies

The Vendor agrees to make the supplies listed below available in sufficient quantities to meet the Purchaser's need for as long as the system supplied under this Agreement is in use by the Purchaser or any assignee of the Purchaser. The price for such supplies shall not be increased by more than _____% for each year from the date of this Agreement.

Maintenance

Warranty and free maintenance

The equipment purchased under this Agreement is warranted for a period of _____ months after delivery against defects in material and workmanship and from failure of operation during ordinary use, and during this period the Vendor will furnish all maintenance, service and parts necessary to maintain the equipment in working order at no cost to the Purchaser.

Provision of on-site maintenance

The Vendor shall provide full-time on-site maintenance from _____ to _____, Monday to Friday [these should be the Purchaser's usual working hours] during the first 30 days after acceptance by the Purchaser. If during such period the downtime for the system exceeds the downtime percentage set out in schedule _____, the Vendor shall continue to provide maintenance under this paragraph until the reliability standards set out in that schedule have been met for any 30-day period.

Thereafter, maintenance shall be provided not more than _____ hours after the Vendor has been notified by telephone by the Purchaser that maintenance is required. All maintenance shall be provided by qualified maintenance engineers employed by the Vendor who are familiar with the types of equipment at the Purchaser's site. The Vendor shall not be entitled to subcontract maintenance provided under this Agreement.

Access for maintenance

The Purchaser shall give access to the system as required by the Vendor's maintenance personnel. In the case of regularly scheduled preventative maintenance, which shall be carried out at the times and in the manner set out in schedule _____, the Vendor shall give the Purchaser _____ day's notice of its intention to carry out such maintenance. The Purchaser may request an adjournment of such maintenance of not more than _____ days, to a date to be mutually agreed.

Continuity

The Vendor agrees to provide the maintenance services as defined in this Agreement to the Purchaser, or to any person to whom the Purchaser has assigned the system, for as long as the system is in use. The price for such services may be increased on each anniversary of this

Agreement by not more than ____% per year. The Purchaser may terminate the provision of maintenance services at any time by at least 30 days' prior written notice.

Remedies

Liquidated damages

The parties acknowledge that the actual damages for the breach of this contract may be difficult to determine with accuracy and, accordingly, have agreed to the following provision for liquidated damages which the parties acknowledge are reasonable estimates of their potential losses.

8 Contracts for Custom Software Development

WHAT IS 'CUSTOM' SOFTWARE?

There is no standard definition of 'custom' software. It is tempting to define it as all software which is not standard, but then 'standard' software can equally be defined as all software which is not custom!

In the context of this chapter, custom software is software, usually a whole system, which is designed and produced for a single client. While many of the component items of the system may have been used before, and therefore are themselves 'standard', the whole system is unique. It is this uniqueness that gives rise to many of the special problems associated with the development of custom software.

The development process usually falls into three stages. The first stage involves an initial analysis by the vendor of the customer's requirements. This process is usually done before the contract is entered into, and often forms part of the tendering process. The next stage involves the preparation of a detailed design for the system. During this stage the vendor must learn from the customer the details of the aspects of the customer's business which will be served by the software, and design a system to meet those needs which will run efficiently on the customer's hardware system. The third stage involves implementing the design by actually writing the software, compiling it to run on the customer's machine, and installing it on that machine. A possible fourth stage is the maintenance of the software once it is installed, but this is usually the subject of a separate contract.

Because each piece of custom development is unique, no one knows at the outset exactly what is being contracted for. It is this uncertainty of scope which gives rise to most of the problems — and associated litigation — connected with the development of custom software. It is usually the case that the client is entering a contract for development for a software system because he does not have the necessary expertise to do the development himself. The parties therefore come into the contractual relationship from two mutually exclusive areas of expertise; the software vendor is an expert in designing and programming software, but knows nothing about the client's business for which the software is needed, and the client is an expert in his own business but knows nothing about software design and production. Both areas of expertise must be combined in order to produce a software system which meets the client's needs.

This process of combining the two areas of expertise is usually an iterative one which takes place continuously during the development process. It is an almost universal experience that one result of this joint learning process is that the scope of the project expands considerably during development unless careful control is exercised. As the client learns more about the software he realises that there are improvements and refinements to his procedures which become possible with a computer. The systems analyst sees enhancements to the original design that would improve the whole system as he learns more about the client's business.

Uncontrolled growth in the scope of the project causes many problems, which can result in a total breakdown of relations between the vendor and the client. The main problems are:

(a)   Increased cost: in the case of a fixed-price contract this can put the vendor in serious financial difficulties, and may even drive him into insolvency; in the case of a time-and-materials contract the client has the financial problems which will make him extremely unhappy even if he is not made insolvent. Typically, an estimate of the total cost will have been given at the outset. The client, who is unsophisticated in the area of software development, will not understand why this estimate bears no relationship to the final cost, and certainly will not understand that at least part of the blame for the increase is due to his own increased expectations.

(b)   Late delivery, which can cause the client serious business losses if the software system is essential to his business.

(c)   More computer time is required for the development, which can seriously tie up the client's facilities.

(d)   Changes made after programming has started can cause problems and bugs in the part of the system already programmed.

(e)   The increased demands on the vendor's staff can cause the vendor to have problems staffing other projects, thus causing difficulties with other clients.

COMMON PROBLEMS IN CUSTOM SOFTWARE DEVELOPMENT

This almost universally experienced expansion in scope of the project during development results in a number of common problems. Other problems result from the nature of the contract, and from the structure of the industry. The most common of these problems involve money. Everybody knows that financial problems are the problems most likely to lead to a breakdown in friendly relations and to litigation in any relationship, including marriage.

Most software development contracts are on some sort of fixed-price basis, the pricing being related to deliverables of some sort. Some vendors charge by line of code, others have methods of dividing the software into modules, and charging according to the number of modules. The vendor will have performed an initial analysis of the system required, usually as part of the bidding process, will have estimated the number of deliverables required, and thereby estimated the price. Here is an immediate source of trouble. The initial analysis is done at the very beginning of the mutual learning process. For this reason the estimate given is almost always too low. Even though an increase in scope during development is the common experience, vendors rarely anticipate the size of this increase. This is partly due to the fact that the estimate is part of a tendering process, and the vendor is anxious for the business. It is also due to the fact that software development is typically done by small, cash-poor organisations who are in a weak position when bargaining with customers. And it is due in part to the usual genuine optimism experienced by business people at the outset of a new business relationship.

It should be immediately obvious that this system of pricing provides false comfort to both sides. The customer believes that he is going to pay a price close to the estimated price for the system he wants. The vendor believes that he will be paid according to output, and that output is a reasonable indicator of costs. The customer's belief is false because the system he wants by the time he has learned about software is unlikely to be the system he thought he wanted when the contract was signed. The vendor's belief is false because the physical size of the resulting programs, whether measured in lines of code or in constituent modules, bears almost no relationship to the costs of developing them. Some of that code, or some of those modules, will be standard subroutines, others will have required enormous numbers of man-hours to develop. Further, even if the increase in scope does result in a matching increase in chargeable deliverables, the vendor then has to deal with a very unhappy customer who has found that the original estimate bears no relationship to the final cost.

Further difficulties are caused by the usual method of payment. As a software development project typically takes several months to complete (even if all goes well), and as the vendor is unlikely to have large financial resources from which the development can be funded, progress payments are commonly provided for in the contract. Although these payments should ideally be tied to deliveries (see the discussion below), so that the customer gets something of value with each payment, this is not easy to do. In the first part of the development, the design stages, a great deal of time is put in by the vendor's personnel, but very little of actual value to the customer is produced. If the contract were terminated for any reason during this stage, a new vendor would have been saved some work, but the hours saved would be small compared to the hours already spent by the first vendor. The new vendor would still have to go through the process of learning about the client's business. Also, no two software houses tackle systems development in exactly the same way, so the first vendor's work would be of limited value to the second.

From what has already been said, the reader should not be surprised to learn that bankruptcy and other business termination is common amongst software developers. It should also be obvious that such a business failure in the middle of the development process is likely to be very expensive for the customer, and could have a disastrous effect on the customer's business. Even after the development is completed, the business failure of the vendor can have serious results if the customer depends on the vendor for software maintenance.

Over-optimism about the scope of the project is typically accompanied by over-optimism about the time needed to complete the project. Late delivery may be very expensive to the customer. If the software was required for a new computer system, that system must be ordered, and a delivery date fixed, well in advance. The customer may therefore find himself making large payments for hardware he cannot use. If the software was required to enable the customer to expand business, or to take on new business, delay in delivery will mean loss of profits from lost business, or expenses in providing outside processing in order to keep the new business.

When software is being developed for use on the customer's existing system, it is usual for much of the machine time needed for the development to be provided by the customer. If the scope of the contract is greatly increased, this could result in excessive demands on the customer's machine time, to the extent that normal business is interfered with. If the development is being done on the vendor's machine, or if machine time is being hired from a third party, there could be a similar result. The increased scope can also cause excessive demands on the time of the personnel of both the customer and the vendor, interfering with business and causing personnel dissatisfaction.

A general problem with contracts for the development of anything, including software, is that it is very difficult to define meaningful quality standards for something before it comes into existence.

Other problems can arise with the staffing of the project by the vendor. Because of the amount of learning that must go on, particularly in the early stages of the development, it is highly desirable that the same personnel be involved throughout the whole development process. While it is not possible for the vendor to prevent its employees from leaving, the customer should at least insist that the vendor does not use outside contract staff, who often do such work merely because they are between jobs.

Ownership of the software, and rights to use it, should be agreed upon at the outset. The customer will generally prefer to have the ownership of, and exclusive rights to, the system. On the other hand, the vendor would like to be able to use the work done if there is an opportunity to develop a similar system for another customer. The vendor may even wish to sell the system as a standard product if there is a market for it. This is particularly true if the vendor has made little or no profit on the development because of an increase in scope.

CONTENTS OF A SOFTWARE DEVELOPMENT CONTRACT

Structure of the contract

One way of dealing with some of the problems referred to above is to split the development process into three stages, and have a separate contract for each stage. These three stages are the initial analysis, preparation of the detailed design, and programming and installation.

Initial analysis
This has been traditionally done at no cost to the customer, as part of the bidding process. While this may appear to be favourable to the customer, it is generally not so. To perform an adequate initial analysis, unless the vendor is already familiar with the customer's business, takes time and money. A vendor who is not sure of receiving any return for this time and expenditure will naturally put the minimum of both into performing the analysis. It would benefit both parties if the customer contracted with one interested vendor for a more detailed initial analysis to be performed. This analysis could then be used as the basis for tenders by any vendor interested in bidding for the development contract. A fixed price could be agreed to for this stage, as it should not be difficult for an experienced vendor to estimate the amount of time needed for such an analysis, and only an experienced vendor should be hired to perform this task.

Preparation of the detailed design
This is the stage where the escalations of scope and cost usually take place. A more thorough initial analysis should do something to limit this, but it is almost impossible to prevent. This is the most difficult stage to prepare an adequate contract for, because it is almost impossible to provide specifications at the outset for the final product. From the point of view of the vendor, this stage is best done on a time-and-materials basis, with regular payments. This is unlikely to be acceptable to the customer, however. These issues are discussed in detail below.

Programming and installation
If the detailed design has been properly prepared, the programming should present few problems. One problem which can arise is that the customer, if he has not understood the design properly, may object that the software does not do what he had hoped for when he actually sees it running. Of course, if the design has not been properly prepared, this is the stage when the deficiencies become evident. Once the programming is completed, installation on the customer's equipment should not present serious problems unless the equipment is faulty, or unless unexpected incompatibilities between the software and the hardware show up. This is possible with a new hardware system, when the software vendor may have had inadequate technical information and insufficient test time.

Maintenance

The relationship between the vendor and the customer rarely ends with the development stages described so far. Even in the best produced software bugs will show up from time to time, which require fixing. It is much easier for the person who wrote the software to fix them than to give the job to an outsider. Therefore, there is usually a fourth stage for which a contract is required — the maintenance stage!

The vendor will usually agree to a warranty period after installation when maintenance is performed free of charge. This is the period when bugs are most likely to turn up. Thereafter, maintenance is usually performed under a separate, renewable contract.

Scope

Initial analysis

Defining the scope of the initial analysis phase should not be difficult. The customer will have given the vendor a preliminary description of requirements, technical details of the hardware system the software is to be used on, and copies of any reports or other documents the software is to produce. It will be necessary for the vendor to perform some further initial data gathering by observing the customer's operations and interviewing key members of the customer's staff. The parties should agree approximately how much time is necessary for this, and the customer should name those of its employees who should be interviewed, and agree to make them available. The vendor will then analyse this data, and prepare an outline design proposal. The customer may request that alternative design proposals are also prepared, so that a choice can be made between them, perhaps on the basis of tenders received for the next stage. A timetable for preparation of these proposals should be set out in the contract. The contents of the outline proposal should also be specified, and should be adequate to allow another software vendor to bid realistically on the development of the detailed design.

Detailed design

It is easy to state what the detailed design documents should contain. It is not easy to define the amount of work required to produce those documents, but this is what costs the money and tends to grow beyond recognition. It is necessary for the contract both to define the work needed and to set out procedures for controlling the amount of work performed.

The amount of work needed is best defined by breaking the development process down into individual steps, and by making a good faith attempt to estimate the time needed to complete each step in the light of the outline design, with an agreed error margin. Control procedures must include regular review and approval by the management of both parties of the work done. This, in turn, requires that those managements are properly educated about what it is that they are reviewing. The vendor should insist that the customer's management approves of the work done in each step, and that that approval is documented. Work in excess of the agreed amount incurred at the customer's request, or the necessity later to re-do work previously approved by the customer, should involve additional payment if the contract is for a fixed price. It is important that the vendor makes the unsophisticated customer (in a data-processing sense) understand that the successful development of the software depends as much upon the customer as it does upon the vendor.

Programming and installation
Once the detailed design has been prepared and approved, the vendor should be able to estimate the amount of time needed to prepare the programs with reasonable accuracy. A fixed-price contract is therefore feasible, although it should provide for additional payments if extra programming is required because of design changes requested by the customer. It is harder to make such an estimate for installation, because that can be affected by hardware problems beyond the software vendor's control. The scope of the work can be defined, however, by setting out the steps to be taken and giving an estimate of the time required to complete those steps if no hardware problems are encountered. Installation and testing also require a considerable amount of cooperation by the customer, both in provision of machine time and in personnel requirements. The expected extent of such cooperation should be agreed beforehand so that, for example, the installation does not prevent necessary day-to-day operation of the equipment. Where the system is to replace an existing system, the customer should be obliged to run the two systems in tandem for a reasonable agreed period, so that a failure in the new system while the initial bugs are being caught does not have disastrous effects on the customer's business.

Payment

Initial analysis
As the scope of the initial analysis stage is accurately estimable, it could be paid for either by a fixed price or on a time-and-materials basis. Assuming that the scope is limited, and this is a matter for agreement between the parties, payment can be made on delivery of the outline design proposal.

Detailed design
The vendor would naturally prefer to have this stage done on a time-and-materials basis so as to be protected against increases in scope. The customer, just as naturally, prefers to have some limit on the cost, and needs to know what the project is likely to cost before embarking upon it. If some sort of fixed pricing is to be used, it is important that both parties have some protection.

To protect the vendor:

(a) The price should be payable in stages, preferably designed so as to match the vendor's expenditure.
(b) The vendor should have a right to stop work if payment is not made.
(c) If the scope of the contract is increased at the customer's request, or because of some act or neglect on the part of the customer, the price should be increased.

To protect the customer:

(a) Progress payments should, as far as possible, be tied to deliverable products. Then, if the vendor goes out of business or the contract is terminated before the development is complete, the customer has something which can be used. Therefore, the specified deliverables should be defined in such a way as to be as useful as possible to the customer in the event of such a termination. This would include adequate documentation, where applicable.
(b) The total interim progress payments should not exceed the vendor's costs. A part of the payment, representing the vendor's profit, should be held back until the system has passed all the acceptance tests.

Programming and installation

The scope of the programming should be reasonably fixed once the detailed design has been approved, and therefore is suitable for a fixed-price contract. Again, there should be progress payments if the process is likely to last more than a month, and these payments should be tied to deliverables. This is easier to do at this stage. The vendor should be protected against changes requested by the customer by a provision for increased payments. As explained above, the installation stage provides more problems for fixed pricing because of the possibility of delays which are the fault of neither party. If the customer insists on some kind of fixed price, there should be provision for increased payments for extra work occasioned by hardware problems. Installation should normally be completed in a relatively short time, so it is unlikely that progress payments will be necessary.

Staffing and resources

Vendor

The success of the project depends upon the calibre of the personnel staffing it. The customer should stipulate the qualifications of the staff to be used, according to the various job categories involved, i.e., systems analyst, programmer.

Success also depends to a great extent on having continuity of staff throughout the project. The learning process cannot be adequately repeated for a new staff member coming in half-way through, and that person is therefore more likely to make errors. While employees of the vendor cannot be forced to remain in their jobs, the vendor can agree to use only full-time employees, rather than contract staff who are more likely to leave at short notice.

The customer should provide some protection against the effects of a business termination by the vendor during the course of the contract by a requirement that the vendor personnel involved will assist in the handover to a new developer. If the contract contains a provision preventing the parties from attempting to hire away each other's employees (see below), that provision should not apply in the event of a business termination by the vendor.

The vendor's personnel should undertake to keep confidential all of the customer's business secrets which they may learn during their work on the software system. They should also agree to comply with all the customer's security provisions while working on the customer's premises. Further, security measures to apply when they are working on the customer's confidential information on the vendor's premises should be provided. Alternatively, the vendor could give an undertaking regarding these matters, provided that the vendor's employees are subject to a suitable confidentiality agreement.

When the vendor's staff are working on the customer's premises the law may require that there is suitable insurance against injury. The responsibility for providing this insurance should be set out in the contract.

When the contract requires the use of the vendor's resources, such as machine time, or the provision of supplies such as magnetic media by the vendor, payment for these resources or supplies should preferably be separate from the payment for the development work.

Customer

The customer must agree to give the vendor full assistance by properly qualified employees. A project manager, whose qualifications have been approved by the vendor, should be named in the contract, and the customer should agree not to remove that person from the post except for reasons of unsatisfactory performance.

There should be a mutual undertaking not to offer employment to each other's employees. This is particularly important for the vendor to obtain, as there is always a temptation to the customer to acquire competent programming staff to maintain the software by making an attractive offer to the people most concerned with the development of the system.

When the contract provides for use of the customer's resources, particularly machine time, there should be a limitation on the amount of time used for the development. The customer should not be obliged to supply resources to the extent that normal business is interfered with.

Timetables

At each stage of the development, it is important to set out each of the steps involved, and to provide a timetable for the performance by each of the parties. This will help to draw attention to delays at an early stage, allowing the parties to correct the problem where possible, or to negotiate a later delivery date. Where the scope of any stage is increased at the request of the customer, the vendor should have the right to adjust the timetable and the delivery date accordingly.

Performance

It is almost impossible to provide meaningful performance standards for the software before the completion of the detailed design and even then it is not easy to give more than general standards which are to be met.

It is possible, however, to monitor performance by adequate testing procedures to be applied during the programming stage of the development. The contract should set out the tests to be performed, the testing schedule, and the responsibilities for providing test data and for approving the results.

The initial level of testing is to determine whether each program operates in accordance with the program specifications. The data for this testing are usually provided by the vendor. The next level of testing is to determine whether each program meets the customer's requirements. The responsibility for producing the data needed for this testing must be with the customer. Similarly, the system as a whole must be tested for conformity with the customer's requirements, again using data supplied by the customer. Any extra work or delay caused by any inadequacy of the customer-supplied test data should be the subject of a contract adjustment, in price or in delivery data, as appropriate. The final testing should be with live data, to ensure that the system operates correctly under normal conditions. At each stage, the customer should approve the test results before further work on development of that program proceeds.

Installation and acceptance

A clear timetable for the installation and acceptance testing should be set out. The acceptance testing procedures should also be set out. Acceptance should be defined to occur when the system conforms to the established performance specifications for the specified acceptance test, otherwise the vendor is at the mercy of a customer who refuses to make the final payments until perfection is achieved. This is a virtually impossible requirement in the software field. Acceptance should trigger the final payment in a fixed-price contract, and marks the beginning of any warranty period.

Ownership and exclusivity

The fact that the customer has paid for the software does not mean that it automatically owns the copyright. As explained in Chapter 13, the copyright in a work is owned by the author unless the work was produced in the course of the author's employment, when it is owned by the author's employer. As the vendor is not an employee of the customer, the vendor will own the copyright in the software unless the vendor agrees to assign that copyright to the customer. The customer should always seek to get an agreement for assignment. However, the vendor may wish to be able to use or adapt the system for another customer in the same business. If the customer is prepared to agree to this, it should be done by an agreement to license the vendor to make such use of the customer's copyright, rather than by allowing the vendor to retain the copyright. In that way, the customer can retain a right of veto if the vendor wishes to use the software in a way that would commercially damage the customer, and any agreement to license should contain such a right of veto.

Ownership of the copyright by the customer does not, however, prevent the vendor from using the same ideas in a different form for another client. If the software represents an innovation which will give the customer a commercial advantage over its competitors, the customer does not want that innovation given to a competitor. In such circumstances the customer should insist that the vendor undertakes not to work for a competitor of the customer on a similar product for a length of time representing the time it would take the competitor, without assistance, to develop a similar system for itself. The vendor should also agree not to go into competition with the customer for a similar period. The customer cannot lawfully insist on too long a period of non-competition, otherwise the whole restriction will be unenforceable.

Documentation

Documentation is important if the customer is to be able to make full use of the software. Unfortunately, documentation is the phase of the project least popular with programmers, and it tends to get neglected. The contract should specify in detail the documentation to be provided and the standards which it is to meet, and a timetable for its production should be set out. If all documentation is not provided before acceptance then part of the final payment should be held back until it is provided.

Warranties

The giving of warranties with respect to something that is not in existence at the time the warranty is given is full of dangers for the warrantor, the vendor. On the other hand, no customer in his right mind would agree to pay a large sum for custom software without some reassurance that what has been paid for will work. Skill and care are needed on the part of the contract negotiators and drafters to reach an acceptable compromise.

Thought should first be given to the possibility that warranties may be implied by law into the contract. The question of the applicability of the law on sale of goods to a contract for the development of custom software has not yet come up for court decision (see the discussion in Chapter 3), and it is likely that such a contract would be treated as one for services, rather than goods. However, this is not certain, particularly in view of the fact that certain taxing authorities have been attempting to levy sales tax, which applies only to sales of goods, on payments for custom software. The warranties implied in the sale of goods under the laws of at least the UK, most of the Commonwealth and the USA, include warranties of merchantability and fitness for purpose. Both these warranties are most unsuitable for custom software, at least from the vendor's point of view. The vendor should therefore ensure that those warranties are expressly excluded, where this is possible, from the contract. It is most unlikely that these warranties would not be excludable, as this type of contract is most unlikely to be a 'consumer' or other protected transaction.

There are certain express warranties that should not be given. A vendor should never warrant that the software will be 'bug free', for instance by giving a warranty such as: 'The Vendor warrants that the Software will be free of program coding errors when installed.'

The first reason why this warranty should not be given is that software of any degree of complexity and sophistication is hardly ever completely bug free, even after years of use. The word processing software being used to write this book is one of the best selling programs which has been on the market for several years, and yet from time to time I come across a bug. The important thing is that the bugs I find are trivial, they may be slightly annoying but they do not interfere with the satisfactory performance of the program. That is all any customer needs; stable software which performs satisfactorily the tasks the customer requires it for.

The second reason why this warranty should not be given is that trivial bugs may be unreasonably difficult and expensive for the vendor to fix. On the other hand, it may be easy, and involve minimal inconvenience to the customer, to alter the operating procedures to eliminate the effect of the bug. A customer who can insist on having the bug fixed at no real expense to himself is less likely to agree to such a change in procedures.

Another warranty which should not be given, but which is unfortunately often seen in software contracts because it has been lifted unthinkingly from a hardware contract, is a warranty that the software will be free from defects in materials and workmanship. Such a warranty, which is suitable and appropriate for a piece of machinery, is unsuitable and inappropriate for software. Particular care over warranty language should be taken when a 'bundled' system is being sold, and separate warranties should be given for the hardware and for the software elements of the bundle.

Probably the best compromise is a warranty that the software will conform to the contract specifications. This, of course, suffers from the difficulty of defining the specifications of as yet undeveloped software in any meaningful way, which is discussed above. However, this warranty will give the customer reasonable protection if the specifications are in a result-orientated, rather than a descriptive form. The customer's interest is in having the software process the payroll or deal with the customer accounts, or whatever, and is not really concerned with how this is achieved.

As has already been seen, the satisfactory development of custom software demands cooperation from the customer. Any warranty that the vendor gives should be in terms which exempt the vendor from liability if failure is caused by lack of timely cooperation from the customer.

Warranty problems will be considerably reduced if the customer has been made responsible for the approval of each step of the development process. Too often, the customer has sat back and waited until the final product is running, and then complained that this was not what was wanted, even though it may conform exactly to the initial specifictions. Disputes over whether the vendor is obliged to make the changes the customer wants under the warranty then arise, particularly when the warranty was vaguely worded. The problem was that, at the beginning, the customer did not really know what he wanted but asked for something, and that was what he got. If the customer is fully involved in the development process, in the manner described above, this problem should not arise.

The vendor should also give a warranty that the software does not infringe a third party's patent or copyright. If any third-party software has been incorporated into the software, the vendor should be responsible for ensuring that such use was properly licensed, even though the parties may agree that the customer should pay any licence fee.

Vendor business termination

As has been stated above, business failures in this field have been regrettably common. The customer should be aware of this risk, and should seek to build as much protection as possible into the contract. The dangers of insolvency happening during the development process are obvious, but it could be just as serious if failure occurred afterwards and the customer was dependent upon the vendor for maintenance.

During development
The importance of being able to secure the assistance of the vendor's staff who have been involved in the project for an orderly handover to a new vendor has already been mentioned. The customer should also have a right to any code and documentation already produced, even if it is incomplete. In order to avoid some of the problems arising from bankruptcy law, the customer should require that title to these items is transferred upon completion of each, as part of the consideration for the progress payments.

Afterwards
Obviously, if the customer has been maintaining the software after installation there is no problem. If, however, the customer has been relying on the vendor, a new source of maintenance will be required. For this, a copy of the source code is needed, with all alterations made to date, and as full documentation as possible. In general, giving the customer possession of the source code does not pose the problems with custom software that it does with standard software (see Chapter 9 for a discussion of those problems). The customer is likely to be the owner of the software, and even if this is not the case there is little risk that the vendor's trade secrets will be given away by the customer in the usual circumstances. Preferably, the maintenance contract should provide that a copy of the source code is to be retained at the customer's premises, and that the vendor undertakes to update that copy every time alterations are made to the programs.

Maintenance

Maintenance after the expiry of the warranty period is usually dealt with by a separate contract, and it is preferable to deal with maintenance in this way.

The agreement should be for a period such as a year, renewable by either party. If the vendor is given the right to terminate without cause, or to refuse renewal, then this should be done on sufficiently long notice to allow the customer time to find an alternative source of maintenance.

As with hardware, the contract should set out a timetable for responding to requests for maintenance. Where possible, the customer should be required to install the necessary communications equipment so that the vendor's personnel can access the system through their own computer. This will mean that the vendor can provide a much faster response than if employees have to be sent to the customer's site. The contract should provide who is to pay out-of-pocket expenses of the vendor's employees while they are at the customer's site.

The customer should agree not to make any modifications of its own to the software. Alternatively, the customer must be obliged to inform the vendor of all such modifications, and the vendor should be entitled to charge extra for work needed because of the customer's modifications. However, it is not always easy to apportion blame in practice, so a complete ban on the customer tampering with the software is preferable.

The customer should also agree to provide facilities necessary for performance of the maintenance. These include machine time, time of customer's employees, and print-outs.

The vendor should agree that, where possible, the maintenance will be performed by people who were involved in the development of the system. It is obviously much easier for these people to provide effective maintenance.

A common problem in the industry is that maintenance services tend to be underpriced. A common formula used is some (usually small) percentage of the cost, or of the licence fee. This bears no relationship to the real cost of providing those services. It is in the customer's long-term interest that the vendor is properly remunerated for maintenance services, otherwise the vendor is likely to go out of business leaving the customer with a major problem. The only realistic method for unique, custom software is to charge on a time-and-materials basis. With standard software it is easier to estimate a realistic annual average cost for service, because that service will be provided to a number of customers.

PRECEDENTS

Payments

Progress payments

The Customer agrees that, at the completion of each stage listed in schedule ＿＿ to this Agreement it will pay to the Vendor the percentage of the total contract price applicable to that stage, less a retention of ＿＿%. The percentages of the contract price applicable to each stage are set forth in schedule ＿＿ to this Agreement. The balance shall be retained by the Customer until final acceptance of the System. If this Agreement is terminated by the Vendor, or by the Customer because of the Vendor's default, prior to final acceptance of the System, the Customer shall be entitled to retain said balances as liquidated damages for the Vendor's breach. In any other event, the balances shall be paid to the Vendor upon termination. The Customer shall not be obliged to pay any such progress payment until it has received from the Vendor a progress report signed by an officer of the Vendor, certifying the completion of the relevant stage and describing the status of progress towards completion of the remaining stages.

Increase in scope at customer's request

If, at any time during this Agreement, the Customer requests any addition to, or modification of, the System as specified in Schedule ＿＿ to this Agreement, such request shall be made in writing and signed by an officer of the Customer. The Vendor shall provide an estimate of the additional expected cost of the modification or addition. The Vendor shall not be obliged to perform any step towards making the modification or addition until the Customer has agreed in writing to pay the estimated additional cost, or such other amount as the parties may agree in writing should be paid.

Staffing and resources

Full-time employees

The Vendor warrants and represents that all persons to be assigned to the performance of this Agreement shall be full-time employees of the Vendor, and that they shall not be transferred from this assignment without the written permission of the Customer.

Right to staff upon vendor business termination

If the Vendor shall cease to conduct business in the area of software development for any reason during this Agreement, the Customer shall have the right to offer employment to all or any of the Vendor's employees assigned to the performance of this Agreement, notwithstanding any provisions in this Agreement or related agreements to the contrary. The Vendor shall notify all such employees of this provision and shall obtain agreement from each of them that, if he or she declines such an offer, he or she will agree to work for not more than 30 days for the Customer as an independent contractor at the same rate of pay as he or she was receiving immediately before his or her employment by the Vendor was terminated, in order to assist the transfer of the work under this Agreement to a new vendor.

Confidentiality

The Vendor agrees to treat as confidential all information received from the Customer which the Customer has indicated in writing to be confidential. The Vendor agrees to disclose this information only to those of its employees who need to know it for the performance of this Agreement, and to ensure that each of those employees has signed an agreement to keep such information confidential. The Vendor further agrees that it and its employees will observe all security regulations in effect from time to time at the Customer's premises, and will comply with the Customer's written security procedures for confidential material. A copy of these procedures is attached to this Agreement as Schedule _____.

Insurance

The Vendor [Customer] agrees, during the term of this Agreement, to maintain at its expense all insurance required by law for the Vendor's employees while working upon the Customer's premises, and to provide the Customer [Vendor] with a certificate of such insurance upon request.

Limitation on usage of resources

The Customer agrees to make available to the Vendor full assistance by the Customer's employees, provided, however, that if such assistance shall seriously interfere with any employee's duties, the employees of both parties in charge of the performance of this Agreement shall agree upon a schedule for the availability to the Vendor of that employee's time.

The Customer shall make available to the Vendor ____ hours of machine time per month, at times to be mutually agreed at the beginning of the month in question between such supervising employees. If, in any month, the Vendor shall require more time than is specified herein, the parties shall negotiate terms for the provision of such time, which may include purchase of time from a third party, or offsetting the sums due under this Agreement by ____ per hour of extra time, less any allowance for machine time allotted but not used in preceding months.

Testing

The following testing shall be carried out in accordance with the timetables contained in Schedule ____ to this Agreement:

(a)   Initial testing. Each program, as completed, shall be tested against data supplied by the Vendor to ensure performance in accordance with the program specifications set out in Schedule ____ to this Agreement.

(b)   Customer testing. Each program, upon successful completion of initial testing, shall be tested against data supplied by the Customer to ensure that the program meets the Customer's requirements as specified in Schedule ____ to this Agreement.

(c)   System testing. Upon successful completion of customer testing for each program, the complete System shall be tested against data supplied by the Customer to ensure conformity with the Customer's requirements.

(d)   Final testing. The final testing shall take place using live data to ensure that the System performs correctly under normal operating conditions.

Acceptance

Upon notification to the Customer by the Vendor that the installation procedures set out in Schedule ____ to this Agreement are complete, the Customer shall perform the acceptance tests described in Schedule ____ to this Agreement. Such tests shall be completed no later than ____ days after the receipt of the notice of installation. It is mutually agreed that as soon as the System performs in the acceptance tests according to the specifications set out in Schedule ____ the software shall be deemed to be accepted by the Customer. If any acceptance test shall disclose deficiencies in the software, the Vendor will correct such deficiencies within ____ days, and the Customer shall thereafter have ____ days to retest the software.

Ownership

All original materials including but not limited to programs, listings, print-outs, flow charts and documentation produced by the Vendor under this Agreement shall belong exclusively to the Customer. The Vendor hereby agrees to assign, and does assign, all copyrights in these materials to the Customer. The Customer agrees that it will, upon written request from the Vendor, grant the Vendor a non-exclusive licence to use the materials in connection with work to be done by the Vendor for a third party, provided, however, that the Customer may refuse to grant such a licence if the Customer reasonably considers that its business interests would thereby be damaged.

Non-competition

During the performance of this Agreement and for ____ months after its completion or termination, the Vendor agrees that it will not enter into any business competitive with that of the Customer and will not develop software for a business in direct competition with the Customer. The Vendor further agrees that it will not make use of, or disclose any information concerning the Customer not already known to the public or any information, methods, systems or other business information created, learned or developed in connection with this Agreement.

Warranty of non-infringement

The Vendor warrants that all materials produced under this Agreement will not infringe any patent, copyright, trade secret or other proprietary right of any third party. To the extent that this material contains matter which is proprietary to a third party, the Vendor warrants that it is licensed by the owner to make such use of such matter, and that it has the right to grant the Customer a sub-licence to use such matter. The Vendor will indemnify and hold the Customer harmless from and against any loss, damage, cost, liability or expense (including reasonable counsel fees) arising out of any breach or claimed breach of this warranty.

Maintenance

Scope

During the term of this Agreement, the Vendor will correct all errors notified to it by the Customer which are attributable to programming errors by the Vendor and which significantly affect the use of the software. The Customer shall notify the Vendor in writing of any modifications made to the software by the Customer, and the Vendor shall not be responsible for correcting errors which arise from such modifications. The Vendor may, at its option, correct errors arising from the Customer's modifications at its usual charges on a time-and-materials basis.

Customer assistance

The Customer shall provide such reasonable assistance as may be required by the Vendor in performance of its duties under this Agreement. Such assistance shall include, but is not limited to, provision of reports on errors and problems, timely provision of all required test data, consultation between technical staffs of the Vendor and the Customer, and provision of machine time reasonably required by the Vendor.

Provision of communications

The Customer shall install and maintain for the duration of this Agreement communications equipment allowing the Vendor to access the Customer's System from the Vendor's premises. Such equipment shall conform to the specifications set out in Schedule _____ to this Agreement. The Vendor may use this equipment for the purpose of performance of this Agreement, and for that purpose only, subject in each case to the prior approval of the Customer.

Staffing

The Vendor agrees that it will use only suitably qualified, full-time employees in the performance of this Agreement. It further agrees that it will, when possible, assign one of the employees involved in the development of the software to the performance of this Agreement.

9 Contracts for Purchase and Modification of Standard Software

WHAT IS 'STANDARD' SOFTWARE?

The answer to the question whether a piece of software is 'standard' software depends upon the context. In terms of retail marketing, a piece of software will be considered standard if a large number of identical packages (which normally include programs and documentation) are sold without any modification. At the other extreme, in terms of software development, any piece of software which is used in essentially the same form by two or more users is standard software, as opposed to custom software. The former type is most commonly encountered in the field of personal computers and microcomputers, whose users generally purchase mass-produced software packages which generally fit their needs, and adapt their particular requirements to the limitations of those programs. The latter type generally exists in connection with larger computer systems, where a software house may be able to provide a specialised software package, such as a hospital accounting system, or an inventory program for an automobile parts stockist, for one user which it has previously developed for a similar user.

Ideally, every user would prefer to have software which fits his exact needs. In the case of mass-produced software, which usually sells for a relatively low price, it is not economical for the producer of that software to supply custom modifications. Further, because such software is usually sold in object-code form only, it is impossible or very difficult for the purchaser to make modifications. Under the circumstances, the user trades some convenience for the lower price that mass sale of standard software makes possible. At the other end of the scale, while some cost savings are involved because the specialised software is usable for more than one customer, it is generally sufficiently expensive to make minor modifications economically possible. In either case, standard software does provide advantages over custom-designed software. Obviously, a major advantage is that of price; mass marketing allows the owner of a personal computer to purchase a sophisticated spreadsheet program, word processing program or data-base management program for a tiny fraction of the costs of developing such a program. Another advantage is that much of the initial debugging should have been completed before the product is marketed, so it can be successfully run immediately after purchase. It is possible to see the system running before purchase in order to determine reliability and suitability. Further, in many cases the manufacturer supplies maintenance information to all users at little or no charge, whereas the costs of maintenance of custom software can be considerable.

The foregoing discussion has been about the purchase of standard software, but in most cases it is to the vendor's advantage to license use of the software, rather than to sell a copy outright. The considerations in a decision to license rather than to sell are set out in Chapter 15. Essentially, a licence, which provides a continuing contractual relationship, gives the software producer greater control over the use of the software, provided the licence can be enforced. In the case of low-cost, mass-marketed software packages which have not involved very large development costs, it is not feasible for the producer to try to enforce licence agreements with each of the purchasers. However, whenever development costs represent a significant capital investment by the producer in that piece of software, efforts should be made to control use, in particular copying, by the user.

LICENSING STANDARD SOFTWARE

The general considerations, and the desirable terms and conditions for a software licence, will depend upon whether the software is sold in large numbers of low-cost standard copies, or is specialised, expensive software of which relatively few copies are sold.

Mass-produced software

General considerations
Mass marketing of software produces some peculiar problems, of which the software producer should be aware. Some of these arise from the

nature of the market; many of the potential customers will be relatively unsophisticated in relation to computer software, and will have little experience of, or understanding of, computer systems. This is particularly true of most of the present purchasers of personal computers, to whom most standard, mass-marketed software is sold. They may very well have unrealistic ideas about what a particular piece of software can do for them. They are unlikely to have any real understanding of the effort involved to produce a reliable piece of software, which means that they often complain about the price of a software package and feel 'justified' in copying it.

Other problems arise because of the newness of the market, which means that the applicable law is not well defined. For example, it has not yet been determined anywhere whether software is 'goods' for the purposes of applying the law relating to sale of goods. It seems very likely that the sale of mass-marketed software in the form of discs or cassettes will be held to come within sale-of-goods provisions, but what is the effect of licensing these software packages rather than selling them outright? A software package usually consists of one or more diskettes or cassettes, together with a manual and other literature. The purchase of a software package under a licence would seem to be analogous to the purchase of a patented article, where part of the price paid is for the article, and part for an implied licence under the patent to use it. The user has no right, because of the patent, to duplicate the article, but nevertheless the sale of the article to the user is a sale of goods. The situation is likely to become even more complicated in the future, as systems for transferring software electronically to the user's computer are now possible, and commercial forms of such systems are being actively worked on.

It is also likely that many sales of mass-marketed software will be consumer transactions, and will therefore come within provisions designed to protect consumers. Examples are the UK Unfair Contract Terms Act 1977, and the US Magnuson-Moss Warranty Act. Vendors of software which is likely to be bought by individuals for personal purposes, such as games, should consult a lawyer familiar with commercial law in the relevant jurisdiction in order to ascertain what provisions such laws may impose upon him.

Because, of necessity, mass-marketed software is sold or licensed under standard form provisions, the purchaser has no opportunity for negotiating contract terms at all. The only choice the purchaser has is not to buy. Therefore, the following discussion relates only to considerations the software producer should have in mind when drawing up a standard contract for the sale or licensing of his software.

Sale of software packages

If it is decided to sell the software package outright, this may be done without any written contract at all. The disadvantage of this course is that all warranties and other terms implied by law or by custom will apply to the sale. This could mean that the seller of a £30 home finance package could be liable for damages hundreds or thousands of times the purchase price if the program is defective and causes losses. Another disadvantage is that most people do not understand the copyright laws, and believe that if they have bought a copy of a program that gives them an unlimited right to copy it. The software producer would be well advised to sell the software package under a simple form of written agreement.

As it will almost certainly be impracticable to require every purchaser to sign an agreement, care must be taken that it will be enforceable under the general contract provisions which have been discussed in Chapter 3. An unsigned contract will only be binding on the purchaser if it was clearly brought to his or her attention at the time of purchase, and if it does not contain unconscionable terms. Further, when the purchase is a consumer transaction, legislation may invalidate some clauses which limit or exclude warranties or liability.

The contract should be in clearly readable type, and should be on the outside of the package so that it can be read before purchase. This requirement will be unpopular with the marketing department, who will want a more attractive package, but a contract which cannot be read until after the package has been bought is completely worthless. Some vendors try to avoid this problem by stating that the package can be returned for a full refund if the contract terms are not acceptable (making the purchase voidable at the purchaser's option). If the contract is on the inside, but accessible before purchase, then attention to its presence should be drawn by some wording on the outside of the package in a place where a purchaser should reasonably be expected to look before purchase.

The contract should contain the following provisions:

(a) Exclusion or limitation of implied warranties. As the degree to which such warranties can be excluded or limited, and the formalities required to make such exclusion or limitation effective, vary from jurisdiction to jurisdiction, a local lawyer familiar with the commercial laws of the jurisdiction should be consulted in the drafting of such provisions. There should also be a provision excluding liability for representations made in advertising or by salesmen.

(b)   Exclusion or limitation of liability for damages. The same comments apply here as under (a).

(c)   Notice of copyright, and description of the relevant provisions of the copyright laws. This may discourage the otherwise honest people who might be tempted to copy the program, and prevents a plea of innocence on the part of apprehended pirates.

(d)   Provisions for replacement of defective discs. While the general law, and good commercial practice, allow for the replacement of discs which were defective when sold, it is advantageous to provide expressly how this is to be done. The seller would be well advised to make such an exchange easy, in order to generate customer confidence, at the same time putting a time-limit on the exchange.

(e)   Replacement of subsequently damaged discs. In order to discourage copying, it is to the seller's advantage to provide his customers with replacements for discs damaged in use at the cost of the basic medium. It is essential to do so in the case of programs which are copy protected, as otherwise only the most unsophisticated purchasers will buy the program in the first place.

Licensing of software packages
In the case of a licence, there must be a written agreement. Without such an agreement, the law will presume the transfer of the software package to the purchaser to be a sale. There are three mechanisms generally used in the industry to ensure that the licence provisions are binding on the licensee/purchaser:

(a)   The 'package' licence, which provides that acceptance of the terms is signified by the purchaser opening the package, or using the program. As with the unsigned sales contract discussed above, this will only be effective if the purchaser has clear notice of the terms of the licence at the time of purchase, or at least before opening the package, and it is clear that the unopened package can be returned for a full refund if the purchaser rejects the contract. There has not yet been any court decision on the effect or validity of such a licence, so there is some uncertainty in choosing this method.

(b)   The 'baited' licence, where the seller seeks to induce the purchaser to sign the licence agreement, and to return a signed copy to the seller, by the promise of the provision of certain goods or services if the signed licence is returned. This usually includes free updates, or the opportunity to purchase new versions of the program at reduced prices, and may also include charts or cards which make use of the program easier. Other 'bribes' include such things as T-shirts and posters, or back-up discs in the case of copy-protected software.

(c)   The distributor-enforced licence. For software that is distributed only through retailers, rather than sold through mail order, it is possible to require purchasers to sign the licence agreement at the time of purchase. This is done by suitable provisions in the distributorship agreements which the software producer has with retail distributors. These provisions should make the distributor liable for obtaining a signed licence for each customer to whom a copy of the software package is sold, and for transmitting a copy of the signed licence to the producer. This type of provision is generally more readily acceptable and enforceable in the case of more specialised, high-cost packages. In addition to the terms suggested above for inclusion in a sales agreement, a licence should include the following provisions:

(i)   Protection of the software owner's proprietary rights. The software producer may wish to protect the programs through trade-secret law, although the dangers of relying on such protection in the case of software produced in a large number of copies is discussed in Chapter 15. In this case, the licence should contain suitable provisions by which the licensee agrees to keep the software confidential. In the more common case of copyright protection, the licence should limit copying to a specified number of back-up copies (in the case of software that is not copy protected) and prohibit or limit user modifications to the software and decompiling of the object-code program (which is the form generally supplied) into source code. The software owner may also wish to limit the number of machines on which the software can be run, or the number of users who can use the software at any one time. In general, any copying of the accompanying documentation should be prohibited. Provisions protecting trade marks and trade names may also be included.

(ii)   Maintenance. The provision of maintenance, in the form of patches to fix bugs, is one means of inducing a purchaser to sign the licence agreement. It is also a means for detecting unauthorised copies because the owners of such copies will not receive maintenance information, and for discouraging the ownership of such copies. If this service is provided, the software owner should disclaim all liability in respect of copies of the software to which unauthorised modifications have been made by the user. For similar reasons, the software owner may wish to provide its licensees with documentation updates.

(iii)   Termination. If the licence is terminated for any reason, the licensee should be obliged either to return or to destroy all copies of the program and documentation in his possession.

Specialised software

Differences between specialised and mass-produced software

The first major difference between specialised and mass-produced standard software is that the vendor sells many fewer copies of specialised software. This has the advantage that it is possible for the vendor to maintain a direct relationship with the customer, making it possible to police use, maintain confidentiality of trade secrets and provide some customisation of the software. It also has the disadvantage that any unauthorised copying represents a much more serious loss to the vendor. The second difference arises from the first: the software is much more expensive. One effect of this is that maintenance becomes economically feasible, as does the cost of customisation. It has the advantage to the customer that the importance of the purchase to both parties makes it possible for the customer to negotiate licence terms. On the other hand, it is likely that the effect on the customer's business of any failure of the software will be much more serious than a similar failure by a mass-produced program. This will make the customer more anxious to have proper warranties, while it will make the vendor anxious to limit liability.

General considerations

Specialised software should always be licensed rather than sold outright. This is because of the economic importance to the vendor of proper control over the use of the software and the protection of trade secrets. It also has the advantage to the customer of providing more flexible means of payment for the use of the software than is possible with a purchase. These matters are discussed below.

Contents of a licence for specialised software

Specifications   The customer should insist on detailed specifications for the software being set out in the agreement. Where the software package is standard, and is already running on third parties' machines, provision of a detailed set of specifications should not prove difficult. Important factors that should be included are facility requirements, run time, programming language and operating procedures. Provision of detailed specifications will require more thought and care where some customisation of the software is to be provided. In the case of the first sale of a package, where the sale takes place before there has been any long-term operational testing of the package, the provision of specifications will present some of the problems found in the provision of specifications in custom software development, discussed in Chapter 8.

Specifications for the documentation should also be included, particularly in the case of a new package, or where some customisation is to be provided. This is less crucial in the case of an established, standard package, where the customer will have had a chance to examine the vendor's standard documentation before deciding on the purchase. If special documentation is to be supplied, the details should be set out in the agreement.

Installation and acceptance   Unlike mass-produced software, which is generally much simpler and supplied in versions designed to run immediately on a specified machine, specialised software will often require installation by the vendor on the customer's machine.

A delivery schedule should be agreed upon. In the case of an established package, this should provide few problems. It can advantageously be done by the vendor agreeing to deliver at the customer's request, upon a reasonable notice period. This allows the purchaser to have the necessary hardware installed before delivery is due, while giving the vendor sufficient notice to arrange for the necessary personnel to install the software. In the case of a newly developed package, delivery and installation timetabling present problems similar to those encountered in custom-development contracts.

After the vendor has certified that the installation is complete, acceptance testing begins. This procedure has been discussed in detail in Chapter 8. In the case of standard software, the vendor may seek to incorporate a standard set of acceptance tests into every contract. The purchaser should carefully review these to see if they fulfil its particular requirements before agreeing to them. It is important for the vendor's protection that objective acceptance criteria are established. It is important for the customer's protection that payments do not become due under the licence until these objective criteria are met.

Warranties The discussion of warranties relating to software development in Chapter 8 applies equally here. The vendor should never give a warranty that the program will be error free, however well established the program.

Because the customer will not know the history of the program's development, the vendor should be required to give a warranty that either it owns the rights to the program or it has the right to sublicense the customer to use any portions of the software owned by others. The vendor should also give an indemnity against infringement of the proprietary rights of others.

Payment Payment for use of the software under a licence can be made in a number of ways. In negotiating payment, the vendor is concerned that it receives a reasonable return on the investment that it has put into the development of the software. The customer, on the other hand, does not want to pay more for the software than it is economically worth to its business.

The most common method of payment, traditionally, is the lump-sum payment at the commencement of the licence. While this method does have the advantage to the vendor that it gets its money immediately, and does not have to worry about the future financial status of the customer, it has a number of disadvantages for both parties. The disadvantage to the vendor is that it has to set an arbitrary price for the software, which in most cases will not reflect the value of that software to the customer. The vendor gets paid the same, regardless of the amount of use that the customer makes of the software. The disadvantages to the customer are clear: it has to pay before any cost savings resulting from the use of the software are realised, and it has to pay the same regardless of the amount of use that it makes of the programs. It also has the disadvantage that a vendor who no longer has any financial interest in the software will be less inclined to exert itself to solve any problems with the software that arise later.

If a lump-sum payment is used, the customer should ensure that the payment is structured to provide the maximum protection. Only part should be payable on delivery, with the remainder payable no sooner than successful completion of the acceptance testing. Preferably, part should not be payable until the expiration of any warranty period, to encourage the vendor to provide prompt service during this period, which is when most of the problems with the software should surface.

One possible way of linking the price of the licence to the use made of it is by setting the price according to the number of users who can simultaneously access the programs. The vendor will generally also limit the licence to a specified CPU, although in this case there should be provision allowing the customer to use the software on a back-up system while the named system is down.

With some types of software it may be possible to link pricing more closely to usage, by means of what is sometimes called 'click' pricing. This means that fees are charged on a regular basis, usually monthly, based on the number of transactions of a particular type which have occurred in that period. For the vendor's protection, there should be some minimum payment in each period. The method of accounting for the sum payable will depend upon the type of software and the transaction chosen as the pricing basis. It may be possible for the vendor to build a 'counter' into the software, either as the primary means of determining the number of chargeable transactions or as a check against the customer's own accounting. This type of pricing has the advantage to both parties that it is based on usage. It would also be possible to combine the two methods, in cases where the vendor preferred some capital return as well as income by setting a lower initial fee in combination with a reduced price per transaction.

The agreement is also likely to involve certain one-time charges, such as those involved in delivery, installation and user training. These charges should be set out in the agreement. Maintenance charges are considered below.

Term and termination   Most software licences are perpetual. If the licence is for a fixed term, then renewal provisions must be agreed upon and included in the licence agreement. If there are periodic payments associated with a renewable licence, then the customer should ensure that these cannot be raised by more than an agreed amount, either a fixed percentage or by a formula which varies with a recognised price index, at each renewal.

In the case of a perpetual licence for a fixed sum, the customer should be able to terminate at any time. In other cases, the customer should be able to terminate upon reasonable notice, or, in the case of a term licence, only upon the vendor's default. The vendor should normally only be able to terminate when the customer is in default, and has failed to cure that default after reasonable notice.

Upon termination, the customer should be obliged either to return the software and documentation, together with all copies of the whole or part of either which it has made, to the vendor, or to certify to the vendor that these items have been destroyed.

Protection of the vendor's proprietary rights   Firstly, ownership of the software should be clearly set out. In the case of standard software, the vendor will properly assert ownership. The case of customised standard software is less clear, but the vendor should normally insist on having full ownership of this too, otherwise complicated problems of joint ownership could arise. The customer who has paid for the customisation may justly demand that the vendor does not supply the customised form of the software to any third party. Such a customer may also wish to recoup some of its costs by licensing its customised software to others; if it does so, it should get agreement from the vendor in the licence agreement that the customer has the right to sublicense such third parties to use the vendor's software, upon payment of an agreed licence fee.

The customer should acknowledge the vendor's proprietary rights, and the fact that the software and documentation contain trade secrets belonging to the vendor. An acknowledgment of copyright should also be made where appropriate, with an agreement to maintain that copyright by placing the appropriate notice on all copies made of the copyright materials.

The vendor should consider including the following restrictions, where appropriate:

(a)   Access to listings and documentation containing confidential information to be limited to those of the customer's employees and contractors who have a need to know such information to carry out their duties. All such persons to sign confidentiality agreements in the same terms as the confidentiality clauses in the licence.

(b)   Prohibit the customer from competing with the vendor's software business, in particular the sale of competing software, or the use of the vendor's software in a service bureau operation, at least without proper payment to the vendor for such use.

(c)   Restrict use of the software to a single CPU at a named location.

(d)   Restrict the copying of either programs or documentation to a specified number of back-ups. Provision should be made for the safe storage of such back-up copies so that they do not fall into unauthorised hands. The vendor should have a right to inspect periodically the customer's storage and procedures to maintain confidentiality.

(e)   Supply object code only, and prohibit recompiling or any other reverse-engineering technique which can yield source code.

(f)   The customer should agree to assist the vendor in tracking down unauthorised users of the software, and to notify the vendor immediately of any unauthorised use which comes to the customer's attention.

Access to source code   It is relatively easy to take another person's source-code program and reprogram it in object code so that it is very difficult to detect that copying has taken place. This is not so for object code — copying of object code is usually readily detected. For this reason, vendors are usually reluctant to part with the source code for their standard programs.

Lack of access to source code is of little concern to the purchaser of a mass-produced, relatively inexpensive program. It is, however, of considerable concern to the purchaser/licensee of a high-cost, specialised program, which may be of considerable importance to its business. This is because it is almost impossible to provide maintenance for such a program without the source code. So long as the vendor is around to provide this maintenance, there should be no problem. If, however, the vendor becomes bankrupt (a not uncommon occurrence in this industry), or if a disaster destroys all the vendor's copies of the source code, the purchaser is in trouble.

It is therefore common in licence negotiations for the purchaser to demand access to the source code, and for the vendor to refuse to grant it. The resolution to this problem may depend upon the relative bargaining strengths of the parties. In general, with a standard software package, the vendor has too much invested to allow control over the software to pass from its control.

One compromise which has been frequently used since it was first proposed is to set up an escrow for the source code. The parties agree that the vendor will deposit a copy of the source code and related documentation with an independent escrow agent, who will release the source code to the customer upon the happening of one or more specified events connected with the ability of the vendor to continue to supply maintenance. The escrow agreement should:

(a)   Define what is to be deposited in escrow.

(b)   Provide for verification of the escrowed materials. This can cause problems, as the vendor will not wish any potential competitors to inspect the deposited source code to ensure that the agreed code and materials have been deposited.

(c)   Provide that the vendor is responsible for updating the escrowed copy each time that the customer's software is repaired, modified or enhanced.

(d)   Agree who is to pay the escrow fees.

(e)   Define the triggering events. These should include bankruptcy proceedings of all kinds. The clause providing for termination upon such events included in Chapter 6 should be consulted for suitable language.

(f)   Provide for the mechanism for releasing the escrowed code, including the possibility that the parties may disagree that a triggering event has occurred.

Such escrow agreements may provide only illusory comfort to the customer. One reason for this is that the bankruptcy laws of the relevant jurisdiction may provide protection for the bankrupt's property and executory contracts which will effectively nullify the operation of the escrow upon bankruptcy. As bankruptcy laws vary from jurisdiction to jurisdiction, a local lawyer should be consulted. So far as the United States are concerned, there is considerable doubt whether escrow provisions will be effective under the provisions of the new Bankruptcy Code.

Another reason for concern on the part of the customer is that the escrow will only be of use if the escrowed code represents the actual software running on the customer's machine at the time that the triggering event occurs. Even with the best organised vendor, it is unlikely that all changes to the customer's object code programs will be matched by immediate changes to the escrow copy of the source code. This is even less likely with a failing vendor, because, in general, business failure does not occur instantaneously. The common pattern is that the vendor, which is usually small and under-capitalised, gets into trouble with a contract, and has to commit more and more of its personnel to trying to meet deadlines. In this emergency situation, routine administrative matters, such as updating escrow code, are pushed aside to deal with the emergency at hand. Eventually, the pressure causes the vendor to fail, and it does so leaving administrative tasks, including the updating of escrowed source code, undone. The customer is likely to find that, even if it does get the source out of escrow without problems from the bankruptcy court, the source does not correspond to the versions of its programs that it is presently running.

One suggestion that has been made to try to get round the bankruptcy-law problems, although it does not avoid the other problems, is to have the source code held in trust for the customer, rather than in escrow. Again, a lawyer familiar with this area of law in the jurisdiction concerned should be consulted before such an arrangement is entered into.

Maintenance   Much of what was said in Chapter 8 with respect to maintenance of custom software applies to the maintenance of specialised software. The main difference is that the cost of the efforts can be spread out over several customers, as a bug fixed for one piece of standard software can be fixed in the same way for all the others.

One problem that often occurs is to define the difference between maintenance and improvement of the program. The vendor may subsequently come out with improved versions of the software, which it then licenses to new licensees at a higher rate. The licensees of the older version should have a contractual right to such improved versions, but the contract must make clear the terms upon which they are to get these versions. This usually involves the payment of an upgrade fee. On the other hand, licensees should receive patches to repair bugs in their existing version under the basic maintenance-agreement payments. Sometimes it is not easy to determine when a repair stops and an improvement begins. It may be possible to arrive at an agreed definition in terms of the function of the software. Ultimately, the licensee must accept that the dividing line is largely in the discretion of the vendor, and at least insist that it is treated on no worse terms in this respect than any of the vendor's other customers.

MODIFYING STANDARD SOFTWARE

Modification of standard software usually occurs with respect to specialised software. Mass-produced software is generally so inexpensive (in software terms) as to make customising modifications uneconomic. Also, the producers of such software rarely allow access to source code, and such access is necessary to make the modifications.

On the other hand, it is common that a piece of specialised software requires some modifications to adapt it to the customer's needs, and it is sufficiently valuable to the customer's business to make customisation economical.

In many cases, the modifications will be made by the software vendor. If the vendor has the capability to do this, then it is almost always best to have the person who wrote the programs perform the modification. An agreement to perform such work has many features in common with an agreement to produce custom software, and Chapter 8 should be consulted for general principles. There should, however, be fewer problems with the adaptation of existing software to produce a custom system than there are with producing a custom system from scratch; for example, the customer will have a more focused view of what it expects because it has a running software system on which it is basing those expectations. It is therefore much easier to define the scope of the system, and to provide performance specifications and acceptance procedures.

If the customer is to make the modifications itself, either by its own employees or by hiring an outside software house, there must be an agreement which permits the customer access to the source code and necessary documentation. In return, the customer must agree to protect properly the vendor's proprietary rights in the software. Also, the vendor should be exempted from liability to repair the software, once modified, and should also exclude or limit its liability for failure of the software unless the customer can prove that such failure was not the result of the modifications to the original code. Without such protection, the vendor would be placed in the almost impossible position of having to prove that failure was caused by things beyond its knowledge, namely the activities of the persons who made the modifications. Similar limitations should be placed on all warranties.

If the customer wishes to allow others to use its modified version of the software, it must obtain the vendor's permission to sublicense. This will usually be on terms of a payment per sublicence granted. The vendor should include in the agreement with the customer an agreement that the customer will only grant such sublicences on specified terms and conditions, and will preferably include as an attachment to the agreement a form of sublicence to be used. This should include terms protecting the licensor's proprietary rights, and should ensure that the sublicensee does not look to the licensor for any warranty or liability greater than those given to the licensee. The customer may wish the vendor to agree that if, for any reason, the licence to the customer is terminated, the vendor will grant licences directly to the sublicensees. Otherwise, under the rules relating to licences, the sublicensees' licences to use the vendor's software terminate automatically when the main licence terminates, and the customer may find it hard to obtain takers for its version of the software without such assurance of continuity.

PRECEDENTS

Package licence

YOU SHOULD CAREFULLY READ THE FOLLOWING
TERMS AND CONDITIONS BEFORE OPENING THIS PACK-
AGE. OPENING THIS PACKAGE INDICATES YOUR ACCEP-
TANCE OF THESE TERMS AND CONDITIONS. IF YOU DO
NOT AGREE WITH THEM, YOU SHOULD PROMPTLY
RETURN THIS PACKAGE UNOPENED TO THE PLACE
WHERE YOU BOUGHT IT FOR A FULL REFUND.

LICENCE
This licence permits you to do the following:

(a)   Use the program on a single machine.
(b)   Copy the program into any machine-readable form for back-up
purposes.
(c)   Modify the program for your own use on a single machine.
(d)   Transfer the program and this licence to another person, if that
person agrees to accept the terms and conditions of this licence. If you
transfer the program you must at the same time transfer to the same
person all back-up copies of the program you have made, or else destroy
them.

You must include the Vendor's copyright notice on all copies and
modifications.
    YOU MAY NOT USE, COPY, MODIFY OR TRANSFER THE
PROGRAM IN WHOLE OR IN PART, EXCEPT AS EXPRESSLY
PROVIDED IN THIS LICENCE. IF YOU TRANSFER POSSES-
SION OF ANY COPY OR MODIFICATION (EXCEPT AS
PROVIDED UNDER (d) ABOVE), YOUR LICENCE IS AUTO-
MATICALLY TERMINATED.

TERM
This licence is effective until terminated. You may terminate it at any
time by destroying the program, together with all copies and
modifications of the whole or any part of the program. This licence may
also be terminated if you fail to comply with any term or condition of this

licence agreement. Upon such termination, you agree to destroy all copies and modifications of the whole or any part of the program.

LIMITED WARRANTY

THIS PROGRAM IS PROVIDED 'AS IS' WITHOUT WARRANTY OF ANY KIND, EITHER EXPRESSED OR IMPLIED, INCLUDING, BUT NOT LIMITED TO THE IMPLIED WARRANTIES OF MERCHANTABILITY AND FITNESS FOR A PARTICULAR PURPOSE.

In some places, under certain circumstances, the law may not allow the exclusion of implied warranties, so the above exclusion may not apply to you. In such a case, the Vendor does not warrant that this program will meet your needs, or that the operation of the program will be error free.

In all cases, the Vendor does warrant the medium on which the program is furnished to be free from defects in workmanship and materials under normal use for a period of ninety (90) days from the date of delivery to you as evidenced by a copy of your receipt.

LIMITATIONS OF REMEDIES

The Vendor's entire liability and your exclusive remedy shall be the replacement of any medium not meeting the limited warranty given above, provided the defective medium is returned to the Vendor or an authorised dealer together with a copy of your receipt. If the Vendor is not able to deliver a satisfactory replacement, you may return the complete package for a full refund.

IN NO EVENT WILL THE VENDOR BE LIABLE TO YOU FOR ANY DAMAGES, INCLUDING ANY LOST PROFITS, LOST SAVINGS OR OTHER INCIDENTAL OR CONSEQUENTIAL DAMAGES ARISING OUT OF YOUR USE OR INABILITY TO USE THE PROGRAM, OR FOR ANY CLAIM BY ANY THIRD PARTY.

In some places under certain circumstances the law does not allow such exclusion of liability, so the above exclusion may not apply to you.

VENDOR'S RIGHTS

Copyright in the program and other materials supplied to you as part of this package belongs to the Vendor. Further, you expressly agree that the program contains information confidential to the Vendor. You agree to take all reasonable steps to protect the Vendor's copyrights and confidential information, including, but not limited to, placing the Vendor's copyright and confidential information notice on all copies or modifications of the program which you make. You also agree that you will not recompile the object code provided to you, or use any other technique to produce a source-code version of this program.

GENERAL

You may not sublicense, transfer or assign this licence agreement except as expressly provided above.

This licence agreement will be governed by the law of ____.

If you have any questions concerning this agreement, please contact the Vendor at the following address: ____.

YOU ACKNOWLEDGE THAT YOU HAVE READ AND UNDERSTAND THIS AGREEMENT AND AGREE TO BE BOUND BY ITS TERMS AND CONDITIONS. YOU FURTHER AGREE THAT IT IS THE COMPLETE AND EXCLUSIVE STATEMENT OF THE AGREEMENT BETWEEN US WHICH SUPERSEDES ANY PROPOSAL OR PRIOR AGREEMENT, ORAL OR WRITTEN, AND ANY OTHER COMMUNICATIONS BETWEEN US RELATING TO THE SUBJECT-MATTER OF THIS LICENCE AGREEMENT.

Multiple-use provisions

Multiple-copy use

This Licence applies to use on a single central processing unit only. If the Customer intends to use the Software, or any part of it, on more than one central processing unit, a separate licence for each such use must be obtained.

Multiple-user use

If the Customer's system is such that multiple users can simultaneously access the system, then the following licence fees shall apply for such multiple use:

Possible simultaneous users	Licences required
1	1
2-5	2
etc.	

Failure to comply with this provision shall be grounds for termination of this licence.

Specialised software licence

AGREEMENT by and between ——— (the 'Licensor') and ——— (the 'Licensee').

WHEREAS, the Licensor is the sole owner of a software system known as the 'Software'; and

WHEREAS, the Licensee desires to use the Software for its own purposes;

NOW, THEREFORE, the Licensor agrees to grant a non-exclusive, perpetual licence to use the Software to the Licensee upon the following terms and conditions:

1 *Deliverables* The Licensor shall deliver to the Licensee the following items:

(a) One complete set of the Software as listed in Appendix A to this Agreement.

(b) One complete set of manuals and documentation as listed in Appendix B to this Agreement.

(c) All data sets necessary to execute the Software as listed in Appendix C to this Agreement.

2 *Payment* The Licensee shall pay to the Licensor the sum of ——— within ——— days from the installation of the Software.

3 *Installation* The Licensor shall supply ——— qualified installation engineers for ——— days upon ——— days' written notice by the Licensee that it is ready for installation. The Licensee shall supply ——— suitably qualified employees to work with the Licensor's engineers for the purpose of installing the Software.

4 *Maintenance and improvements* Maintenance of and improvements to the Software shall be provided by the Licensor under the Licensor's standard Maintenance Agreement which does not form part of this Licence Agreement.

5 *Warranties* The Licensor gives the following warranties to the Licensee:

(a) That the Software is an unencumbered asset of the Licensee [or, that, to the extent that the Software is owned by third parties, the

Licensor has the right under licences from such third parties to license the Licensee to use the Software, and that the Licensor is not in breach of such licences].

(b)   That the Software will be free from significant defects in design, operation and usability in the Licensee's environment and will be in substantial accordance with the description of the Software contained in Appendices A to C of this Agreement.

THE FOREGOING WARRANTIES ARE IN LIEU OF ALL OTHER WARRANTIES, EXPRESS OR IMPLIED, INCLUDING BUT NOT LIMITED TO, THE IMPLIED WARRANTIES OF MERCHANTABILITY AND FITNESS FOR A PARTICULAR PURPOSE.

The extent of the Licensor's liability under these warranties shall be the correction or replacement, at the Licensor's option, of the defective items.

6   *Liability*   The Licensor shall not be liable for any loss or damage that may arise through the use by the Licensee of the Software, including any indirect, special or consequential damages, in connection with or arising from the performance or use of the Software, except such loss as shall result directly from the wilful misconduct or gross negligence of the Licensor or its agents.

7   *Indemnity*   The Licensor shall indemnify and hold the Licensee, its employees and agents harmless from any loss, damage or liability for infringements of any patent, trade mark or copyright with respect to the use of the items delivered hereunder, provided that the Licensor is promptly notified in writing of any suit or claim against the Licensee, and provided further that the Licensee permits the Licensor to defend or independently settle the same, and the Licensee gives the Licensor all reasonable information, assistance and authority to do so.

8   *Confidentiality*   Both parties agree that all material and information which has or will come into the possession or knowledge of each in connection with this Agreement and which consists of confidential and proprietary data whose disclosure or use by third parties would be damaging to the owner of such material or information will be held in the strictest confidence, and that no use will be made of the same other than in performance of this Agreement. Such material or information will be disclosed only to those employees or agents of the disclosing party who have a need to know, and only after such employee or agent has entered into a confidentiality agreement in substantially

the same terms as this paragraph. It is agreed that if either party shall breach the provisions of this clause, the other party shall have the right, in addition to such other remedies as may be available, to injunctive relief, it being acknowledged that legal remedies are inadequate.

9   *Proprietary information*   It is expressly understood and agreed that Software contains computer programs, documentation, information and data proprietary to the Licensor. The Licensee agrees to maintain all data and information contained in the Software, including system programs, documentation, modifications and conversions, in strictest confidence for the Licensor. The Licensee agrees that it will not disclose or allow to be disclosed any such information or data, and will take all reasonable steps to ensure that no unauthorised person shall have access to the Software, or any proprietary information contained therein.

10   *Restrictions on use*   The Licensee agrees to use the Software only on the computer system described in Appendix D to this Agreement. The Licensee further agrees that it will only make such archival copies of the Software as are necessary to ensure safe storage for a copy of the Software and proper operation of the Software on the specified system. The Licensee shall, on written demand by the Licensor, certify to the Licensor the number and location of such archival copies. The Licensee agrees that it will not modify the Software, nor will it make a source-code version of the Software, by recompilation or any other method.

11   *Destruction on termination*   Upon termination of this Agreement for any reason, the Licensee will either return to the Licensor or destroy all copies of the Software, including programs, documentation and data sets, supplied under this Agreement, and all archival copies thereof. The Licensee shall, within one month of the date of such termination, furnish the Licensor with a certificate of compliance with this paragraph, and agrees that, if such certificate is not furnished within the time stated, the Licensor shall have the right, in addition to such other remedies as may be available to it, to seek injunctive relief.

[Standard termination, notice, merger clauses, etc. should be added. See Chapter 6 for precedents.]

Conversion by customer

Licence grant
The Licensor grants the Licensee a non-exclusive, perpetual licence to use and modify the Software, and to sublicense the Software so modified to third parties.

Sublicences

The Licensee may grant sublicences to third parties to use versions of the Software modified by the Licensee in the form contained in Schedule A to this Agreement. With respect to each such sublicence granted, the Licensee shall, within 10 days of the date of execution of such sublicence, supply a copy of the executed sublicence to the Licensor, and shall pay the sum of _____ in respect of that sublicence.

Copyright

The Licensee acknowledges that all copyrights in the Software belong to the Licensor, and agrees to reproduce and include a copyright notice or proprietary legend, as appropriate, referring to the Licensor's ownership on all copies of the Software which it makes. Any modified versions of the Software produced by the Licensee shall be treated as derivative works, and appropriate copyright notices and proprietary legends, to be approved by the Licensor, shall be placed by the Licensee on all copies of such modified versions.

Warranties

THE LICENSOR GRANTS NO WARRANTIES, EXPRESS OR IMPLIED IN RESPECT OF THE SOFTWARE, INCLUDING BUT NOT LIMITED TO ALL WARRANTIES OF MERCHANT-ABILITY AND FITNESS FOR PURPOSE. THE LICENSEE TAKES THE SOFTWARE ON AN 'AS IS' BASIS.

Exclusion of liability

The Licensor shall not be liable for any loss or damage of any kind that may arise, including any indirect, special or consequential damages, in connection with or arising from the performance or use of the Software, except such loss as shall arise directly from the wilful misconduct or gross negligence of the Licensor. It is further expressly agreed and understood that the Licensor has no liability to make modifications to, or to perform maintenance upon, the Software, in either the form licensed or any modified version.

10 Contracts for the Use of Another's Computer

There are several kinds of arrangements for using another person's computer. At one extreme, there is the provision of machine time only, with no other services. The next step is the provision of 'enhanced' machine time, in which the computer owner also provides personnel, and possibly also supplies items such as paper, magnetic tape, etc., the customer supplying the programs. Time-sharing arrangements permit the customer to use not only the computer, but also the supplier's programs, with the customer inputting the data to be processed. At the other extreme is the service-bureau contract, in which the supplier also inputs the customer's data, and supplies the output in final usable form such as reports, payroll cheques or invoices.

Machine-time contracts present few problems, and are not considered here.

TIME-SHARING CONTRACTS

In the most common type of time-sharing contract, the customer uses a terminal at its premises to access the vendor's computer. This access may be to obtain information from a data base, or to use the vendor's programs to process data input by the customer. The following matters should be dealt with in a contract for time-sharing services:

(a) The terminal:

(i) Who provides it? As the terminal must be compatible with the vendor's computer, it is usual for the vendor to supply the terminal. The user may be able to obtain a terminal more cheaply elsewhere, but in this case the specifications of the terminal must be set out. The vendor should provide that it is not liable for problems arising from hardware incompatibility if the terminal is supplied by a third party.

(ii)   Who owns it? When the terminal is supplied by the vendor, it must be decided whether the user will rent it or buy it outright. Normally, the owner is liable for insurance on the terminal, so if a non-owning user is to be liable for insurance this must be expressly provided in the contract.

(iii)   Who installs it? Installation usually involves a third party, the phone company, because the communication between the user's terminal and the vendor's computer is generally over a phone line. The contract should provide who is responsible for getting the phone line installed, and for hooking the terminal up to it. Where the vendor is responsible for installation, which should be the usual situation because it is the vendor who has the necessary expertise, the user should ensure that there is a timetable that the vendor must comply with, and that the standards for acceptable installation are spelled out. If possible, no payments under the contract should be due until after satisfactory installation.

(iv)   Who maintains it? If the terminal is rented from the vendor, the rental agreement usually contains maintenance provisions. In any event, the user should ensure that it has an adequate maintenance contract with the vendor or some competent third party. The maintenance contract should provide for a specified response time to maintenance calls, target repair times, and provision for the supply of alternative equipment if a repair cannot be effected within a reasonable time. What is reasonable will depend on the use that the user is making of the facility, and other factors such as alternative terminals already on the premises.

(v)   What can it be used for? In the case where the terminal is supplied by the vendor, the user may wish to have a specific provision that it is free to use the terminal for other purposes.

(b)   Charges. Charging for time-sharing services can be done in a number of ways. Charges may be for various things, almost always on a time/usage basis. These charges may include:

(i)   Connect time, the time that the terminal is actually in contact with the computer.

(ii)   Computer time, the time that the computer is actually processing the user's data or performing data-base searches for the user.

(iii)   Storage charges, for storage of the user's data by the vendor when this is more than temporary storage during processing.

(iv)   Line charges, the cost of providing the link-up lines when this is done by the vendor.

(v)   Equipment charges, for terminals and modems where these are supplied on a rental basis by the vendor.

(vi)   Program charges, where there is use of programs belonging to third parties for which the vendor pays a fee based on usage.

It is important that these charges are clearly set out in the contract. The user should also obtain an estimate from the vendor of the likely monthly charges based on anticipated usage before entering the contract, rather than finding out at the end of the first billing period that it has taken on something which is not cost effective for its business.

(c)   Performance. The contract should set out an expected and a maximum time for response to input data. The expected time is the average of typical responses for this particular type of usage, the maximum is the longest time acceptable to the user. There should be provision for penalties, such as a rebate in charges, if more than a small percentage of response times exceed the maximum. The user would also be advised to insist on a right to termination if more than a certain percentage of responses over a specified period exceed the maximum, or if the normal response time consistently deteriorates.

The contract should also provide that if machine down time exceeds a specified amount in any particular billing period, the charges should be appropriately reduced, and should give the user the option to terminate if machine down time exceeds a specified amount in each of two or more consecutive months. Ideally, the vendor should be able to supply a back-up machine so that down time is not a problem to the user, but frequently this is not possible.

(d)   Security. When the contract involves storage by the vendor of the user's data, there should be adequate provisions to ensure that no other user of the service can access these data.

The contract should also specify who is responsible for making back-up copies of the user's data. If this is the vendor's responsibility, then there should be provisions for the security of these back-up copies, and for safe storage off the vendor's site for at least one copy. The contract should also provide that the data are owned by the user, and that all copies must be delivered to the user upon termination of the contract. The user must also be free to access or inspect copies of the data at any time during the business hours of the vendor.

(e)   Programs. To the extent that special programs are developed for, or modified on behalf of the user by the vendor, provision should be made for ownership of these programs. If ownership is to be vested in the vendor, then there should be a provision for licensing these programs to the user if the contract is terminated and it wishes to use another time-sharing service or to take the work in-house. Such a provision should also specify the hardware requirements to run such programs, and guarantee compatibility with this hardware.

The user should always seek an indemnity against copyright or other claims by third parties in respect of the programs it uses which are supplied by the vendor.

SERVICE-BUREAU CONTRACTS

In the days, not too long ago, when computers were large, very expensive mainframes, only the largest businesses could afford to own a computer. Smaller businesses generally obtained computer services through a service bureau, which performs the same functions that a data-processing unit does in a large organisation. The bureau not only provides a suitable computer, but it also provides programming and data-entry services, taking the raw data from the customer and returning finished reports or whatever other end-product is required. As computers have shrunk in both price and size, more and more small businesses are able to afford a computer suitable for their needs. It is likely, therefore, that service bureaux will become increasingly less used in the next few years, mainly providing specialised services, and allowing businesses to get experience of computerising their operations before actually purchasing their own equipment.

The main problems that occur with the use of a service bureau, from the user's point of view, are defining and enforcing standards of performance, and ensuring an orderly and speedy hand over in the event that the user decides to take its computing in-house or to use another bureau. Other problems that can arise which should be provided for are loss of data by the bureau, and the need to ensure confidentiality of the user's data and output reports.

The following areas should be covered in a service-bureau contract. Most bureaux have a form of standard contract, but most of those which have come to the author's attention have been woefully inadequate. The user should insist at least on adequate protection against failure to provide an adequately speedy and reliable service, and against loss of data or of confidentiality.

Performance

Products
The products to be delivered by the bureau should be described in detail in the contract. This description should include the type of product (e.g., reports, invoices, customer accounts), the content of each product, preferably by a sample attached to the agreement as an exhibit, and their frequency (e.g., daily, weekly, monthly).

Time of performance
For each of the products to be delivered by the bureau, there must be a specified time of delivery. This should preferably be expressed both in absolute terms, for example, all monthly reports to be prepared within five days from the end of the month concerned, and as a period relative to the time of delivery of the information by the customer to the bureau, for example, monthly reports to be delivered no later than three days after receipt of the information. Particularly where daily reports are concerned, any exceptions to the specified turn-around time, such as holidays, should be set out.

Quality
Quality standards for the products should be set out in the agreement. These should include a definition of the allowable error percentage, penalty provisions including termination if this percentage is exceeded, and a mechanism for detecting and correcting errors. There should also be defined standards for the appearance of the completed products, particularly where these are items intended to be sent to the user's customers, such as invoices.

Protection of user's information

Confidentiality
There must be a guarantee by the service bureau that the confidentiality of all the user's information will be maintained. This should cover such things as preventing third-party access to the user's data and files, both in electronic storage and in hard-copy form. Preferably, the bureau should have developed a system of controls to prevent unauthorised access, and this system should be defined in the contract to permit the user to determine whether the system is being followed. The output from the bureau should similarly be protected. In the case of confidential

reports which are produced in multiple copies by means of interleaved carbons, the user should get the bureau to agree to destroy all such carbons, or to deliver them to the user for destruction. If this is not done, and the carbons merely thrown away, it is possible to read the data printed on the forms from the carbon.

Loss of data

The bureau should undertake to make back-up copies of all the user's files and data at specified intervals. There should also be a provision for storage of at least one back-up copy in secure storage off the bureau's premises. This helps to minimise the loss if the bureau's premises are damaged or destroyed by flood, fire or a natural disaster. The bureau should undertake to pay the costs of replacing all data lost as a result of the acts or negligence of its own personnel, and should also agree to insure against accidental loss, theft, catastrophe and the like. It should also undertake to keep this coverage in effect during the life of the contract.

Inspection

The user should have a right to inspect both the bureau's own premises and the off-site storage at any time to ensure that the security precautions are being followed.

Term of the contract

Either the contract should be for a relatively short term, renewable only by the user, or the user should be able to terminate on short notice, no more than 90 days. This allows the user to cease using a bureau that is providing unsatisfactory service before it starts to suffer damage to its business caused by that unsatisfactory service. The bureau will probably also want a right of termination in this case, but that should be on a much longer period of notice, at least six months, in order to give the user time to make suitable alternative arrangements and to effect an orderly transition.

Pricing

The system of pricing should be clearly set out in the contract. As in the case of a time-sharing arrangement, an estimate of expected average monthly costs should be obtained before the contract is entered into.

The industry practice is usually to provide for a fixed price only for a limited period, such as the first year, and to provide for price escalations at regular intervals thereafter. This should be according to a clear formula, and notice of the proposed increase should be given to the user well in advance. The user should also seek a right to terminate if the price increase is unacceptable.

Termination

As discussed above, the user should have a right of termination if performance consistently falls below the specified standard, if there are breaches of security or if the price is unacceptably increased. The user should also ensure that it has a right to terminate in the event of financial instability of the bureau, a regrettably common occurrence in this industry. This should include the normal termination provision discussed in Chapter 6, and should also include provisions protecting the user's files and data from levy by creditors of the bureau. Such provisions are also discussed in Chapter 6.

Generally, when the user terminates the contract, the bureau is unhappy. If it is short of business, it may be considerably more than unhappy, because the loss of this customer could mean that it is unable to make payments due on its equipment. In this atmosphere, the user may encounter considerable difficulties in making the transition to a new bureau, or to in-house processing, because the cooperation of the outgoing bureau is required to effect this transfer. Therefore, provisions for transition should be clearly set out in the contract, with a timetable and penalties for lateness in performing any of the hand-over procedures. If the user is entering the contract as a step towards its own in-house computerisation, this should be made known to the bureau at the outset, so that it expects the termination.

The contract should also provide that the user owns its files, and the media on which they are stored, and ownership of any programs which have been specially written or adapted for the user should be provided for. If they are not owned by the user, then there should be a clear provision giving the user the right to use them after termination, upon agreed terms and for an agreed fee. In order to assist transition to an in-house system or to another bureau, if the user is given rights to the programs, the contract should set out the equipment specifications required to run the progams. Similarly, the processing steps required to process the data using the programs should be specified.

Other terms

Some of the terms suitable for time-sharing contracts are also suitable for service-bureau contracts. In particular, the bureau should indemnify the user against any third-party claims arising from the use of the bureau's equipment or software.

Provisions for the training of the user's personnel who are to provide the data, and for the bureau's personnel who are to provide special programming or other services related to the user's special needs are desirable. Where it is necessary to train the bureau's personnel, the user should try to get the bureau to undertake that it will keep those personnel available to deal with problems experienced by the user.

Whenever the user is legally required to have an audit in the regular course of its business, there should be provisions requiring the vendor to cooperate with the user's auditors. Similarly, if the user is subject to government regulations which affect how its data are processed or its reports produced, the contract should contain specific provisions to ensure that these regulations are complied with.

The user may also wish to seek protection against disclosure of its information by the vendor under a legally enforceable demand without notice, giving it a chance to take legal proceedings to protect itself.

PRECEDENTS

Time-sharing contracts

The terminal
Ownership by vendor   All terminals required by the User for the performance of this Agreement shall be supplied by the Vendor, and shall remain the property of the Vendor. [If the user is to insure the terminals: the User shall at all times during the term of this Agreement maintain a policy of insurance with an insurer approved by the Vendor insuring the terminals supplied under this Agreement against all normal commercial risks. If, at any time during the term of this Agreement, there is no such insurance policy in force, the Vendor shall be entitled to take out such a policy and to charge all costs and expenses of such policy to the User.]

Ownership by user   The User agrees to obtain all terminals required by the User for the performance of this Agreement. Such terminals shall comply with the specifications set forth in Appendix ____ to this

Agreement. The Vendor shall not be liable for any performance delays or failures caused in any way by the terminals.

Installation   The Vendor [or, the User] shall be responsible for the installation of all necessary communication means at the User's premises. Within _____ days from the date of installation of such communication means, the Vendor shall install all terminals at the User's site and shall certify their readiness for use. [If the user is responsible for installation of the phone lines etc., there should be a provision for notifying the vendor of such installation so that it can start installing the terminals.] No sums shall be payable under this Agreement [other than the initial payment provided for by paragraph _____ of this Agreement] until such certificate of readiness has been provided.

Maintenance   The Vendor shall maintain and repair all terminals, so as to keep them in good working order. The Vendor agrees to respond to all requests for repairs within _____ hours of the time that it is notified by telephone that the terminal is not operating properly. If the Vendor is not able to perform such repairs as are needed within _____ hours, the Vendor agrees to provide the User with a replacement terminal until the repairs are completed.

Use   The User is hereby granted the right to use the terminals supplied under this Agreement for any purpose whatsoever, provided such use is not deleterious to the terminal. Such purposes may include, but are not limited to, use with other time-sharing services, such as a Telex or TWX terminal, or as part of the User's own computer network.

Performance
The Vendor warrants that the system will supply a response to an entry made by the User within the following times from the time the entry is received at the Vendor's installation:

_____ a.m. to _____ a.m.: _____ seconds [etc.]

Such time shall in no event exceed a maximum of _____ seconds. If more than _____% of responses in a one-month period exceed such maximum time, the User shall be entitled to a percentage reduction in the service charges for that month equal to the percentage by which the responses which take more than the said maximum to the total number of responses exceeds _____%. The Vendor shall not be responsible for delays in response time caused by transmission difficulties, or other circumstances beyond the Vendor's reasonable control.

The Vendor agrees that if machine down time in any one month exceeds _____ hours, the service charges for the month will be reduced in proportion to the number of hours of down time in excess of the said agreed period as compared to the total number of hours billed to the User in that month.

Security

Protection from unauthorised access   The Vendor agrees that all data belonging to the User which is stored in the Vendor's installation or at the Vendor's premises in any form whatsoever will be maintained in strictest confidence, and that the Vendor will take all reasonable precautions and security measures to ensure that the User's data cannot be accessed by any unauthorised third party.

Back-up copies   The Vendor will make copies of the User's data stored in the Vendor's installation at least once a _____, and will store those copies at a secure location off the Vendor's premises. [Insert detailed provisions for safe storage, where necessary.] Upon request, the Vendor shall inform the User of the location of such storage, and shall permit the User to make security inspections of such storage at any reasonable time, without notice to the Vendor.

Access   The User shall be permitted access at all times to all data belonging to the User which is stored in the Vendor's installation or on the Vendor's premises or in safe storage. All such data, and the media on which such data are stored shall be and at all times remain the property of the User, and the Vendor shall mark and store such data and storage media containing such data in such a manner as to give notice to third parties of the User's ownership of them.

Termination   Upon termination of this Agreement for any reason whatsoever, the User shall be entitled to obtain immediate access to and to remove all data belonging to the User stored in the Vendor's installation or on the Vendor's premises, subject only to a liability to pay reasonable costs for any storage media not previously paid for under the terms of this Agreement.

Programs

Supply to user   The Vendor will, at the request of the User, furnish to the User copies in both source and object code of all programs developed for, or modified on behalf of the User by the Vendor upon payment of the charges set forth in paragraph _____ of this Agreement. The Vendor warrants that said programs will run on hardware conforming to the specifications set forth in Appendix ____ to this Agreement.

Copyright-infringement indemnity The Vendor warrants and represents that all software not owned by the Vendor used by the Vendor in respect of the performance of this Agreement has been procured by the Vendor under valid licences from the owners thereof, and that the Vendor is not now, and will not be during the term of this Agreement, in default under any such licence. The Vendor will not in performance of this Agreement utilise any software which might cause the User to be subject to a suit for the infringement of the rights of a third party in connection with the User's use of such software. The Vendor will indemnify and hold harmless the User from and against any loss, cost, liability or expense (including reasonable attorney's fees) which the User may incur by reason of any breach or claimed breach of such warranties and representations.

Service-bureau contracts

Performance
   Products and delivery The Vendor agrees to deliver to the User, at the User's premises, the following products and reports at the frequency and times shown below:

Exhibit A Reference No.	Product or report	Frequency	Day (or date) and Time of delivery
1			
2			

Each of the products and reports listed above shall be in the same form and contain the same types of information as the samples attached to this Agreement as Exhibits A1 to A____ inclusive. When any date of delivery set out above falls on an official holiday, delivery shall be due the next business day thereafter. A list of such official holidays is set out in Exhibit B to this Agreement.

It is expressly agreed and understood that the above schedule of delivery dates is dependent upon the timely delivery by the User to the Vendor of the input data. The Vendor shall not be liable for late delivery caused by late delivery of input data by the User. In the event of such late delivery by the User, the Vendor agrees that it will provide the products and reports set out above in the following times from receipt of the input data:

Product	Time of delivery after receipt (hours)
X	X

For the purposes of this paragraph, the following periods shall be excluded from the computation of elapsed time [include any period when service is not normally provided, such as nights, weekends].

Quality   The Vendor hereby warrants that the products and reports produced under this Agreement shall be free from errors. The User shall be responsible for checking the accuracy of the products and reports delivered by the Vendor, and all errors shall be promptly corrected by the Vendor at its own expense. The Vendor further agrees that if the percentage errors, to be determined by dividing the total number of output lines which are correct into the total number of output lines which are incorrect, exceed the following percentage for each type of product and report for any period set out below, the charges to the User for that period shall be reduced by the same percentage as the percentage errors.

Product or report	Maximum percentage error	Period
X	X	X

It is further agreed that, if the maximum percentage error is exceeded for any product or report for _____ consecutive periods, the User shall be entitled to terminate this Agreement under the provisions of paragraph _____ [the termination clauses] of this Agreement.

The Vendor further warrants that the products and reports shall be uniform in appearance, and in accord with generally accepted industry standards.

Protection of information

Confidentiality   The Vendor agrees that it will keep all information belonging to the User in the strictest confidence, and that it will not disclose such information to any third party, nor permit any third party access to such information without prior written permission from the

User. The Vendor further agrees that it will ensure that any of its employees who have access to the User's information execute a secrecy agreement to the same effect. The Vendor shall take all reasonable precautions to prevent unauthorised access by any third party to the User's information, whether in electronic or hard-copy form, and shall provide the User upon request with a copy of the procedure used by the Vendor to prevent such access. The User shall, upon request from the Vendor, supply the Vendor with a list of persons authorised by the User to have access to the User's information. The Vendor further agrees to destroy all intermediate and work files used in the processing immediately upon completion of the processing, and to destroy immediately by burning or shredding all carbons removed from reports produced under this Agreement [or, to deliver to the User all such carbons at the same time as the reports are delivered].

Back-up copies   See the corresponding provision for time-sharing agreements on page 166.

Access   See the corresponding provisions for time-sharing agreements on page 166.

Term
The term of this Agreement shall be 12 months, which may be renewed by the User for like periods by giving at least 60 days' written notice of such intention to renew to the Vendor.
OR
The term of this Agreement shall be ____ years, provided however that the User may terminate this Agreement without cause at any time after the end of the first six months of the term by giving at least 60 days' written notice to the Vendor, and the Vendor may terminate this Agreement without cause at any time after the end of the first 12 months of the term by giving at least six months' written notice to the User.

Pricing
The charges to be paid to the Vendor by the User for the services provided hereunder are set out in Exhibit X, provided that the minimum charge payable by the User in any one month shall be ____. The charges set forth in Exhibit X may be increased on each anniversary date of this Agreement upon at least 90 days' written notice to the User, who may within the 30 days following such notice give notice of termination of this Agreement in accordance with paragraph ____ above. [It is desirable to have some limitation on the increase, rather

than relying solely upon the right of termination as protection against a massive price increase by the vendor. This could be a fixed percentage, or it could depend upon some well recognised price index.]

Termination

Termination for cause   See Chapter 6 for precedents.

Cooperation on termination   Upon expiry of this Agreeament, or upon termination for any reason, the Vendor agrees to cooperate fully with the User and any party who will thereafter provide data-processing services to the User in providing services necessary to an orderly transfer of the User's data-processing requirements to the new processor. Such services shall include, but not be limited to, provision of all files and intermediate materials in the format defined by the User, and provision of all supplies, media and other property owned by the User. All services provided under this paragraph shall be charged at the rate in effect at the date of termination or expiry. The transition shall proceed according to the timetable set out in Exhibit Y to this Agreement, and for every delay in the performance of this timetable caused by the Vendor, the Vendor shall pay to the User the sum of ____ per day of delay.

Conversion to in-house processing   The User has informed the Vendor of its future intention to have its data processing performed in-house. The User may begin such in-house processing at any time during the term of this Agreement upon six months' notice to the Vendor. In the event of such notice being given, the Vendor agrees to grant the User a perpetual, fully paid-up licence to use the software used by the Vendor to process the User's data under this Agreement for the sum of ____. The specifications for the hardware needed to run this software are set out in Exhibit Z to this Agreement.

Other terms

Copyright-infringement indemnity   See the corresponding provision for time-sharing agreements on page 167.

User training   The Vendor will supply all necessary instruction to enable the User to supply the required input data and to utilise the products and reports supplied under this Agreement, including, but not limited to, a training program of at least ____ duration for the User's personnel, to be conducted at a mutually agreed upon time at the User's site by qualified Vendor's personnel at the Vendor's expense. If the User requires further personnel training, the Vendor shall supply such training at the User's expense, at the Vendor's standard rates set out in Exhibit ____.

User audit cooperation The Vendor agrees to make all records relating to the User available at all reasonable times to the User's auditors and to prepare such reports, grant computer usage, and permit such programming examination and access to facilities and personnel as may be necessary to meet the User's audit requirements. The User agrees to pay all reasonable charges for the services supplied by the Vendor in connection with such audit requirements.

Disclosure under process of law If the Vendor receives any legally enforceable demand for disclosure of any of the User's information, it shall immediately inform the User of such receipt and, to the extent that the Vendor deems legally possible, it shall refrain from complying with such demand until the User has had a reasonable opportunity to advise the Vendor of the User's position regarding such compliance. The User shall indemnify and hold harmless the Vendor from any consequences of following the User's instructions with regard to compliance. If the User fails to instruct the Vendor promptly with regard to compliance, or if criminal sanctions may be imposed upon the Vendor, its officers or employees as a result of non-compliance, the Vendor may act in accordance with advice given to it by its legal adviser without liability of any kind to the User or to any party claiming through the User.

11   *Computer-related Services*

CONSULTANCY AGREEMENTS

The assistance of a consultant may be required in a number of computer-related matters. A business considering computerising its operations may seek advice about the hardware and software it requires. A business wishing to upgrade its computer system requires assistance in choosing a system with hardware and, preferably, software that is compatible with its existing system. It may also be a good idea to hire a consultant to perform the initial outline system analysis for custom software, discussed in Chapter 8.

Consultants are usually paid on a time-and-materials basis. The client may, however, wish to put some sort of ceiling on the total cost. It is probably not feasible to have a flat limit on either time or cost, but there should be provision for regular notification of the accrued fees and costs, and an option for the client to terminate the agreement after a certain cut-off point. The client may also wish to keep some control over the chargeable expenses, such as travel costs, by including in the agreement a schedule of the amount of travel that is to be undertaken in any period, any additional travel only to be undertaken at the client's written request. It may also be possible to agree the maximum amount of each such expense, or at least to agree the class of travel and of hotels to be used, and to limit the meal expenses on a per diem basis.

Total cost is also controlled by controlling the scope of the work to be done. This involves having a detailed specification in the contract of what is to be done by the consultant. This specification should also define what reports and other documentation are to be produced.

When the consulting is to be performed by a firm or corporation, then the client should consider insisting that only named individuals, which it should have an opportunity to interview first, perform the contract. If this is not possible, the agreement should specify the qualifications of the individuals who are to perform the work. As in software development, the client should also seek an assurance that the persons originally assigned to the contract are not withdrawn, except for reasons approved by the client. The client should also have the right to approve all persons assigned to the contract, either originally or as substitutions.

The consultant will almost inevitably learn business secrets of the client, so a confidentiality clause must be included in the agreement. It may be more difficult to get an agreement to a non-competition clause, such as the one set out in Chapter 8, but at the very least the consultant should agree not to work for a competitor of the client during the term of the contract and for a period, at least three months, thereafter. On the other hand, even if the consultant is willing to agree to a non-competition clause, care must be taken that it is not too restrictive. Non-competition clauses are examined in more detail in Chapter 12, in the section dealing with employment contracts.

The agreement should also provide for ownership of work produced. As explained in Chapter 13, copyright in copyrightable work will belong to the consultant unless there is specific assignment or agreement to assign. As this is custom work performed for the particular client, the client should insist on ownership of all work produced specifically for it. There may be problems if this work includes matter regularly used by the consultant in his business, as joint copyright is awkward to administrate in these circumstances. In such a case, it may be better for the consultant to grant a licence to the client to use the material, and for the consultant to agree not to use for work with other clients the parts developed for this client alone.

PROGRAMMING CONTRACTS

It is not uncommon for software developers to hire freelance programmers on a contract basis to deal with the fluctuating workload of their business. It is also possible, but less common, that a computer user will hire a programmer on a contract basis to work on the development or customisation of a particular piece of software. Chapter 8, on custom software development, and the section in Chapter 9 on customising of standard software should be consulted for matters that should be included in such contracts.

Most of the comments relating to consultancy contracts apply here. However, because this is a relationship which more closely resembles employment because it is the provision of contract labour, rather than the provision of professional advice as in the consultancy contract, care must be taken to comply with any local employment laws which may apply to the situation. Where it is desirable that the relationship should clearly not be one of employee and employer, whether for tax or other purposes, a lawyer specialising in the area of employment law in the jurisdiction concerned should be consulted.

One problem with hiring contract programmers for a particular project is that, while it is clearly desirable to have them continue working on the project until it is complete, it is often not possible to specify precisely at the outset how long the project will take. However, the programmer may not wish to be tied for an indefinite period, particularly if he or she is simply filling in between regular employment. On the other hand, it is possible legally to have a contractor agree to work for a particular period without the right to terminate, while most jurisdictions do not allow an employee to make a similar agreement — lack of freedom to change employment is too close to slavery. This difference partially arises from the fact that an employer is presumed to be in a position of influence over an employee, and the law does not permit such a position to be abused. On the other hand, there is the presumption that an independent contractor deals at arm's length, and there is no presumption of influence, even though economically the independent contractor may be in a weaker bargaining position than many employees.

Non-competition agreements for independent programmers should be drafted with the same restraint-of-trade considerations in mind as apply to employees (see Chapter 12). The clause should not be so restrictive that it effectively prevents the programmer from earning a living using his or her programming skills and expertise, including expertise acquired on this particular job.

PRECEDENTS

Limitation of expenses

Allowable expenses incurred by the Consultant and payable by the Client under this Agreement shall consist of the following:

(a)   Air travel, at coach fare rates, between the Consultant's base office and the Client's site.

(b)   Hotel, meals and local transportation, not to exceed _____ per day.

All such expenses shall be evidenced by receipts. The Consultant shall notify the Client at monthly intervals of the Consultant's allowable expenses under this Agreement. Such expenses shall not exceed ____ per month, without the prior written consent of the Client.

Client approval of substitute staff

The Consultant shall not make any changes in the staff listed in [paragraph listing approved assigned individuals] without the Client's prior approval, which will not be unreasonably withheld. If such a change is approved by the Client, the Consultant shall submit to the Client the names and qualifications of three proposed substitutes, and shall permit the Client an opportunity to interview these proposed substitutes; the Client shall notify the Consultant within three days from the last of such interviews which of the proposed substitutes it has selected. If the Client fails to make such notification within the time allowed, the Consultant shall make the selection.

Confidentiality

The Consultant acknowledges that in the course of performing this Agreement it will learn confidential and trade-secret information proprietary to the Client, and may learn confidential and trade-secret information proprietary to the Client's customers. The Consultant will keep all such information in the strictest confidence, and will take all reasonable precautions against disclosure of such information to third parties during or at any time after the term of this Agreement. The Consultant agrees that it will only disclose such information to those of its employees and agents who need to know it in the performance of their duties with respect to this Agreement, and will ensure that each of those employees and agents signs a written confidentiality agreement in the same terms as this paragraph. At the termination of this Agreement, the Consultant will promptly return to the Client all copies of information furnished by the Client, and all information prepared by the Consultant for or in connection with this Agreement.

Non-competition

The Consultant agrees that it will not, during the term of this Agreement and for ____ thereafter, engage in any business in direct competition with the Client, or perform services similar to those performed under this Agreement for any organisation in direct competition with the Client, except with the Client's prior written consent.

Ownership of work produced

The Consultant agrees that, with respect to the Consultant's work under this Agreement, any works produced by, or any developments made by the Consultant or under the Consultant's direction shall be the sole and complete property of the Client, and the Consultant hereby agrees to assign and does assign all rights to patents, copyrights and all other proprietary rights in said works and developments to the Client.

12   Contracts for Manufacturers

The heading of this chapter is not entirely accurate, because all of the types of contract to be discussed here could also be made by businesses which are not 'manufacturers', at least in the usual sense of the word. However, the chapter deals with contracts from the point of view of businesses in the field of supplying computer-related goods and services, rather than that of consumers of those goods and services.

The contracts considered in this chapter have another thing in common: they are all contracts which could have serious adverse affects on the business concerned if they are not properly prepared, and they involve complex areas of law, in particular antitrust and employment law. These are not areas for 'do-it-yourself': a lawyer experienced in such areas of law should be consulted in the negotiation and preparation of such contracts. The purpose of this chapter is to point out the factors that should be kept in mind when dealing with these types of agreements in the computer field.

OEM CONTRACTS

'OEM' is the standard abbreviation for 'original equipment manufacturer'. OEM contracts deal with a sale of a complete system by the manufacturer of one part of the system, which involves combining items produced by third parties with items which it produces. There are two common types of computer-related OEM contracts:

(a) A hardware manufacturer adds third-party software to its hardware to produce a bundled system.

(b) A software house supplies its customer with third-party hardware on which to run software supplied by the software house. In fact, it is common in such arrangements for the software house also to supply third-party software, such as an operating system or standard database management software, together with its own custom or customised software.

From the point of view of the third party, the OEM acts as a distributor. The next section of this chapter deals with distributor agreements. The OEM's concern must be that it is not left with liabilities to its customers for the third-party-supplied items greater than those it can pass on to the third party. The OEM should consider including provisions on the following matters in its customer contracts:

(a) *When hardware is supplied by third parties:*

(i) Warranties should match the warranties given by the third-party supplier to the OEM. If the warranties for different pieces of the hardware differ, then the contract should specify which warranties apply to which items.

(ii) The period of warranties on the hardware should match the period of the warranties from the supplier (and will normally start to run on shipment from the supplier to the OEM).

(iii) The OEM should exclude liability for the hardware in its customer contracts to match any exclusion of liability contained in its contract with the suppliers.

(iv) There should be a *force-majeure* clause which excuses the OEM from delays caused by matters beyond its reasonable control, and this should expressly include delays caused by the third-party suppliers.

(v) If the contract between the OEM and the supplier includes a penalty for cancellation, the OEM/customer agreement should include a provision by which the customer undertakes to indemnify the OEM against such penalties if they are incurred because of cancellation or change of requirements by the customer.

(b) *When software is supplied by third parties.* The above provisions for hardware apply equally to third-party software. Other provisions that should be considered include:

(i) Where the software is to be supplied to the customer in exactly the same form that it was received by the OEM, the only maintenance provided should be that supplied by the third-party supplier.

(ii) Installation dates and acceptance procedures should be specified separately for each piece of software. Standard software, whether supplied by the OEM or by a third party, will normally be installed and pass the acceptance tests much more rapidly than the custom software. The customer should not be able to hold up payment on the whole package, or reject the whole package, simply because one piece of custom software is late or is initially unacceptable, at least when that piece of software is not essential to the running of the whole system by the customer.

(iii)   Where part of the hardware is by agreement to be supplied later, but the system is operative before it is supplied, it should be provided that acceptance will be complete on the satisfactory completion of acceptance testing on the original system. Work needed to get the software running on the extended system should be separately described and paid for.

DISTRIBUTION CONTRACTS

It is very common in all fields for the chain of commerce to include one or more levels of distributors between the manufacturer and the end consumer. It is also a sad fact that there is probably more litigation over distribution contracts than over any other kind of contract involving the sale of goods. This is partly because the manufacturer has to have confidence in the ability of its distributor to sell its products. Disappointing sales, for whatever cause, tend to sour the relationship. The manufacturer also has to trust the distributor to report sales correctly for royalty purposes.

The relationship is also complicated in jurisdictions with antitrust or competition laws because the parties are potential, if not actual, competitors. Therefore, any agreement between them will be carefully scrutinised. In fact, many of the cases involving questions of competition or antitrust law, at least in the USA, arise out of actions in which a disgruntled distributor sued its principal.

Some particular problems that arise with the distribution of software are as follows:

(a)   The distributor may wish or need to modify the software to meet the needs of a particular customer. In this case, the distributor will need to have access to the source code. The vendor should license the distributor to make the modifications, so as to be able to exert control over disclosure of proprietary information and to protect its rights in the software. This type of licence is discussed in Chapter 9. The distributor will then grant its customers a sublicence to use the modified software.

(b)   When the software to be distributed is standard software which is sold unmodified, the vendor may wish to make the distributor liable for ensuring that the end user signs a licence agreement. The vendor may also wish to have the distributor's assistance in detecting and preventing unauthorised use or copying of the software.

(c) The vendor and the distributor should agree who is to be responsible for providing maintenance and updates to the end users. Again, where this is the distributor's responsibility, it will require access to the source code.

(d) Where the distributor modifies or maintains the software, it will be necessary to provide for ownership of the improvements made by the distributor. If the vendor cannot obtain agreement that all such improvements belong to the vendor, at least the distributor should be obliged to inform the vendor of all such improvements and to give the vendor a licence for its own use and use by its other customers.

(e) The vendor must be careful to exclude liability for unauthorised representations made by, or warranties given by, the distributor.

(f) The distributor must be given training in the use of the software, and be given full documentation so that it is capable of at least properly advising its clients and, if necessary, installing the software on a client's system. The distributor may also need to be taught how to train the end users in the use of the software.

(g) When the distributor sells the software as part of a bundled system, and the distribution agreement provides for royalties payable on a percentage of the sale price of the software, problems can arise in allocating the amount of the system price that is to be attributed to the vendor's software. This is because the system is generally sold for a price that is less than the sum of its parts, or the price includes service aspects as well as the hardware and software. If this situation is likely to arise, it should be discussed and a formula negotiated before the distribution agreement is entered into. This means that the distributor, when bidding to supply a bundled system, will be able to make a proper allowance for the royalty element. If agreement is not reached on royalties at the outset, the vendor will often try to insist on its full royalty, with the result that the distributor may end up making a loss and feeling bitter towards the vendor.

(h) There are a number of problems that may arise if the agreement is terminated, particularly if it is terminated by the vendor for failure to meet a minimum sales or similar performance provision. If the distributor has been maintaining software for its customers, the usual termination provision that all copies of the software are destroyed or returned to the vendor will not work unless the vendor is willing and able to take over the distributor's maintenance responsibilities. If the distributor is in the process of customising the software for a particular customer when termination occurs, it should be allowed to complete this work, which involves leaving it with a copy of the source code. On the other hand, if the distributor has licensed the vendor to use the improvements it made, it is unlikely to want the vendor to continue using those improvements, particularly if the licence was royalty-free, after termination.

EMPLOYMENT AGREEMENTS

The law relating to employment agreements can be complicated, and varies from jurisdiction to jurisdiction. Therefore, this section contains only general guidance, and a lawyer with knowledge of the relevant requirements of the local law and the restrictions that an employer may place upon employees should be consulted in drawing up an employment agreement.

Why it is desirable to have a written employment agreement

In most common-law jurisdictions, the law treats the relationship of employer and employee as being governed by an implied contract, and implies certain terms into such contract. From the employer's point of view, one of the most important of these implied terms is an implied obligation of confidence, preventing an employee from disclosing or misusing his employer's trade secrets. The law also implies an obligation of loyalty, which prevents an employee carrying on a competing business during the term of his employment. The specific statutes dealing with patent and copyright law may also provide for ownership by the employer of certain inventions and works made by the employee during his employment.

There are a number of reasons, however, why it is unwise to rely solely on these implied provisions, at least for any employee who is likely to have any access to the employer's trade secrets or who could possibly come up with an invention or other protectable work or idea. One good reason for having an agreement with express confidentiality provisions is that the existence of such an agreement is one of the factors which help to persuade a court that the information concerned is, in fact, kept secret. It also puts the employee on notice that secrets are involved, and allows the imposition of particular provisions designed to protect the trade secrets from inadvertent disclosure. With regard to patents and copyrights, the case-law does not make clear the exact circumstances in which provisions giving the rights in inventions and works by employees to their employers apply. Further, those provisions vary from jurisdiction to jurisdiction. In addition, these provisions will not cover the ownership of valuable, but unpatentable, ideas and uncopyrightable works.

A written employment agreement has the following advantages:

(a) It can clarify ownership of ideas, inventions, works and improvements made by the employee, and provide for a procedure for notifying the existence of such ideas, etc., to the employer and for assigning rights in those which by agreement belong to the employer.

(b) It can clarify the ownership of ideas, etc., made by the employee before his employment commenced.

(c) It can include detailed provisions providing for protection of the employer's trade secrets.

(d) It can include an acknowledgement by the employee that these secrets were not previously known to him, to undermine a later defence in an action against the employee regarding the employer's trade secrets that the matter was not, in fact, secret.

(e) It can include non-competition provisions going beyond the implied obligation of loyalty. This is the only way in which post-employment restrictions can be imposed.

(f) It can provide a written assurance by the employee that he is not under any prior contractual obligations which would prevent his employment or interfere with his performance of his duties. This is useful to provide a defence against a claim by the employee's former employer that the employee accepted the new employment in breach of a restrictive covenant and that this breach was knowingly induced by the new employer.

(g) It clearly defines terms of employment, in particular the term and grounds for termination. In some jurisdictions, by law, the employee must be given written notice of certain terms and conditions of the employment.

(h) It can include provisions for dealing with employee grievances and employer dissatisfaction, and for arbitration of disputes.

General considerations

It must be decided whether the company policy will be to require all employees to sign an employment agreement, or only certain employees. If all employees are to have a written agreement, then it will probably be necessary to have more than one form of agreement, with provisions suitable to the various grades of employee. For example, a restrictive covenant which would be valid and enforceable against a senior manager or a research scientist or systems analyst would probably be too wide, and therefore unenforceable, against a secretary or an assembly-line worker. On the other hand, if the decision is to use a standard agreement, but to require only certain levels of employee to sign it, then there must be a carefully thought-out policy on which employees have to sign. For example, although secretaries are unlikely to make an invention, they may learn trade secrets through their work. It is advisable to require all employees to sign a confidentiality agreement, even if only senior employees sign an agreement containing non-competition and assignment-of-invention clauses. This is because almost any employee could come across a trade secret in the course of his employment, and this fact should be drawn to his attention. Also, a consistent policy on the protection of confidential information is of great assistance in proving that the information was, in fact, kept as a trade secret by the business concerned.

There is generally not much difficulty in getting a new employee to sign an employment agreement, and consideration for the agreement is the employment itself. In the case of new employees, however, the employee should be notified of the requirement that the agreement must be signed as a condition of employment at the time the offer of employment is made, and he should be supplied with a copy. The employer will have to consider its response if the employee seeks to negotiate the terms of the agreement, or if the employee refuses to sign.

More problems are encountered when an employer who has not previously used written employment agreements seeks to impose them on its existing employees. A legal problem is the question of what consideration is given by the employer for such an agreement by the employee. This is usually recited to be the continued employment of the employee, but this may be illusory unless the employer has the right to terminate the employment immediately if the employee refuses to sign the agreement. The employer may not have this right, either because of contractual obligations to the employee, or because of the general employment law of the jurisdiction concerned. In such cases there should be some separate, valuable consideration, such as a bonus, a promotion or increased vacation time. There may also be human

problems, for example, the employee may feel that his trustworthiness is
being called into doubt.

In every case, it is important to have an agreement which can be read
and understood by the employee. It should be kept as short as possible,
and should be written in clear layman's language, avoiding 'legalese'.

Non-disclosure of confidential information

As mentioned above, the common law implies an obligation of
confidence into the relationship between employee and employer.
Written agreements for non-disclosure, the advisability of which is
discussed above, are generally treated by courts in common-law
jurisdictions as being statements of this general obligation. The
obligation continues to be enforceable after the termination of the
employment, for as long as the information concerned is, in fact, a secret.

The employer should have a written, standard code of conduct setting
out procedures for protecting its confidential information. The existence
of such a code is of the greatest assistance in persuading a court that the
information is to be treated as trade secrets. The employee agreement
should contain a specific agreement to carry out the code provisions, and
an acknowledgement that the employee has been provided with a copy
of the code, and has read it. This helps to prevent any later attempt to
argue that the code was not brought to the employee's attention.

The agreement should also contain provisions dealing with the
protection of confidential documents, and for their return at the
termination of the employment. This is particularly important for
technical staff, who are likely to have important documents such as
laboratory notebooks or program code and comments. It should be
made clear from the outset that such employees are not permitted to
take copies of such items with them when they leave without specific
permission from the employer.

It is most advisable to have an 'exit interview' with each employee
immediately before leaving the employment, regardless of the reason for
termination. At this time, a check should be made to ensure that all
confidential documents, and all copies of such documents, have been
returned. The employee should be reminded of any obligations that
continue after the termination of his employment, including the
obligation of confidentiality, and there should be a standard procedure
that he signs a statement that he has been given this reminder.

Problems can arise with the enforcement of non-disclosure

agreements after termination of employment in the case of employees whose employability depends upon their highly technical knowledge and skills. Some of that knowledge will have been derived during the course of their employment, and will probably include trade-secret matter. If the employee is put in the position that a non-disclosure agreement makes him effectively unemployable in his field, then it may be at least partly unenforceable under the rules against restraint of trade, discussed below in the context of non-competition agreements. This situation is particularly likely to arise in the computer industry. The courts tend to distinguish between knowledge which the employee developed himself during the course of his employment, and knowledge which he merely acquired from the employer, being more reluctant to deprive him of the use of the former than of the latter. The courts have attempted to devise compromise solutions, such as that reached in *The Telex Corporation* v *International Business Machines Corporation* 367 F Supp 258, 363 (N.D. Okla.1973), trade-secret aspects affirmed 510 F 2d 894 (10th Cir. 1975), certiorari denied 423 US 802 (1975). The court required Telex to keep former IBM employees from assignment to projects developing products functionally equivalent to those they had worked on at IBM for two years after termination of their employment with IBM.

Non-competition agreements

During employment
The common-law implied obligation of loyalty covers employment with a competing concern during employment. A specific agreement not to enter such employment is enforceable, even in jurisdictions which severely limit post-employment non-competition provisions. The employer may wish to extend the written agreement to cover non-competing outside employment as well, in order to ensure that he gets the employee's full attention and energies, and this is also generally enforceable. However, the courts have not in general extended the common-law obligation to prevent an employee preparing to set up a competing business before he leaves, at least where the employer's trade secrets are not involved. The employer may wish to obtain a specific agreement from the employee not to start such organisation while still employed. It is questionable whether an injunction would be granted, at least where trade secrets are not involved, but the employer may still be able to obtain damages.

After employment

Restrictions on the post-employment activities of employees come within the general area of covenants in restraint of trade, which are the subject of common-law rules and, in many jurisdictions, statutory provisions.

The general common-law rule is that such covenants are unenforceable unless reasonable, the court being the final arbiter of what is reasonable in any particular case. Post-employment non-competition provisions in employment agreements are generally more carefully scrutinised than, for example, such provisions in the contract for the sale of a business. This is because the law has traditionally viewed the employee as being in a weaker bargaining position with respect to an employer than a vendor of a business is with respect to the purchaser. Of course, in industries with strong trade unions, this may not necessarily be true.

It is for the employer to show that the restraint is reasonably necessary to protect some proprietary interest which it owns. However, even if the restraint is reasonably necessary to protect such an interest, it will not be enforced if the effect of doing so is to deprive the employee of any opportunity of employment in the field in which he is skilled or experienced, because he is then forced to choose between staying with his employer or unemployment. Also, the employee cannot be restrained from using the body of knowledge and skill that he has acquired in his work, even if some of that knowledge and skill was acquired during the employment in question. As discussed above, the interaction of this provision with the protection of the employer's trade secrets can lead to problems in the case of employees who possess advanced technical skills and are employed to develop new products or to do research.

While what is reasonable in each case depends on the particular circumstances, there are certain guidelines which have been developed by the courts. If the employer is engaged in more than one business the employee can only be prevented from competing with the particular business of the employer in which he was employed. The period of the restriction must be reasonable with respect to the interest being protected, so that the employee in possession of short-lived trade secrets can be restrained for a much shorter period than the employee in possession of information with a longer period of value. The area of the restriction must also be reasonable, so a sales representative can only be prevented from taking a competing sales job in the area which he covered for his former employer. These factors are all related, so, for example, a wide area restriction will only be reasonable if it is for a short time, and vice versa.

Because of the difficulty of estimating the reasonableness of a non-competition covenant at the time it is entered into, it is advisable to have a severability clause (see Chapter 6) to ensure that the rest of the agreement remains valid even if the non-competition covenant is held to be unenforceable. In some jurisdictions the courts may at their discretion, rewrite an invalid covenant to make it valid and enforceable, but the majority of common-law jurisdictions do not permit this.

A number of states in the USA have statutes that deal with restrictive covenants. In some states (including California, a major centre for the computer industry), post-employment restrictive covenants are not enforceable by statute, and in others the case-law is so restrictive as to, in effect, make such covenants invalid. In a number of other states, including New York, the general common-law rule applies, but the courts will not modify an invalid restriction to make it enforceable. In the remaining states, including Texas and Massachusetts, the courts will rewrite the restriction to make it enforceable.

Even in the case of jurisdictions with statutory provisions, the law relating to restrictive covenants is constantly being considered and developed through case-law, and a lawyer in the jurisdiction who is experienced in this area of the law should be consulted whenever a post-employment non-competition provision is to be inserted into an employment agreement.

In difficult cases, it may be possible to make an otherwise unenforceable agreement enforceable by providing for payment to the ex-employee of sums representing lost salary if he is unable to obtain other employment because of the restriction. This is a solution that clearly only makes business sense for an employee with knowledge which would be particularly damaging to the employer in the hands of a competitor. Another possibility is to have the employee agree to enter a post-employment consultancy agreement upon termination of his employment, but this is probably unenforceable unless the employee is willing to do this *at the time of termination* and trade secrets are involved. The compensation must be adequate.

Ownership of ideas, inventions and works

The general common-law rule is that ideas, inventions and the like made by employees are owned by the maker unless they are made 'in the course of employment', when they are owned by the employer. In general this only occurs, in the absence of any agreement to the contrary, when the employee's job includes the making of inventions or the creation of works. Inventions relating to the employer's business made by employees in senior management positions may also belong to the employer, even if those employees are not 'employed to invent', on the ground that such employees are in a special position of trust and under particular obligations to further their employer's interests. In the case of patentable inventions, this may be modified in certain jurisdictions by the 'shop right' doctrine, which gives the employer a royalty-free licence to any patent resulting from an invention made by an employee who was not employed to invent but who did the work in his employer's time, or using his employer's materials.

Inventions

UK.   Ownership of inventions made in the UK after 1 June 1978 is covered by s. 39 of the Patents Act 1977, which provides:

(1)   Notwithstanding anything in any rule of law, an invention made by an employee shall, as between him and his employer, be taken to belong to his employer for the purposes of this Act and all other purposes if —

(a)   it was made in the course of the normal duties of the employee or in the course of duties falling outside his normal duties, but specifically assigned to him, and the circumstances in either case were such that an invention might reasonably be expected to result from the carrying out of his duties; or
(b)   the invention was made in the course of the duties of the employee and, at the time of making the invention, because of the nature of his duties and the particular responsibilities arising from the nature of his duties he had a special obligation to further the interests of the employer's undertaking.

(2)   Any other invention made by an employee shall, as between him and his employer, be taken for those purposes to belong to the employee.

It can be seen that this essentially codifies the common-law rules. However, s. 42 changes the law by making unenforceable any contract which diminishes an employee's rights to inventions, save for agreements to keep trade secrets confidential. This means that an agreement for the assignment of future inventions to the employer contained in an employment contract is now invalid, in respect of post May 1978 inventions. The Act also contains provisions awarding compensation to an employee for an invention which belongs by law to the employer and on which a patent has issued, based upon the value of that patent to the employer.

USA. The US Patent Act does not contain any provisions regarding ownership of employees' inventions, so the common-law rules apply in general. Clauses in employment agreements assigning rights in future inventions to the employer are common. However, the law in certain states limits the enforceability of such provisions, and the courts in some states have also developed rules governing such provisions.

The court-made rules generally consider the fairness of the provision in the particular circumstances. Such a clause in the contract of a low-paid worker is less likely to be fair than in the contract of a highly paid engineer or manager. Similarly, the courts tend to disfavour agreements which require the employee to assign inventions made after the termination of the employment, particularly if that would make it difficult for the employee to find other employment. An agreement to assign inventions not related to the employer's business is also of questionable validity, particularly in the case of an employee not employed to invent.

A number of states have statutory provisions invalidating provisions that require the assignment of inventions made in the employee's own time and which do not relate to the employer's business. These states include California and Washington. Federal legislation has been proposed to the same effect, as has federal legislation to compensate employees for inventions owned by or assigned to their employers as a result of the employment relationship, patterned on the German law.

Copyright works
UK. The ownership of copyright in literary, dramatic, musical and artistic works is governed by s. 4 of the Copyright Act 1956. The copyright in works made in the course of the author's employment under a contract of employment belongs to the employer, although there are some special provisions relating to contributions by employee journalists, which need not concern us here. The term used in the Act,

'in the course of the author's employment', has been interpreted to mean 'within the scope of the duties of his employment'. The Act permits agreements altering this rule, so an agreement by an employee to assign the copyright in future works made outside the scope of his employment would be valid, unless a court found it to be oppressive, as would an agreement by a person not under a contract of employment, such as a consultant.

USA. The Copyright Act provides for ownership by an employer of a 'work made for hire', 17 USC s. 201(b). These are works made by employees within the scope of their employment. Certain specially commissioned works also come within this provision. Congress specifically excluded inclusion of a shop right similar to that which applies to patents when it was considering the Copyright Act 1976, so s. 201(b) is the sole provision for employers' rights in copyright works produced by employees. Employment agreements can provide for assignments to the employer of employees' works outside of works-for-hire, and there do not appear to be any state statutes limiting the enforceability of such provisions similar to those relating to inventions, discussed above. The courts would probably apply the same tests of fairness in evaluating the validity of any such provision.

PRECEDENTS

Employment agreements

Introduction
The Employer is dedicated to a policy of exerting a significant influence in its chosen fields through technical innovation and creative administration and marketing. The competitive success of this policy depends to a large extent on the Employer's ability to capitalise on the creative talents of its employees, and to maintain a free flow of pertinent information among its employees. For this reason, all key employees are required to sign the following Agreement, under which:

(a) Requirements for avoiding conflicting outside activities are specified.
(b) The Employer is assured of exclusive rights to ideas, works and inventions that relate to company business.
(c) The Employer is protected against unauthorised disclosure of proprietary information.

Confidentiality

In consideration of my employment or the continuation of my employment by the Employer:

(a) I agree that all research notebooks and other research records, technical data, drawings and the like, prepared by me or which come into my possession during my employment by the Employer are, and shall remain, the property of the Employer and at the termination of my employment with the Employer I will return all such documents, and all copies of such documents to the Employer.

(b) I also agree that I will not divulge to others, except officers and senior management of the Employer who should reasonably and in the normal course of business be given such information, any information I may obtain during the course of my employment relating to the inventions, trade secrets, ideas and improvements to such inventions, trade secrets and ideas belonging to the Employer, whether developed by me or not, without first obtaining from the Employer written permission to do so.

Non-Competition

During employment   During the term of my employment, I will not, without the prior approval of the [suitable officer] of the Employer, (i) engage in any other professional employment or consulting, or (ii) directly or indirectly participate or assist in any business which is a current or potential supplier, customer or competitor of the Employer, except that I may invest to an extent not exceeding one per cent of the total outstanding shares in each of one or more companies whose shares are listed on a national stock or securities exchange.

After employment

(a) I agree that, for a period of _____ immediately following termination of my employment for any reason, I will not engage in any business or perform any service within a radius of _____ miles from the place of my employment with the Employer which directly or indirectly competes with any business of the Employer.

(b) I also agree that, for a period of _____ immediately following termination of my employment for any reason, I will not, for myself or on another's behalf, solicit or service in any way any customer of the Employer with whom the Employer has done business in the period of _____ years immediately preceding the termination of my employment.

(c) If any court shall determine that if any provision in the above paragraphs is unenforceable for any reason, the provision shall be deemed amended to the extent required to make it valid and enforceable. It is further agreed that the foregoing provisions are severable, and that if any provision is held to be invalid and unenforceable, the remaining provisions shall not thereby be invalidated.

Disclosure and assignment of inventions

(a) I will disclose promptly to the Employer all ideas, inventions, works of authorship (including, but not limited to, computer programs, software and documentation), improvements or discoveries, patentable or unpatentable, copyrightable or uncopyrightable, which during the term of my employment I may conceive, make, develop or work on, in whole or in part, solely or jointly with others, whether or not reduced to drawings, written descriptions, documentation, models or other tangible form, and which relate to any product, service, research or development fields in which the Employer or any of its affiliates is actively engaged, or to my employment activities; and all such ideas, inventions, works, improvements and discoveries shall forthwith and without further consideration become and be the exclusive property of the Employer, its successors and assigns.

(b) I will assist the Employer in every way necessary, including the signing of any and all papers, authorisations, applications and assignments, and making and keeping of all proper records, and the giving of evidence and testimony (all at the Employer's expense), to obtain and to maintain for the use of the Employer, its nominees, successors and assigns, patents, copyrights and other protection for any and all such ideas, inventions, works, improvements and discoveries in all countries.

(c) As a matter of record, Schedule A attached to this Agreement contains a complete list of all ideas, inventions, works, improvements and discoveries, patented or unpatented, copyrighted and not copyrighted, and completed prior to my employment with the Employer, which I desire to have excluded from the operation of this Agreement.

13 Protection of Computer Products: General Concepts

Ralph Waldo Emerson is reported to have said, 'If a man write a better book, preach a better sermon, or make a better mousetrap than his neighbour, though he build his house in the woods, the world will make a beaten path to his door.' Unfortunately, in a free-enterprise society, that path will barely be trodden down before copies of his book, sermon or mousetrap will appear on the market at a cheaper price to lure away his customers. Unchecked, this behaviour, which may in the short term benefit the public, will in the long term work to the public's disadvantage. This is because the author or inventor, who may have expended a great deal of time and money in producing his book or developing his mousetrap, can easily be undercut by those who did not bear this expenditure. This can result in financial loss, and discouragement from further efforts at authorship or invention. Most modern societies have recognised the benefits that human ingenuity and intellectual efforts bring to us all, and have developed laws which encourage such inventiveness by helping the inventor and author to profit from their efforts. In general these laws achieve this result by preventing others from profiting at the author's or inventor's expense.

There are a number of legal concepts which can be used to protect the products of human ingenuity. In common-law systems, and most other legal systems, the most common of these concepts are patents, copyrights, trade marks, trade secrets and unfair competition (sometimes known as 'passing-off'). Because they are all designed to give a kind of ownership, or property right, to the fruits of the human mind, they are often referred to collectively as 'intellectual property'. This chapter will examine the various kinds of intellectual property which are relevant to the computer field. Subsequent chapters will discuss the application of these principles to various types of computer product and give practical advice on methods of protection.

PATENTS

History of the patent system

The history of the common-law patent system is usually traced back to the Statute of Monopolies 1623. That statute was itself a landmark in the long period of English history during which power gradually shifted from the monarch and nobility to a body of elected representatives. It became clear at an early stage in this history that whoever controlled the purse-strings ultimately controlled the country. Parliament had at an early stage arrogated to itself the right to approve any taxes to be levied; the struggle between the Stuart monarchs and Parliament that led to the Civil War in the 17th century was marked by frequent attempts by the king to raise money by means other than taxes. One such method, widely used by other European monarchs and by the Tudors, was the sale of monopolies. An individual would be granted a monopoly for the manufacture or import of a certain commodity; the monopolist could then charge high prices, and could afford to pay the Crown handsomely for this privilege. Parliament therefore had two reasons for wanting to get rid of monopolies: they imposed financial burdens on the people and they provided uncontrolled revenue to the monarch. The Statute of Monopolies 1623, which outlawed such grants of monopolies, was the result. However, even at that time, the importance of incentives for technological progress was realised, so the statute exempted limited monopolies for new inventions from the overall prohibition.

Why are such monopolies to inventions called 'patents'? This is an abbreviation of 'letters patent', the means whereby the Crown granted rights or privileges which were of public concern. 'Patent' means 'open', and such a grant was made by a letter which was not sealed shut, but was left open with the seal attached at the bottom.

The importance of encouraging authors and inventors was also recognised by the early English colonists of America. After independence this became enshrined in the Constitution: article 1, section 8, clause 8, empowers Congress to 'promote the progress of science and useful arts by securing for limited times to authors and inventors the exclusive right to their respective writings and discoveries'. Today, almost all countries have some system of protection for inventions, including most Third World and Communist countries. Probably the last major country without such a system is the People's Republic of China which will inaugurate one in 1985.

Patentability

There are certain basic concepts which are common to almost all patent systems. In general, protection is given to an inventive idea by prohibiting others for a limited period from making, using or selling the invention without the permission of the inventor. The protection period for inventions is generally in the region of 15 to 20 years. What is meant by 'inventive'? In order to qualify for protection, most systems require that the invention be new, not obvious to those working in the field, and useful. Certain things are almost always excluded from patent protection, such as scientific laws and mathematical principles. Some systems also exclude from protection anything used to treat human illness, but most countries allow patents on pharmaceuticals.

The requirement that the invention must be new is usually referred to as 'novelty'. In outline, an invention has novelty if there are no prior patents for the same thing, no prior publications by third parties disclosing the same thing, and the inventor has not made the invention public himself by selling, showing or publishing it to the public. The technical requirements of novelty, such as whether patent applications or only published patents count, whether foreign-language publications are to be considered, and what constitutes publication by the inventor, differ from country to country. It should be particularly noted that, under UK law, any publication by the inventor results in loss of patentability, whereas under US law the inventor can apply for a patent any time within a period of one year from his first publication of the invention. Anyone considering obtaining patent protection for an invention should consult a local expert in patent law before doing anything that could disclose the invention to the public before the patent is applied for.

Under most systems an invention only fails the novelty test if all the features of that invention are to be found in one single prior source. It is, however, permissible to combine several prior sources, each showing some of the features of the invention in question, to show that the invention was obvious. This requirement of 'non-obviousness' is the one that causes most problems for the inventor, both in getting the patent application allowed and in any subsequent litigation. The most common reason for applications being refused and litigated patents being found invalid is obviousness.

While the exact wording of the test or tests applied to determine whether an invention is obvious varies from country to country, the tests themselves are in general very similar. A general statement would be that an invention is unpatentable for obviousness if it would have been obvious, at the time it was made, to a person skilled in the field of technology the invention relates to, who had before him all the relevant prior art. It will be clear to the percipient reader that, ultimately, this test is subjective, and, as with all subjective tests, it is difficult to predict in advance what result a trier of fact in a legal process will reach in applying the test to the facts of the case. Often the greatest inventions are the simplest, and simple inventions tend to look obvious in hindsight. A number of subsidiary factors are often put forward to persuade the judge or patent examiner that, at the time, the invention was not obvious to the person skilled in the art. Amongst these factors are repeated failures, by the inventor or others, to achieve this result, considerable effort needed to make the invention, a long-felt need which had previously been unmet, and commercial success of the invention.

The requirement of usefulness is usually the easiest to meet. In practice the only things that are excluded from patentability on the ground of non-usefulness are perpetual motion machines (unless the inventor can produce a working model!) and inventions that can only be used for an illegal or immoral purpose.

Advantages and disadvantages of patents

The main advantage of patent protection is that it provides protection for the underlying concept, even against a later independent development of the same invention. The main disadvantage of patent protection, especially for the individual inventor and small business, is that it is expensive to obtain and even more expensive to protect. Patent litigation is notoriously expensive, and the outcome is always uncertain. The plaintiff who sues for infringement of his patent may emerge with that patent having been held to be invalid. This has been a particular risk in the United States where, at least until very recently, the Federal judiciary has tended to be anti-patents, regarding them as dangerous monopolies which must be limited as far as possible. It is hoped that the recent creation of the Court of Appeals for the Federal Circuit, to which all appeals from district courts on patent matters must go, will be more sympathetic to the patentee, and will produce some consistency in patent law.

Obtaining a patent

Patent protection is a matter of national law, and a patent must be applied for in each country in which it is desired to obtain patent protection. There are, however, some international patent conventions and treaties which make it easier to apply in other countries once the first national application has been filed, and these are discussed below.

The central document in any application for a patent is the patent specification. This is the document which describes what the invention is and how it works, and sets out the exact limits of the monopoly claimed. The exact structure of this document and the rules for drafting it vary from country to country, but most jurisdictions demand a detailed description, accompanied by drawings in most cases, sufficient to enable a person familiar with that particular area of technology to practise the invention without undue experimentation. This requirement stems from the basic nature of the patent grant — in return for the limited monopoly the inventor makes his invention open to the public, who can practise it freely once the monopoly expires. If the inventor were to be allowed to conceal essential factors needed for the working of the invention he would not be keeping his part of the bargain. The other general requirement of a patent specification is that it contains a section, called 'claims', where the boundaries of the area for which the monopoly is sought are exactly delineated, just as a conveyance of land must delineate the exact boundaries of the land conveyed. These claims are usually required to be written in a formalised manner, and are interpreted according to set rules. A patent will only be held to be infringed if the allegedly infringing device or process or composition falls within the limits of the claims.

This technical nature of the patent specification, and the importance of having the invention claimed precisely, means that it is extremely dangerous for the lay person to draft his own specification unless he has extensive experience in this area. To give an example of these dangers from the writer's own experience while practising at the patent bar in England: the invention was a stair lift for use in the home. The inventor, who had very little money but who was a very skilled and experienced engineer, had written his own patent application. He had disclosed his invention to the defendants, a manufacturing company. After at first expressing interest, they then told the inventor that they had decided not to proceed with the idea. To the inventor's dismay and fury, he later found that this company was making and selling a chair lift identical to his patented lift. The company then came out with a second model, which used the same principles but had a slightly different mode of operation. At trial the judge held that the first model infringed the inventor's patent, but that the second did not, because the patent claims were unnecessarily limited to the exact embodiment the inventor himself had used. Thus, although the inventor was awarded damages for the first model, and for the use of his trade secrets revealed in confidence to the defendants, he was unable to prevent them continuing to manufacture, royalty free, the second model.

In most countries the individual who does not choose to write and prosecute his own patent application must use the services of a person qualified to prosecute patent applications in the patent office of that country. In some countries, such as the USA and Germany, there are two sorts of qualified persons, those who are, and those who are not, also qualified lawyers. In others, such as the UK, the professions of patent agent (qualified to prosecute patent applications) and of lawyer are separate and it is not possible to practise both at the same time.

All countries which have a patent system have a government agency, the patent office, which is responsible for processing patent applications and for the issuance of patents. In broad terms there are two approaches to the role of the patent office. In some countries the only role of the patent office is to ensure that the patent application complies with the formal rules. If it does, then a patent is granted, and the question of validity is left entirely up to the courts. In the other system, which is used by most of the industrialised nations, the patent office also has a responsibility to examine the application for validity, and to refuse to grant a patent for an invention it finds to be unpatentable. As might be expected, in such countries it is usually a much more expensive process to obtain a patent, especially if the process of appealing a refusal by the patent examiner to allow an application is proceeded with.

International patent conventions

The oldest international convention relating to patents and other intellectual property, and the one that applies to the largest number of countries is the International Convention for the Protection of Industrial Property, usually referred to as the Paris Convention after the city where it was signed in March 1883. The countries to which the Convention applies constitute a union for the protection of industrial property.

The main provision of the Paris Convention is that all members of the union agree to give nationals of other members the same rights to protection of industrial property (an older term for what is now more commonly called 'intellectual property') as they give to their own nationals. In practice, the most useful provision of the Convention is art. 4, which provides that the filing of a patent application or utility model registration in any member nation within one year (six months in the case of an industrial design or trade-mark registration) of the date of an earlier application for protection of the same invention or design in another convention country will be given the same priority date as the earlier application.

The Paris Convention merely deals with reciprocal rights under the national laws of its members. The other two international patent conventions, the Patent Cooperation Treaty and the European Patent Convention, provide a form of multinational patent application.

Under the Patent Cooperation Treaty (the PCT), the applicant files his application, designating the countries for which he desires a patent, in a 'receiving office', which is usually his national patent office. The receiving office checks that the formalities are correct, and then transmits one copy of the application to the International Searching Authority, and another to the International Bureau of WIPO (World Intellectual Property Organisation). Applications filed in French, German, Japanese or Russian are translated into English free of charge by WIPO, those filed in any other of the official languages are translated by the International Searching Authority. The International Searching Authority then conducts a search for relevant prior art. The applicant may amend the claims once during the international stage of the proceedings, then the international application is published. The application and search report are then forwarded to the patent offices of the designated countries, and the application is then processed like an ordinary national application. It is possible for the applicant to demand an international preliminary examination before transmittal to the national offices. This examination provides a preliminary, non-binding opinion of the patentability of the invention.

Currently, the provisions of the PCT apply to 33 countries who have ratified the treaty. The evidence is that its provisions are being little used at present. This may be partly due to unfamiliarity, as the Treaty only came into operation in the first signatory countries in 1978.

The European Patent Convention (the EPC), although in operation for approximately the same length of time as the PCT, is being widely

utilised. This goes one step further than the PCT in that the whole
process of patent prosecution is carried out by the European Patent
Office (EPO), although at the end of the process the patents which issue
are still national patents. It is planned that eventually it will be possible
to obtain an EEC patent, which will be a unitary patent covering all of
the European Community countries. There is in existence a Community
Patent Convention, but it has not yet been ratified, and ratification
appears to be some years off.

An application under the European Patent Convention is filed in one
of the three official languages, English, French and German, with the
EPO in Munich. Applicants from a member state whose language is not
one of these three may file the application in their own language, but
they must also file a translation into one of the official languages.
Whichever official language is selected, that language is used for all
subsequent proceedings in the EPO. The application must specify
which of the member states it is desired to obtain patents in. After the
application has been checked to ensure that the formalities are correct, a
prior-art search is carried out by the Search Department, which is
located in the Hague, and the application is published. The applicant
then has six months in which to request substantive examination of the
application. Failure to request examination within the time-limit or any
extension that may be allowed results in abandonment of the
application. The applicant is given the opportunity to respond to any
objections made by the examiner, and to make amendments to
overcome objections. If after the examination process is complete, the
application is allowed, a bundle of national patents for the designated
states issue, and these patents are thereafter governed by the national
laws of the states concerned.

COPYRIGHT

History of Copyright

The law of copyright, at least in England, owes its origins to attempts by
the authorities to control the potentially subversive new technology for
dissemination of information, called printing. It is a sign of the vitality
and inventiveness of the common law that we are now attempting to
adapt the same system for use with the next world-changing,
revolutionary information technology, namely, the computer.

Copyright originated as a perpetual monopoly to the publisher of a printed work, supported by a system of government licensing which was designed to control what was printed. The monopoly was largely due to the control exercised by the printers' guild over members of the trade. As the powers of the guilds decreased and literacy increased, in the late 17th century, the monopoly broke down, and a large number of pirate publishers started to put out cheap editions of popular works. The first copyright statute, passed in 1709, sought to control this by conferring on the author of a book and his assigns the sole right of printing that book for a term of 14 years from the day of first publication.

Copyright protection for other types of works was added piecemeal. Engravings were the first artistic works to be protected, under the Engraving Copyright Act 1734. Fabric designs were given copyright by 27 Geo 3, c. 38 (Designing and Printing of Linens, etc., 1787). Sculpture was added by 38 Geo 3, c. 71 (Copyright, 1798), replaced by the Sculpture Copyright Act 1814. Protection for dramatic works was added by the Dramatic Copyright Act 1833. The Copyright Act 1842 repealed the 1709 Act, extending the period of protection to the life of the author plus seven years or 42 years, whichever was the greater, gave the term 'book' a broad definition to include a single sheet of print or music and included maps, and extended the 1833 Act to musical works. Various Acts dealing with industrial designs of various kinds were passed during the mid 19th century. Finally, other fine arts were brought within the scope of copyright protection in 1862. This patchwork of statutes was unified finally in 1911 by the Copyright Act of that year. This excluded industrial designs, which came under the Patents and Designs Acts of 1907 and 1946. The present UK statute is the Copyright Act 1956, together with the Registered Designs Act 1949 and the Design Copyright Act 1968 which deal with industrial designs.

The importance of protecting the works of authors was recognised by the framers of the Constitution of the United States of America, in the same article that provided for patents. Copyright law in the USA was recently revised, after a long process of consultation, and the present statute is the Copyright Act 1976.

The right of authors to protection from copying was also recognised at an early stage by most civil-law systems. However, with respect to both copyright and patents, the civil-law systems have tended to have a theory of the basis of such protection different from the common-law theory. Common law tends to view these rights as being granted by the state for the general public benefit. Civil law tends to view them as fundamental rights arising from the exercise of human creativity. This different basis has produced rights in civil-law copyright systems which do not form part of common-law copyright. These are the '*droit moral*', an author's 'moral right' to control use made of, and adaptations made to, his works, even after he has parted with title to them. The second is the '*droit de suite*', the right of the author's heirs to benefit from the copyright, even if it had been assigned during the author's lifetime.

What is protected by copyright?

In very general terms, copyright is designed to protect the results of human creativity other than inventions (in the sense that the term 'invention' is used in patent law). Like all generalisations, this is not much use as practical guidance on whether a particular item is within the scope of copyright.

For an exact definition of what is protected by copyright, it is necessary to study the copyright statutes and law of the particular country concerned. Like patents, copyright law is a national matter, although there are international conventions dealing with it which are discussed below. However, there are certain broad categories of works which are universally the subject of copyright. These are literary works, dramatic works, music, drawings, photographs, maps, charts and plans, and sculpture. Most systems also protect gramophone records, tape recordings and cinematograph films.

The category of 'literary works' is a very broad one. As well as including such things that would be recognised by the layman as a literary work, such as novels, non-fiction books, pamphlets, magazine articles and the like, it also includes timetables, directories and football pool coupons! There is no requirement of aesthetic merit for copyright protection in the majority of systems. There is not even a requirement that the literary work be in words; mathematical tables and secret codes have been held to be proper subjects for copyright. All that is required is that some intellectual effort went into the compiling of the document.

Protection of 'dramatic works' covers protection of the text of the work, which includes plays, the words of a musical play, and choreography, if reduced to a system of notation. In most systems the actual performance of the work is not protected by copyright, although some systems provide a form of protection for performances. In the UK an unauthorised reproduction of a performance, such as by showing a film of a live performance, is a criminal offence under the Performers' Protection Acts 1958 to 1972. There is no equivalent legislation in the

USA, although a performer may have a remedy through the rapidly developing tort of wrongful appropriation of his right of publicity.

'Artistic works' generally include drawings, engravings, lithographs, photographs, paintings and sculpture. Again, there is no requirement of aesthetic or artistic merit; the courts long ago realised that the legal process was not equipped to deal with issues as highly subjective as these. The UK Copyright Act 1956, expressly states that the following 'artistic works' are protected 'irrespective of artistic quality': paintings, sculptures, drawings, engravings and photographs. Other categories of artistic works which may be protected are architectural works and 'works of artistic craftsmanship'. The latter category is one that has caused problems; in the UK the courts have required artistic merit for protection under this category, in *George Hensher Ltd* v *Restawile Upholstery (Lancs) Ltd* [1976] AC 64, HL. The US law requires artistic features which are separate from the utilitarian aspects of the article, and only those artistic features are protected by copyright.

'Musical works', like dramatic works, are the manuscripts. Live performances are not copyrightable subject-matter, and recordings are regarded as being a separate category of copyright. Cinematograph films, other audiovisual works and radio and television broadcasts were all latecomers to copyright protection, and are generally treated as being separate categories of copyrightable subject-matter.

In order to determine whether a particular work is subject to copyright protection, it must first be determined whether it is within one of the categories of copyrightable subject-matter. Common-law systems in particular have shown flexibility in attempting to fit new types of works into the existing categories, at least in recent times. A good example of this process can be seen in recent US decisions regarding video games, which are discussed in Chapter 15.

The next requirement is that the work is 'original'. The degree of originality required for copyright protection is very much lower than the degree of novelty required for patent protection. Usually, all that is required is that the work has not been copied from another source. Any degree of intellectual effort is enough to give a copyright, although that copyright may be dependent on the copyright in the work from which it was derived. The main reason for this difference between patent and copyright is that copyright does not confer a true monopoly as a patent does; it merely provides protection from piracy.

The third requirement is that the work is fixed in some form. Even though the poet may have composed the poem in his head, it does not become a copyright work until he writes it down, or (in most systems) fixes it in some other form, such as reading it into a tape recorder. A number of problems with the requirement of fixation which particularly affect the computer field have arisen in the past. A major question is whether this fixation must be in some form which is readable by humans. This question does not seem to have directly arisen in any reported case in the UK, and the Copyright Act 1956 does not clearly provide what type of fixation is necessary. In s. 48(1), 'literary work' is defined as including 'any written table or compilation', on the other hand, s. 49(4) of the Act provides that:

> References in this Act to the time at which, or the period during which, a literary, dramatic or musical work was made are references to the time or period at or during which it was first reduced to writing *or some other material form* (emphasis added).

Under the previous US copyright statute, the Copyright Act 1909, federal copyright only extended to published works, so the question of fixation did not arise as such. However, the Supreme Court, in *White-Smith Music Publishing Co.* v *Apollo Co.* 209 US 1 (1908), held that a 'copy', or 'reproduction' had to be in human-readable form to come within the federal copyright laws. That case concerned a piano roll for a player piano, and was used by the District Court judge in the first US case concerning copyright in the program in a ROM chip, *Data Cash Systems Inc.* v *J S & A Group Inc.* 480 F Supp 1063 (N.D. Ill. 1979), to hold that copying the ROM chip itself was not an infringement of copyright. This rule was expressly abrogated by the Copyright Act 1976, which provides, in s. 102(a), that 'Copyright protection subsists, in accordance with this title, in original works of authorship fixed in any tangible medium of expression, now known or later developed, from which they can be perceived, reproduced or otherwise communicated, either directly or with the aid of a machine or device.' It should be noted that the 1976 Act extends federal copyright to unpublished as well as published works, so the issue of fixation is now relevant.

Ownership of copyright

In general, copyright in a work is owned by the author of that work. There are three exceptions to this general rule under most systems:

(a)   When the author is an employee, and he creates the work as part of his job ('in the course of his employment' is the official legal phrase), the copyright belongs to the employer. In countries with a *droit moral*, the employer's ownership is subject to the employee's *droit moral*.

(b)   In certain limited circumstances, depending on the national law, when an independent contractor is paid to produce a work. It should be noted that, under UK law, these circumstances are very limited, being confined to the commissioning of a photograph, a portrait or an engraving. This is one of the areas where there is general misconception of the law by those not familiar with it — most people (including many lawyers) believe that if they have paid for a work to be created they automatically own the copyright. This is not so in most cases. If you want the copyright, you must get the author to agree to assign it to you.

(c)   When the author assigns all, or some, of his rights in the work.

In the case of joint authorship, where the contributions of the two authors can be separated, for example, where one person writes the words and the other the music of a song, they each have a separate copyright in his own part of the work. On the other hand, where their contributions cannot be separated, they jointly own the copyright in the entire work. Under UK law, one joint owner cannot exploit the copyright for his own benefit without accounting for the profits, and one co-owner may be able to restrain the other from exercising the copyright without his consent. Under US law, each joint owner may separately license the copyright, but must account to the other for profits received.

What protection does copyright provide?

The basic right given to the copyright owner is to prevent others from copying his work. This is, however, usually expressed as the positive exclusive right to reproduce the work, and to do related acts. For example, under the UK Copyright Act 1956, 'copyright' means the exclusive right to do and to authorise others to do, certain acts in relation to that work (s. 1(1)). Those acts, in relation to literary, dramatic and musical works, are set out in s. 2(5), and are reproduction in any material form, publishing, broadcasting, performing in public, making an adaptation, and the doing of any of the above acts in relation to the adaptation. Similar exclusive rights are given in respect of other kinds of copyright works. Similarly, s. 106 of the US Copyright Act 1976 lists the exclusive rights reserved to the owner of the copyright, which are essentially the same as those under UK law.

Because the rights are limited to the author's work, they do not prevent others from using the ideas contained in that work, nor can the author restrain use of an identical work which was independently conceived. On the other hand, if only identical copying could be restrained, the rights given by copyright would be worthless. Provided a sufficiently substantial part of the work has been copied, differences between the two works will not avoid liability for copyright infringement on the part of the copyist. The difficulty is to determine the dividing line between copying sufficient of the author's expression to infringe his copyright, and merely using his ideas, which may inevitably require expression in similar language. There is no easy, universal way of determining where this line is to be drawn. Where the expression of the idea and the idea itself are almost identical because of the simplicity of the idea, only an almost exact copy of that expression will infringe. On the other hand, where the expression is complex and highly original, copying of a small amount of that expression will be sufficient. It should also be noted that an author cannot claim protection for passages in his works which are not his copyright because they are copied from others or are in the public domain.

The term of copyright is determined by national laws, but it tends to be a long one. Copyright in the UK, and in the US for works which are governed by the 1976 Copyright Act, is the life of the author, plus 50 years.

How is copyright acquired?

In the majority of countries, including Britain and the Commonwealth, no formalities are required to acquire a copyright. Copyright comes into existence as soon as a copyrightable work is fixed in some material form. In others, such as the USA, certain formalities are required to protect the copyright in works once they are published.

In the USA the only formality required to maintain the copyright in a published work is the inclusion of a copyright notice on published copies of the work. This notice must be in the required form, which is the symbol ©, or the word 'copyright', or the abbreviation 'copr', the year of first publication and the name of the owner of copyright in the work. This notice must be affixed in such a manner as to give reasonable notice of the claim to copyright. Under the previous law there were rigid provisions about the location of the copyright notice, and copyright could be lost if they were not complied with, but the new law is much less rigid. For phonorecords the correct symbol is ℗ rather than ©. Under the

1909 Act, the omission of this notice on even a single published copy of the work was fatal to the existence of copyright, but the new law gives an opportunity to correct an accidental omission of the notice if the omission was on a relatively small number of published copies, or if the work is registered within five years from the publication without notice and reasonable efforts are made to add the notice to all copies distributed without the notice. An error in the name or date does not affect the copyright, but omission of either is treated as being equivalent to publication without notice.

While only the notice is required to preserve copyright, the copyright owner cannot sue for copyright infringement unless the work is registered with the US Copyright Office. Registration is a simple and cheap procedure, and involves filling in a form, paying a $10 fee and depositing (in most cases) two copies of the work concerned. The Copyright Office determines that the details on the form are correct and that the material is copyrightable subject-matter. If everything is correct, it issues a certificate of registration, usually within about six weeks from the filing of the form. The existence of registration operates as a rebuttable presumption that a valid copyright exists in the work named in the certificate.

The formalities in other countries which require them are in general very similar to those in the USA. However, certain South American countries require the copyright notice to contain the words 'All rights reserved' in addition to the contents required under US law. A full copyright notice should be placed on all works whenever there is any chance at all that they may be published or distributed abroad, so as to protect the copyright fully in all countries.

International copyright conventions

There are two main international copyright conventions, the Berne Convention and the Universal Copyright Convention (usually referred to as the UCC), together with the Rome Convention, which deals with the protection of performers, producers of phonograms and broadcasting organisations.

Of these, the Berne Convention is the oldest, dating from 1887, and provides the widest protection. In the version of the Convention by which the UK is bound (i.e., the one revised at Brussels in 1948), art. 4, which applies to literary and artistic works, provides that:

(1)   Authors who are nationals of any of the countries of the Union

[nations that have signed or acceded to the Convention] shall enjoy in countries other than the country of origin of the work, for their works, whether unpublished or first published in a country of the Union, the rights which their respective laws do now or may hereafter grant to their nationals, as well as the rights specially granted by this Convention.

(2)   The enjoyment and the exercise of these rights shall not be subject to any formality; such enjoyment and such exercise shall be independent of the existence of protection in the country of origin of the work. Consequently, apart from the provisions of this Convention, the extent of protection, as well as the means of redress afforded to the author to protect his rights, shall be governed exclusively by the laws of the country where protection is claimed.

Article 6 extends this protection to authors who are not nationals of a member of the Union, provided the work is first published in one of the countries of the Union, although this protection may be restricted if the author's country of nationality similarly restricts the rights of nationals of other countries of the Union.

The United States was unable to join the Berne Convention because of the provisions of art. 4(2). Largely to bring the USA into an international convention, the UCC was set up in 1952. This similarly requires reciprocal rights for nationals of a member country in all other member countries, but provides that national law relating to formalities must be complied with. There is a considerable overlap of coverage of the two conventions. The UK is both a party to the UCC and a member of the Berne Union.

The effect of these two conventions is that works by a national of a country that is party to one of them are automatically protected in a large part of the world, particularly if the author is a national of a country that is a party to both conventions and the author uses a proper copyright notice.

TRADE SECRETS

What is a trade secret?

A trade secret is any piece of commercially valuable information which is not generally known and which is kept from becoming generally known by its possessor. This type of information is often referred to as 'know-how'. There is no limitation on the type of information that comes within this definition, and within the scope of legal protection for trade secrets. It could be a patentable invention, and the circumstances in which trade-secret protection may be preferable over patent protection are discussed below. More usually, it is information which is not patentable, but which may give its owner a considerable competitive advantage, such as the optimum operating conditions of a chemical plant, or a list of all potential customers in an area for a particular product.

While a trade secret is not a true legal monopoly as a patent is, so long as it is kept a secret it, in effect, gives its owner a monopoly in that information. In some circumstances it may be possible to maintain this 'monopoly' for much longer than the life of a patent — the recipe for chartreuse liqueur has been kept secret by the monks who make it for over 200 years! Trade secrets may be commercially very valuable, often more so than patents, and are often licensed to others, on their own or in conjunction with a patent licence.

How to protect your trade secrets

Protection of trade secrets in common-law systems depends upon two legal concepts, the law of contract, and equitable duties of confidentiality and good-faith dealing which are implied in certain circumstances. Civil-law systems do not in general have the latter concept, so trade-secret protection is weaker in those systems.

The first step in protecting a trade secret is not a legal one. It is the practical step of keeping it a secret in the first place. A court will not restrain a breach of confidentiality or a misuse of a trade secret unless it is first convinced that the information is truly confidential. Once the secret is out, anyone is free to use it.

Protection should start with your own employees. While, in most systems and in all common-law systems, the law implies a duty of confidentiality with respect to an employer's trade secrets, it is much better to have all employees sign a written confidentiality agreement. An example of such an agreement can be found at the end of Chapter 12. This makes their responsibilities clear, in case of later dispute, and also draws to their attention their duty of confidentiality. You should also, whenever possible, make it clear to them what you regard as secret and coming within that agreement.

Secondly, reasonable precautions should be taken to protect your secrets against outsiders and dishonest employees. Industrial espionage has become a major problem in recent years, particularly in areas of fast-moving technology such as computer hardware and software. Secret information should only be given to employees who really need to know it in order to do their job. In the case of hardware, areas where new products are being developed should be protected by a security system, should only be accessible to authorised employees, and visitors should only be allowed in under careful supervision, and after signing a confidentiality agreement. The degree of security, should, of course, depend on the value of the secrets to be protected — the law only looks for *reasonable* precautions. In the case of software, an important precaution is to keep track of all copies of the source code for a secret program, and make sure that none of them leave the possession of the employees engaged on the project. Protecting unauthorised access to your computer system is important, remembering that this access can come from outside as well as inside.

When an employee who has had access to your trade secrets leaves your employ, he should be interviewed before he departs and reminded that his obligation to keep your secrets confidential continues after he ceases to be an employee. Checks should be made to ensure that all confidential material in his possession has been returned. Unfortunately, with the ready access to means of copying documents and software now open to all, it is very difficult to prevent the dishonest employee from taking unauthorised copies with him when he leaves.

You may wish to keep your secret for your own use, but in most cases you will want or need to reveal it to outsiders. The trade secret may be manufacturing know-how which cost you a lot to develop, and you may wish to maximise your return by licensing others to use the know-how in return for payment. Or, the trade secret may be embodied in an object, such as a piece of software, which has been developed for the purpose of sale to others. In order to continue to keep the information secret, the outsider must also be obliged to keep it secret.

This obligation is imposed by agreement. This should always be an express, written agreement, although the common law (or, more correctly, equity, a concept peculiar to common-law systems) will, in certain circumstances, imply such an agreement. An agreement will be implied in circumstances where the imparter of the information made it clear that the information was confidential, and it would amount to fraud on the part of the recipient to allow him to breach that confidence. Because such an obligation will only be implied if a court thinks the circumstances merit it, it should never be relied upon. Further, civil-law systems do not imply such an obligation, so in those countries a written contract must be used.

The contract should, at minimum, contain an agreement by the recipient of the information to keep it secret, to impart it only to those of its employees who need to know it, and only after those employees have signed a secrecy agreement if they do not already have one with their employer, and not to impart it to third parties without the prior, express, written consent of the owner of the trade secret. An example of a confidentiality agreement for software can be found at the end of Chapter 15.

Policing such an agreement for compliance is not usually too difficult in the case of a licence for the use of manufacturing know-how, and in any case the licensee has an incentive to keep the information secret because he is deriving commercial advantage from its secrecy. It is very much more difficult to police such an agreement where the trade secret is contained in an object being sold or leased. As a general principle, if it is anticipated that a significant number of the objects concerned will be distributed, it is very unwise to rely solely upon trade secrets for protection. What this number is depends upon the circumstances — it may be relatively easy to police confidentiality agreements with 100 owners of a mainframe computer; it would be difficult to do the same with 100 owners of a software package. It is important that you do take steps to enforce compliance by any licensee who breaches the agreement, otherwise you will be deemed to have waived your rights and you will have lost your secret. It will be easier to take such steps in the case of a license to use, rather than an outright sale, as you can provide in the agreement for self-help in the form of a right to terminate the agreement and recover possession of the object if the confidentiality obligations are breached. Otherwise, it will be necessary to commence legal proceedings for an injunction in order to prevent loss of confidentiality.

Which protection should you choose?

If you have an invention which is secret, and which fulfils the requirements of patentability, you have a choice between two, mutually incompatible, means of protection of that invention. You can apply for a patent, which reveals your invention to the world, but gives you a monopoly to exploit it for a limited period. On the other hand, you can keep it secret, but your protection lasts only so long as it remains secret, and you cannot prevent someone from exploiting the same invention if independently derived.

The following factors should be taken into account when making the choice:

(a)   If the invention is likely to be of little commercial value, it may not be worth the considerable expenditure that is entailed in obtaining a patent.

(b)   If the invention is likely to have a commercial life of less than five years, it is probably not worth applying for a patent, which usually takes a minimum of two to three years to obtain.

(c)   If the invention contains fundamental principles, which will be used in most future developments in the same field, a patent should be obtained, because this will cover those future developments. Keeping the information secret will not prevent others from independently developing and using the principle.

(d)   If the invention is readily reverse-engineered, that is, the invention can readily be ascertained by study of objects containing the invention which are put on the open market, patent protection should be sought, as the trade secret will only last until the reverse engineering is complete.

(e)   Conversely, if the invention is such that reverse engineering is almost impossible, and there is a good chance of keeping the information secret, then trade-secret protection can last very much longer than a patent.

(f)   If an invention which is not readily reverse-engineered is patented, its details are revealed to competitors, who may be able to design around the claims of the patent and come out with a competing product. Without the information in the patent, had the trade secret been maintained, competitors may be unable to produce a competing product, or only be able to do so after considerable development expenditure.

In the case of trade-secret matter which is not patentable, there may be a similar choice between trade-secret or copyright protection. In the computer field, this particularly arises in the case of software, and the factors concerned in making that choice are discussed in detail in Chapter 15.

TRADE MARKS

What is a trade mark?

A classic common-law definition of a trade mark is the following by Sir Duncan Kerly:

> A trade mark is a symbol which is applied to or attached to goods offered for sale in the market, so as to distinguish them from similar goods, and to identify them with a particular trader or with his successors as the owners of a particular business, as being made, worked upon, imported, selected, certified or sold by him or them, or which has been properly registered under the [Trade Mark] Acts as the trade mark of a particular trader.

This definition is still correct in the UK, but in countries, such as the USA, which permit registration of service marks, the words 'or services' should be added after the word 'goods'. A system of service-mark registration for the UK has been proposed, but has yet to be put into effect.

Trade marks are probably as old as trade itself. Archaeologists have uncovered Greek pottery 'factories', containing large numbers of almost identical pots, all of them bearing a particular mark. While the importance of trade marks in an area or at a time when very few consumers were literate is obvious, they remain of equal importance in modern societies, at least in those with free markets. Modern advertising practices have made a distinctive, easily recognisable trade mark a valuable asset. Almost anywhere in the world, the name 'Coca-Cola', the distinctive script in which the word is written, and the distinctive shape of its bottle are recognised by most consumers as indicating a cola soft drink from one particular source.

Acquiring trade-mark rights

At common law, trade-mark rights are acquired by actual use of the mark on the goods concerned. The first to use has, prima facie, the superior right to the mark. While most countries have a system of registration of trade-marks, discussed below, in common-law countries an earlier, unregistered trade mark can defeat a later user who has registered. This is not generally the case in civil-law countries.

In general, only actual use on goods, or (for service marks) in connection with services, in the market-place counts. Acts preparatory to use, such as pre-release advertising, do not usually give any rights in the mark concerned, although there are recent US cases in which an earlier user who had conducted extensive advertising and had received substantial orders for the goods concerned but had not yet shipped goods was granted priority as against a later user who had actually shipped goods bearing the mark.

In some countries, trade-mark rights can also be acquired by registration, without prior use. This is the case in the UK. An unused mark may be registered, subject to removal on the grounds of non-use. In other countries, for example the USA, a mark cannot be registered until it has actually been used on or in connection with the goods or services concerned.

Trade-mark registration

The method of registering a trade mark depends on the law of the country concerned. There are, however, some general principles. The first is that a mark is registered in respect of the particular goods or services in connection with which it is used. Secondly, goods and services are divided into various classes, and there is an international classification, drawn up at an international conference in London in 1943, which is used by many countries, including the UK and the USA. A separate registration is generally required for each class into which the goods or services in respect of which the mark is used fall.

In order to be registrable, the mark must be capable of distinguishing the goods or services offered by the trade-mark owner from similar goods and services offered by others. In this connection, reference is often made to 'generic' and 'descriptive' marks. The phrase 'generic mark' is in fact a contradiction in terms, because the generic word for an object can never serve to distinguish one producer of that object from another. On the other hand, while a word which is descriptive of the particular goods cannot generally provide this distinguishing function, it may eventually do so if it is sufficiently widely used that consumers come to associate that mark with a particular manufacturer. To give a theoretical example of the difference between the two terms, it would never be possible to use the term 'piano' as a trade mark for the musical instrument whose full name is a pianoforte, because that is a generic term for the object. On the other hand, the word 'harmonious' is descriptive of the characteristics (one hopes) of the instrument. On its own, it is not distinctive. Further, there is a considerable reluctance on the part of courts and trade-mark registrars to allow a trader to pre-empt an ordinary word which should be open to all piano manufacturers to use when describing their wares. However, if one manufacturer puts sufficient time and effort into his use of the term as a trade mark, he may eventually make the name sufficiently distinctive in the market-place to be entitled to have it registered. A number of systems, including the UK and the US have a subsidiary category of registration for marks which are descriptive but have some distinctiveness. If the mark for which registration is sought is distinctive when considered as a whole but contains descriptive matter, the applicant is usually required to state that he does not claim any rights in the descriptive matter.

Another important requirement for registration is that the mark is not confusingly similar to a mark already registered for the same or similar goods or services. A considerable body of law has grown up in common-law systems regarding the meaning of the term 'confusingly similar' or its equivalents, because this is also the test for infringement of a trade mark, and, in addition, it is a factor in the tort of unfair competition (generally called 'passing off' in the UK). This law is discussed more fully below.

In general, registration is only initially for a limited period, with a right of renewal. Renewal generally is only granted upon proof of continued use. Third parties with a sufficient interest in the matter may oppose registration of a mark, or institute proceedings to have an improperly registered mark deleted from the register. The most common ground for opposition is that the mark for which registration is sought is alleged by the opposer to be confusingly similar to the opposer's own mark.

A trade mark which was initially properly registered may later become ineligible for registration, and can be removed from the register. This removal may be at the request of a third party who has some interest in the removal, or it may be done by the trade-mark office on its own motion. In both cases the registered proprietor has a chance to argue against removal before the decision is taken. The main grounds for removal are that the proprietor has ceased to use the mark and does not intend to use it again, that the mark has become separated from its associated goodwill by reason of assignment, and that the mark has ceased to be distinctive of the proprietor's goods or services. In general, the latter ground is not available in the case of marks which have been registered for some statutory minimum period, except in the case of a mark which has in fact become the generic name for an item. The owner of a trade mark for an item which is the first, or predominates in its field must take special care that this mark is not allowed to become the generic name. For example, The Xerox Corporation devotes a considerable budget to reminding people by advertising and other means that the word 'Xerox' is not a synonym for a photocopying machine, and should never be used as a verb instead of 'to photocopy'. An earlier example of the dangers of success is the 'Singer' trade mark, which was held at the end of the 19th century to have become generic for sewing machines. After several years, and considerable efforts, the Singer Manufacturing Company managed to re-establish judicially the distinctiveness of the mark.

The effect of registration is that it provides prima facie evidence of validity. Many systems further provide that, after registration for a certain period, this changes to a presumption of validity which can only be rebutted in limited circumstances. In the UK this presumption arises after seven years, and thereafter the only challenges to the validity of the mark can be that the registration was obtained by fraud, or that the mark was not entitled to registration because it was deceptive or its registration was otherwise contrary to public policy. Registration is usually a prerequisite to commencement of litigation for trade-mark infringement. Unregistered trade-marks can only be protected through the law of unfair competition.

Assignment and licensing of trade marks

A trade mark is not in itself a complete piece of property, because its validity depends upon its use in relation to goods (or services, where service marks are also protected) to indicate origin. The common law insisted that a trade mark could only be assigned in connection with the assignment of the goodwill of the proprietor's *entire* business. This strict rule has generally been modified by statute to allow assignment with only that part of the business to which the mark in question relates. The UK Trade Marks Act 1938, s. 22(7), does provide for assignment of the mark without the goodwill of the business provided the provisions of that section, which include advertising of the assignment, are met.

This association of trade marks and indication of origin provides particular problems in connection with licensing. If there is no real connection between the licensor's and the licensee's businesses except that a royalty is paid for the use of the mark, then there is a real possibility that the public will be deceived. At common law this rendered such a licence ineffective, and continued use by the licensee could result in the licensor losing its rights because the mark had been rendered non-distinctive by the dual use. This was held to be the result of such a licence in a leading case, *Bowden Wire Ltd* v *Bowden Brake Co. Ltd* (1914) 31 RPC 385, HL, affirming (1913) 30 RPC 580, CA. Unlike its predecessor, the 1938 Act provides for registration of users other than the proprietor of the mark under s. 28. This section is not very clearly worded but has generally been regarded as protecting against loss of the mark under the common-law rule when the user is registered and complies with the statutory provisions. These do require a 'connection in the course of trade' between the proprietor and the user, which is generally provided by quality-control provisions in the licence. A recent decision of the House of Lords has cast doubt upon the effectiveness of quality-control provisions alone as the 'connection in the course of trade'. This is *Re American Greetings Corporation's application*, [1984] 1 WLR 189, HL. The applicant sought to register 'Holly Hobbie', the name of a fictional character, as a trade mark for a range of goods other than the greetings cards which were the applicant's sole use of the mark. The Holly Hobbie character is in fact one of the most valuable pieces of character merchandising at present, and a large number of manufacturers have been licensed to produce a wide range of goods bearing the representation of the character and the name 'Holly Hobbie'. The applications for registration were accompanied by registered user agreements which had comprehensive provisions for quality control. The Registrar of Trade Marks had refused the applications under the rather obscure s. 28(6), which provides that:

> The Registrar shall refuse an application under the foregoing provisions of this section if it appears to him that the grant thereof would tend to facilitate trafficking in a trade mark.

The House of Lords agreed with this refusal, holding that the quality-control provisions were not a sufficient 'connection in the course of trade' to prevent these applications falling into the 'sin' of trafficking in trade marks. This decision casts doubt upon the validity of a large number of UK trade-mark licences, and it is to be hoped that it will be reversed by legislation.

Trade-mark licences have generally been recognised as valid in the

United States, provided that the licensor controls the quality of the goods marketed under the licensed mark.

Infringement of trade marks

Registered trade marks are protected by giving the trade-mark owner a right to sue for trade-mark infringement. If infringement is found, further use of the infringing mark can be restrained by injunction, and the trade-mark owner can be awarded damages. In the United States, where the British rule that the loser pays a large proportion of the winner's total costs of the litigation does not apply, the trade-mark owner is also entitled under the statute to an award of attorney's fees.

The essence of trade-mark infringement is the probability that the accused mark will confuse customers. Within this simple statement, however, lies a vast body of case law. What types of confusion will cause a mark to infringe? Must it be exactly the same as the registered mark? Must it be used on exactly the same goods? What customers have to be considered? Do they have to know the identity of the owner of the mark? The courts have had to come up with answers to these and other questions. Because of the central importance of this concept of confusion to both the law of trade marks and the law of unfair competition, it will now be examined in some detail.

Actionable trade confusion

Under s. 4 of the UK Trade Marks Act 1938, a registered trade mark is infringed by the use of a mark which is either identical or so nearly resembles it as to be likely to deceive or cause confusion in the course of trade in goods of the same type as those for which the mark is registered, provided that such use is a trade-mark use, that is, one which can be taken to indicate origin. Similarly, under the US Lanham Act, 15 USC s. 1114, there is a cause of action for infringement where there is use, without the registered owner's consent, of a reproduction, counterfeit or colourable imitation of the registered mark in connection with the sale, distribution or advertising of goods or services in circumstances in which such use is likely to cause confusion or to deceive purchasers about the source or origin of the goods. Most other trade-mark statutes have similar provisions.

The question whether a particular mark 'is likely to deceive or cause confusion' is ultimately one of fact, and can only be decided upon consideration of the particular facts of each case. There are, however, a number of judicially erected guideposts to help the trier of fact to reach a determination which is not purely subjective. The most important of these are as follows:

(a)   Who is likely to be deceived? Common sense, and judicial precedent, suggest that a sophisticated purchaser of expensive goods is likely to take much more care over selecting those goods and investigating their origin than a busy shopper picking an inexpensive item, such as a tube of toothpaste or a can of beans, off a supermarket shelf. Therefore, the latter will be much more easily deceived by a trade mark than the former. Similarly, the ultimate consumer will be more readily confused than a wholesale or retail merchant who is familiar with the goods. Marks which may not be confusing to educated English speakers may be so to illiterate or non-English-speaking consumers. On the other hand, the fact that a few unusually careless or stupid people (the 'moron in a hurry', a legal personality who first appeared in the judgment of Foster J in *Morning Star Co-operative Society Ltd* v *Express Newspapers Ltd* [1979] FSR 113) may be deceived is not enough to outlaw a mark.

(b)   The comparison should be made under the circumstances in which it would be made in practice. In most cases, certainly in the case of marks on consumer goods, it is most unlikely that the purchaser will make a detailed side-by-side comparison of the two marks, or even be able to make such a comparison. Confusion is therefore likely to occur if the general impression on the senses left by the two marks is the same, even if there are various differences between them when viewed side by side.

(c)   The more distinctive the mark, the greater the likelihood of confusion. When a mark is unusual and well known, it is much more likely that consumers, seeing a mark that resembles it in some way, will think that those goods come from the same source. On the other hand, where there are a number of similar marks owned by different entities in use for the same or related goods, comparatively small differences will make the accused mark non-infringing. For example, it is common for trade marks for butter and other dairy products to include the words 'meadow' or 'pasture' or to have a depiction of a cow; such items appearing in both the marks to be compared will, on their own, have little weight as evidence of likelihood of confusion.

(d)   Sound, as well as appearance of the marks must be considered. Confusion can arise when goods are ordered by telephone as well as when they are picked off a shop shelf. On the other hand, mere phonetic similarity is unlikely to be confusing where the ideas conveyed by the two words are different.

(e)   While it need not be shown that the defendant intended to cause confusion, evidence that that was his intention in selecting the mark tends to raise a presumption that his mark is, in fact, likely to confuse.

Originally, there was only an action for trade-mark infringement if the infringing mark was used on goods which competed directly with the goods carrying the registered mark. This was because the only actionable damage was loss of sales by reason of the defendant's deceitful diversion of the plaintiff's business by his use of the deceptive mark. This rule arose from the fact that the action for trade-mark infringement developed historically from the action on the case for deceit. In modern law, the extent to which use on goods which do not directly compete is an infringement depends on the wording of the particular statute concerned. The UK statutory provision, s. 4 of the 1938 Act, refers to 'goods in respesct of which it [the mark concerned] is registered'. This means that an action for trade-mark infringement can only be brought in respect of use by the defendant of the accused mark on goods for which the plaintiff has in fact registered his mark. As there is no requirement of actual use before registration, the registration can cover goods on which the proprietor does not use the mark but which would be close enough to his goods to make use of a similar mark by others objectionable. The danger of too wide a registration, however, is that the defendant may successfully challenge the validity of the registration. The only remedy which may be open to prevent use on non-registered goods is a passing-off action. In contrast, the US provision is much wider, referring to use on 'related' goods, and it has been generally given a wide interpretation by the courts. A court will generally find trade-mark infringement under the Lanham Act if it is convinced that consumers are likely to think that the defendant's goods or services are somehow connected with the plaintiff, even if there is no direct competition between the parties. The damage to the plaintiff is not lost trade, but potential damage to its reputation and loss of control of its identifying mark.

International trade-mark conventions

Trade marks come within the provisions of the Paris Convention, already discussed in relation to patents. This provides that each country retains its own system of registration and protection, but that nationals of the other member countries are equally entitled to such national protection and registration with that country's own citizens. The convention also provides that members will protect 'well known' marks by refusing to register applications for the same or similar marks by third parties, and that they will refuse to register marks containing national flags, emblems and coats of arms of any of the member countries. It also gives the right to a proprietor of a mark in one country to prevent unauthorised registration of that mark by his agent or distributor in another country. This is an important provision in practice, as it is relatively common in some countries for an agent to register in its own name the marks of its foreign principal in order to try to gain, or retain, exclusivity in that country against the principal's wishes.

There is not yet any European trade-mark registration system corresponding to the European patent system, but a system of EEC common trade-mark registration is in the process of being set up. It is, however, likely to be a long time before this system is finally in operation, because there are many more problems to be overcome, including linguistic problems, than there are with a supranational patent system.

UNFAIR COMPETITION

Unfair competition: a rapidly developing concept

The use of the law to control the behaviour of competing businesses is both very old, and very new. Old, in that there have been several previous historical periods when business competition was controlled, usually in the interests of the business owners rather than of the general public. The mediaeval system of guilds was a very comprehensive and effective means of controlling the conduct of business at that time, including regulation of prices, work conditions and entry into the market place. As society became more mobile and more industrialised, the guilds withered and died, remaining generally only as ceremonial bodies and social clubs. The concept of an ordered business structure was replaced by the doctrine of *laissez-faire*, which taught that business should be left completely free to compete in any way possible. This system created considerable wealth, but at the expense of the misery of many, and gradually the need for some sort of regulation of the competitive process came to be realised. The result was the development, largely in the 20th century, of the contrasting but related concepts of antitrust or competition law, which prevents distortions of the competitive process from being used to stifle competition, and unfair competition law, which protects against the excesses of untrammelled competition.

Unlike established legal concepts such as patents, trade marks and copyright, there are very few general principles of unfair competition law which are common to the national laws of the industrialised countries. The scope of unfair competition law varies greatly from country to country. As a result, it is not possible to do more here than to indicate some very general principles, and to describe in a little more detail the law as it is at present in England and in the United States.

Most industrialised countries now have some statutory provisions controlling unfair competition, varying from very limited scope (e.g., the United Kingdom) to very detailed and wide ranging (e.g., Austria). In addition, the common-law countries have developed a judicial system of unfair competition law using developments of established torts. This process has gone much further in the United States than elsewhere, with England having probably the least developed judicial competition law of the common-law countries.

Probably the only common principle is that a business is not allowed to be promoted by misrepresentations, particularly those which harm another trader. This includes innocent as well as deliberate misrepresentations, and misrepresentations by conduct, or by the appearance of goods (often called 'get-up'), as well as misrepresentations by spoken or written words.

United Kingdom

Most of the UK statutes dealing with unfair business practices are aimed at protecting the consumer in various types of transactions where the individual is at particular risk from unscrupulous traders, in particular those involving loans or consumer credit, and at preventing misrepresentations and misleading statements to consumers. The most important of these statutes are the Trade Descriptions Acts 1968 and 1972, and the Fair Trading Act 1973. Control of practices forbidden under these statutes is by criminal prosecution instituted by various authorities, not by civil action instituted by the victim.

Civil action can be brought under tort law. The main tort concerned with unfair competition is passing off. The essence of the tort is activity by a trader which causes the public to believe that his goods or business are the goods or business of the plaintiff. The leading authority on passing off is now the decision of the House of Lords in the Advocaat case, *Erven Warnink BV* v *J. Townend & Sons (Hull) Ltd* [1979] AC 731. The plaintiffs were producers of a drink called 'advocaat', manufactured from eggs and a spirit called '*brandewijn*' in Dutch. The defendants were an English company and a partnership firm which produced a drink made from eggs and fortified sherry, which they sold as 'Keeling's Old English Advocaat'. This bore a lower excise duty, and therefore could be sold for a lower price than the plaintiff's drink. The evidence was that an egg and fortified wine drink such as the defendants' was properly called 'egg flip' in English, so the use of 'advocaat' in connection with the defendants' product was deceptive. The question before the House of Lords was whether the plaintiffs could sue in passing off, even though there was no suggestion that the defendants had ever done anything which could lead to the belief that their goods were produced by any of the plaintiffs. The Lords held that they could, that passing off extends to misuse of a word distinctive of a class of goods, rather than of a particular producer of those goods.

According to the Advocaat case, the essentials which must be proved to establish passing off are (1) a misrepresentation (2) made by a trader in the course of trade (3) to prospective customers of his or ultimate consumers of goods or services supplied by him (4) which is calculated to injure the business or goodwill of another trader (in the sense that this is a reasonably foreseeable consequence) and (5) which causes actual damage to a business or goodwill of the trader by whom the action is brought or (in a *quia timet* action — an action brought before damage is sustained to prevent such damage occurring) will probably do so. The damage will occur, or be likely to do so, if the misrepresentation causes the relevant customers to be confused or deceived. In effect, infringement of a registered trade mark is a special case of the general law of passing off. It is well established that there is no need to prove *actual* intent to deceive, an innocent deception is enough to found an action in passing off, although remedies are more limited in the case of innocent deception.

Confusion and likelihood of confusion have been discussed above in the section of this chapter dealing with trade marks. One of the reasons why the English tort of passing off has not developed so far towards providing a general remedy for unfair competition as other common-law systems is that most cases, at least prior to the Advocaat decision, required proof of an extra element before finding confusion or likelihood of confusion. This element is generally referred to as 'a common field of activity' between the plaintiff and the defendant. In other jurisdictions, such as the United States and Australia, the existence or non-existence of a common field of activity between the plaintiff and the defendant is merely one element to be considered when deciding whether or not there is actionable deception or likelihood of deception. It is a matter of common sense that confusion is more likely when both parties are in the same business, but damaging confusion can occur in other circumstances. To give a fictional illustration, suppose the plaintiff manufactures cakes and biscuits which are sold under the trade mark 'Yummy' (probably unregistrable as being descriptive). If the defendant started to sell soft drinks under the same name, it is possible that a person who knows of the plaintiff's products will think that this is a new product line — increasingly likely in these days of corporate conglomerates and diversification. If the defendant's soft drink tastes bad, or makes a purchaser ill, that purchaser is likely never to purchase anything sold under the 'Yummy' brand again. This obviously damages the plaintiff's business, even though he is not in the same line of business as the defendant. One of the clearest examples from actual case law of this limitation is the Kojak case, *Tavener Rutledge Ltd* v *Trexapalm Ltd* [1977] RPC 275. Riding upon the success of the television series about the lollipop-sucking, New York detective called Kojak, the plaintiffs were marketing and selling 'Kojakpops', without licence from the owners of the television series. When the defendants, who had such a licence, started to sell 'Kojak lollies', the plaintiffs sued for passing off, and succeeded. Although most people might think that it was the plaintiffs who had competed unfairly by taking a 'free ride' on the success of the defendant's licensor, the court held that the plaintiff could not be sued by the licensor for passing off because there was no common field of activity between the plaintiff (confectionery) and the licensor (television programmes). Therefore, the licensor had no rights to transfer to the defendant, and as the plaintiff was first in the market, it could prevent the defendant from putting its confusingly similar product on the market.

A recent Court of Appeal decision may indicate a trend towards broadening passing off towards a wider protection against unfair competition. This is *Sony KK* v *Saray Electronics (London) Ltd* [1983] FSR 302. The plaintiff, a well known manufacturer of electronics goods, markets its goods in the UK through carefully chosen and trained authorised dealers. These dealers can provide full back-up and repair services, and only they are authorised to give the Sony guarantee over and above the statutory rights. Sony's advertising lays stress on its dealer network and the guarantees. The defendants, who are not authorised Sony dealers, and who have a history of bad trading practices, had been holding themselves out as authorised Sony dealers and purporting to give the Sony guarantee. On the plaintiffs' application for an interlocutory injunction, the Court of Appeal not only ordered the defendants to refrain from holding themselves out as authorised dealers and from giving the guarantees, but it also ordered them to affix a notice to each piece of Sony equipment sold by them stating 'Sarays are not authorised Sony dealers and Sony equipment sold here is guaranteed by Sarays but not by Sony'. This decision, even though interlocutory, shows that the court was ready to protect a method of trading under the tort of passing off; there was no passing off of goods in this case.

The only other common-law causes of action which relate to unfair competition are the group of torts dealing with malicious falsehood. These include slander of title and slander of goods. Slander of title involves deliberate falsehoods regarding a vendor's title to the property he is offering for sale, which prevent or hinder the sale. Slander of goods covers deliberate lies disparaging the quality of a trader's goods which prevents their sale. It is an essential element of all this group of torts that there is a false statement which is known to the maker to be false, and which is deliberately intended to do harm. This requirement that the plaintiff must prove actual malice on the part of the defendant means that these actions are rarely of any practical use.

United States

Unfair competition law in the USA is generally state law, although the 9th circuit (which covers the Pacific Coast states) has held that the federal trade-mark statute, the Lanham Act, 15 USC s. 1125(a), provides a general federal action for unfair competition. Other circuits do not agree.

An increasing number of states have statutory provisions dealing with at least some types of unfair competition, but generally it is a common-law action, a branch of tort law.

In contrast to the narrow and cautious view taken by the English judiciary, the American judges have made unfair competition an extremely broad cause of action. To quote from one of the leading books on the subject, J. Thomas McCarthy, *Trademarks and Unfair Competition* (Rochester NY: Lawyers Co-operative Publishing Co., 1973), vol. 1, p. 11:

> It is no easier to define the shape and contour of the law of unfair competition than to define the shape and contour of a constantly changing and shifting fog bank . . .. The word 'unfair' is no more precise than many other legal terms whose purpose is to give discretion to a judge, such as, for example, 'reasonable' or 'adequate'.

One reason for this is the decision of the Supreme Court in *International News Service* v *Associated Press*, 248 US 215 (1918) that the action for unfair competition is not restricted to 'passing off', the substitution of one trader's goods for another's by misrepresentation or deliberate switching. Another reason is that, for constitutional reasons, American judges feel freer to create new law to deal with new social problems than their British brethren, who are bound to enforce legislation enacted by Parliament, and who tend therefore to wait for Parliament to deal with a new problem.

Because of the breadth of the action for unfair competition, and its constant development through the case law, it is very hard to deal with it comprehensively in an outline such as this. Unfair competition is basically any competitive tactics which a judge can be persuaded are unfair. These include such things as infringement of unregistered trade marks and of trade and business names, dilution of the goodwill in a trade mark, appropriation of literary titles and of literary and entertainment characters, simulation of container configuration, packaging or 'trade-dress', 'bait-and-switch' selling, palming off, trade-secret theft, competition by the seller of a business against a buyer, use by a former employee of business secrets belonging to his ex-employer and deceptive advertising. The common thread that runs through all of them is that there is some act or representation which misleads the consumer and which thereby causes damage to a competitor. This is very closely related to the test for trade-mark infringement, discussed above.

The one limitation on the breadth of US unfair competition law is the doctrine of federal pre-emption, which means that the states cannot legislate on the same matter that Congress has legislated on. The Constitution gives Congress the sole power to enact laws relating to patents and copyrights. The Supreme Court held, in a pair of cases usually referred to as *Sears-Compco* (*Sears Roebuck & Co.* v *Stiffel*, 376 US 225 (1964); *Compco Corp.* v *Day-Brite Lighting Inc.*, 376 US 234 (1964)), that state unfair competition law could not be used to give protection to items which were unprotectable under the federal patent and copyright laws. When these decisions first came down, many commentators feared that state unfair competition law would be drastically cut down by pre-emption, but in practice this has not proved to be the case. A number of decisions have held that unfair competition protection can only be denied when Congress has made it clear that there is to be no protection, not in cases where Congress has not spoken on the matter.

14   Protection of Hardware

The protection of hardware presents few legal problems, as compared to the protection of software and firmware. This is because hardware is, in general, recognisable as a machine, even though it operates by electricity rather than moving parts. Machines are objects which the law is used to dealing with, and for which it has developed a recognised set of rules.

PATENT

Machines are a class of objects which have been eligible for patent protection throughout the history of the patent system, and which are patentable under all national patent systems. There are numerous patents already in existence for computers, peripherals and their components. Patenting is probably the best protection for any hardware component which meets the requirements for patentability described in Chapter 13.

COPYRIGHT

Under the copyright laws of most countries, copyright is a concept which does not have much application to machines. Copyright in drawings and sculpture is generally confined to works of an artistic nature, and drawings and objects of a utilitarian nature are excluded. For example, the term 'pictorial, graphic and sculptural works', as used in the US copyright statutes, is defined, (by 17 USC s. 101), as including:

'works of artistic craftsmanship insofar as their form but not their mechanical or utilitarian aspects, are concerned; the design of a useful article, as defined in this section, shall be considered a pictorial, graphic, or sculptural work only if, and only to the extent that, such design incorporates pictorial, graphic, or sculptural features that can be identified separately from, and are capable of existing independently of, the utilitarian aspects of the article.'

A 'useful article' is defined by the same section as 'an article having an intrinsic utilitarian function that is not merely to portray the appearance of the article or to convey information'. The legislative history of the United States Copyright Act 1976 makes it clear that Congress did not intend industrial products to be protected, even though their shape may be aesthetically pleasing. If, however, an article primarily artistic in nature is incorporated into an industrial product, that article can be protected; in one leading case the US Supreme Court held that a lamp base in the form of a Balinese dancer was eligible for copyright protection (*Mazer* v *Stein*, 347 US 201 (1954)).

This is not the case in the UK and certain Commonwealth countries which have followed the British law. As a result of certain key judicial decisions interpreting statutory law, the present position is that, in Britain and its followers, industrial products for which a design drawing was made may be protected by copyright for the full period of the life of the author of the drawing plus 50 years. This should be contrasted with a 15-year protection period for articles which qualify for registration as industrial designs because they appeal to the eye and their shape is not dictated by the function they have to perform. This means that purely functional objects, such as car spares, receive a much longer period of protection than objects which incorporate an artistic design.

How did this anomalous situation come about?

It is largely the result of a statutory system which separated copyright in designs from other sorts of copyright, and sought to ensure that there was no overlap between the two systems. This was necessary because the two systems did provide different types of protection: a registered design was given a patent-type monopoly protection for a relatively short period, in contrast to the negative, 'ability to prevent copying' protection conferred by ordinary copyright, as explained in Chapter 13.

The possibility of overlap first arose with the Copyright Act 1911, which brought together under one statutory 'roof' various types of works which had previously been protected under separate statutes. The 1911 Act counteracted this possibility by s. 22, which provided:

(1)   This Act shall not apply to designs capable of being registered under the Patents and Designs Act 1907, except designs which, though capable of being so registered, are not used or intended to be used as models or patterns to be multiplied by any industrial process.

(2)   General rules under section 86 of the Patents and Designs Act 1907, may be made for determining the conditions under which a design shall be deemed to be used for such purposes as aforesaid.

Rules were subsequently introduced under this section, and one of these rules dealt with the meaning of the phrase 'used as a model or pattern to be multiplied by any industrial process'. This rule provided that:

A design shall be deemed to be used as a model or pattern to be multiplied by any industrial process within the meaning of section 22 of the Copyright Act 1911 —

(a)   when the design is reproduced or is intended to be reproduced in more than fifty single articles, unless all the articles in which the design is reproduced or intended to be reproduced together form a single set of articles.

This section and rule were considered by the House of Lords in the 'Popeye' case, *King Features Syndicate Inc.* v *O & M Kleeman Ltd* [1941] AC 417. The defendant had made certain items in the form of Popeye the Sailor, who had become a well known cartoon character on both sides of the Atlantic by that time. The owners of the copyright in the cartoons sued for copyright infringement. There was no design for the Popeye character registered. At the time that the author first produced the drawings he had no intention of industrialising them, but he had later granted licences for the manufacture of articles in the form of the character. The House of Lords held that a later industrialisation did not take the copyright out of the protection of the Copyright Act 1911 by operation of s. 22. The relevant intent was the intent at the time of the creation of the design.

The law of copyright was substantially amended by the Copyright Act 1956, which is the current British copyright statute. The provisions of this statute regarding overlap with registered designs are complicated, but essentially provide that, for any work which is capable of being registered as a design, the period of copyright protection is the same as that under the Registered Designs Act 1949 (i.e., 15 years from the first industrialisation), so that the relevant type of protection no longer depended solely on the author's intention at the time the work was created. An artistic work would enjoy normal copyright protection until it was applied industrially. Overlap of protection under the 1956 Act was prevented by providing that it would not be an infringement of copyright in the work to do anything which would be within the scope of protection given by the registration of the design. Therefore, once the design was industrialised, its protection depended upon getting a design registration.

This situation has been somewhat changed by the passage of the Design Copyright Act 1968, which provides for dual copyright and registration protection of a registrable design. For articles which have been industrialised, and which have or could have been registered under the Registered Designs Act, the copyright expires 15 years from the date of first marketing of the industrialised design.

It is an essential requirement for registration of a design that the design feature is something that appeals to, and is judged solely by, the eye. An object whose shape or configuration is 'dictated solely by the function which the article made in that shape or configuration has to perform' is not registrable as a design (Registered Designs Act 1949, s. 1(3)). The result of this provision, the courts have held, is that an unregistrable design remains protected by the general copyright law, even if it has been industrialised (*Dorling* v *Honnor Marine Ltd* [1965] Ch 1).

The other unusual feature of British copyright law which produces copyright protection for useful, industrialised objects, is the provision that reproduction of a copyright work includes producing a three-dimensional version of a two-dimensional work, and vice versa. The only qualification on this is the curiously worded s. 9(8) of the Copyright Act 1956, which provides that:

> The making of an object of any description which is in three dimensions shall not be taken to infringe the copyright in an artistic work in two dimensions, if the object would not appear, to persons who are not experts in relation to objects of that description, to be a reproduction of the artistic work.

Section 3 of the 1956 Act provides for copyright in artistic works, which includes drawings 'irrespective of artistic quality'. This means that industrial drawings such as blueprints are protected, and therefore three-dimensional reproductions of those blueprints are also protected, provided that the 'non-expert' can recognise the three-dimensional object to be a reproduction of the two-dimensional work. The non-expert is, in fact, the judge who tries the claim that a three-dimensional object produced by the defendant infringes the plaintiff's copyright in its drawing, and it is rare for a claim of copyright infringement to be refused on this ground.

The result of these provisions is that the maker of industrial objects, such as car parts, can prevent others from manufacturing substantially identical parts for over 50 years. As objects such as car parts have to be substantially identical to the original manufacturer's parts if they are to work, this effectively gives the original manufacturer a monopoly in the supply of spare parts. There have been a few, very limited, judicial restrictions on this surprisingly broad curb on free competition. One such limitation is that a reproduction in three dimensions of an article shown in the drawings of an expired patent is not a copyright infringement because such drawings have, in effect, been dedicated to the public on expiry of the patent. There have also been proposals for the statutory reform of this situation, in particular the Government's green paper entitled *Reform of the Law Relating to Copyright, Designs and Performers' Protection*, published in July 1981. This recommended that industrial articles which are three-dimensional reproductions of drawings will not themselves be protected by copyright unless they come within a proposed expansion of 'works of artistic craftsmanship', which are protected under s. 3(1)(c) of the Copyright Act 1956, to include works whose appearance is not solely dictated by the function they have to perform. However, Parliament has yet to act on these proposals.

There is one type of computer hardware for which copyright protection could be relevant and useful. This is the integrated circuit, the so-called 'silicon chip'. An integrated circuit consists of an array of electronic components, such as transistors, resistors and capacitors, which are formed by a thin pattern of conducting material on a thin wafer of a semiconductor material, usually silicon. In fact, it would be more correct to say 'a series of patterns', because modern integrated circuits contain a very complex array of circuitry, produced by overlaying a whole series of patterns.

In outline, the following steps are used in the manufacture of an integrated circuit. First, the circuit must be designed to fulfil the purpose the chip is to be used for. This is a complex and highly skilled task, and the design of some chips, such as modern 32K and 64K microprocessors, can take several man-years of design effort to produce. The design is then translated into engineering drawings, another highly skilled task, which are then entered into a computer by means of special computer graphics and a machine called a digitiser. The output of the digitiser is used to drive a drafting machine, which produces a reproduction of the original engineering drawing, reduced by several orders of magnitude. From this reproduction a series of master masks are prepared, which are used to produce the desired patterns by means of photolithography on a wafer of almost pure silicon cut from a single crystal. Finally, the wafer is tested to ensure that its circuits are good, and the good circuits are each assembled into a package, which is usually ready to be connected into an electronic device by means of connectors on the exterior of the package.

It will be readily appreciated that design and mask production for complex integrated circuits are very expensive processes. On the other hand, methods exist which allow this design to be copied from a chip and reproduced on other chips in a matter of a few weeks for a fraction of the original production cost. If such copying is not prevented, these copy chips can be produced for much less initial outlay, and therefore marketed at a lower price, within a few weeks from the first release of the original chip on to the market. This type of competition makes it impossible for the original manufacturer to recoup its design costs, and therefore discourages innovation. So this seems to be a classic example of a situation where the efforts of the original designer should be protected in the general interest of encouraging further innovation. But is there such a protection?

Many integrated circuits are not eligible for patent protection, as they are obvious variants on known themes. Trade-secret law does not provide much protection because the chips readily give up their secrets to anyone with access to the means of deciphering them, and are sold in circumstances making contractual protection almost impossible. This would appear to be a good case for copyright protection — protection of the considerable intellectual effort that has gone into the design, while leaving others free to incorporate the same ideas into their own designs. There is, however, considerable doubt about whether integrated circuits are protected by copyright under existing laws.

It seems clear that, in the UK, the original engineering drawings will be protected under the existing law, as explained above. The mask patterns, derived from these drawings, will also be protected. However, the chip produced from these masks will only be protected if it satisfies the s. 9(8) test, described above: would the statutory 'non-expert' recognise these as three-dimensional representations of the original drawings? This must remain in doubt until there is a judicial determination of the question — as explained above, the 'non-expert' is in practice the judge or other tribunal which has to rule on the copyright issue. Given the present leaning of the English judiciary to protect copyright in situations such as these, there is a better than even chance that the decision will favour copyright protection for integrated circuits. This is also a likely result in other countries which follow UK copyright law.

An alternative argument for the copyrightability of integrated circuits and the masks from which they are manufactured under UK law is that the integrated circuits are 'engravings' and the masks are 'photographs'. An 'engraving', for the purposes of the Copyright Act 1956, is defined as including 'any etching, lithograph, woodcut, print or similar work, not being a photograph' (s. 48(1)). As stated above, the chips are produced by a process of photolithography, and would therefore seem to come within this definition. A 'photograph' is defined by the same section as meaning 'any product of photography or of any process akin to photography, other than part of a cinematograph film'. The actual masks used to make the chips are produced by a photographic process. This argument has the major advantage of avoiding the problems of s. 9(8), but there is a point that may be raised against it. Copyright protection is, by s. 3(2) of the Copyright Act 1956, extended to *original* artistic works, which include engravings and photographs. The masks are, in effect, exact photographic reproductions of the engineering drawings, as are the integrated circuits produced using the masks; it is possible that a court would hold that therefore there is no 'originality' in the masks and chips sufficient to give a copyright separate from the copyright in the original drawings.

The position in the USA, the world leader in integrated circuit design, is much less clear. The Copyright Office has been accepting engineering drawings and masks for copyright registration, but has generally been refusing registration of the chips themselves, on the ground that they are 'useful articles', and therefore not copyrightable. One of the leading American producers of integrated circuits, Intel Corporation, sought to force the Copyright Office to register an integrated circuit device produced from registered drawings. Unfortunately, no decision resulted from this case, as the action was dismissed without prejudice on the basis that the Copyright Office would hold a public hearing on the question.

This hearing took place in connection with bill HR 1007, which was introduced into Congress by three Representatives from California. The purpose of the bill was, in effect, to extend copyright protection to integrated circuits by adding them to the definition of 'pictorial, graphic and sculptural works' under the existing copyright statute. The witnesses at the hearing, held in San Jose, California, in April 1979, were divided about the desirability of these provisions. In particular, even the witnesses from the semiconductor industry itself were divided about the sort of protection that their products should have. Bill HR 1007 failed to pass Congress, but these events spurred the semiconductor industry in the USA to consider the matter and reach a consensus that some protection against copying should be given for a limited period, provided innocent purchasers of infringing chips are given some protection. A new bill, HR 1028, has recently been introduced into Congress, which would give a ten-year period of copyright protection to the owners of mask designs, but would allow innocent users of infringing chips to use them under a royalty-free licence. This bill is widely supported by the semiconductor industry as providing a good balance between protection and competition, although it was opposed by the Copyright Office at a recent hearing by the Senate subcommittee considering the bill, on the grounds that it complicated the relatively simple scheme of copyright under the 1976 Act. The Copyright Office's preference is for an entirely new form of statutory protection for integrated circuits.

TRADE SECRETS

As explained in Chapter 13, trade-secret protection depends on being able to keep the information secret. The law will protect the trade-secret owner from unauthorised divulgence of the secret by third parties, and from unauthorised use by others while the information remains secret. However, once the information lawfully becomes public, there is no more protection.

In many cases, the information is effectively made public by putting an object incorporating that information on the open market. A competitor is free to purchase the object and, if he can, obtain that information by the process of 'reverse engineering'. Simple mechanical objects are readily reverse-engineered, complex chemical mixtures may not be unscrambled for many years — the exact formula for Coca-Cola is still a trade secret.

Most computer hardware is vulnerable to reverse engineering, although this process will probably require a considerable expenditure of time and money by the competitor. With items usually sold in small numbers, such as mainframe computer systems, it is possible to prevent the secret getting out by contractual provisions with each customer. This solution is not possible or practicable with devices sold in large numbers, such as standard integrated circuits.

TRADE MARKS

While the use of trade marks cannot prevent copying of the hardware itself, or prevent others from appropriating the underlying ideas, they can be of value. This is particularly true of marks used by an established manufacturer, whose reputation causes members of the public to buy products with that trade mark. It was not chance that caused a foreign manufacturer of a cheap copy of the Apple personal computer to attempt to market it as a 'Pineapple' computer. That attempt was quickly prevented by assertion of the rights residing in the 'Apple' trade mark.

15   *Protection of Software*

The protection of software, unlike the protection of hardware, presents many legal and practical problems. The reader can probably discern this simply by comparing the length of this chapter to that of the preceding chapter. It is also of much greater practical importance, because of the difference in nature between the two. Hardware is in general a relatively expensive item to produce, even if it is copied directly from somewhere else. It is not susceptible to copying by consumers at home. On the other hand, software is cheap to copy, in most cases the only cost being the minor one of the magnetic medium for the copy. It can, in many cases, be copied at home by the consumer, requiring no equipment apart from the computer the consumer must already own if he is to have any interest in software. With the recent, rapid growth of the personal computer industry, and the matching growth of a software industry supplying products for use with personal computers, these problems have become of major economic importance.

PATENT

Any discussion of the patentability of software centres almost entirely on the question whether software is patentable subject-matter at all. The answer to this question depends to some extent on the wording of the particular national patent statute concerned. The discussion below deals in particular with the current position under the law of those countries which are signatories to the European Patent Convention, which includes the United Kingdom, and under United States law.

European Patent Convention

Article 52(2) of the European Patent Convention (EPC) provides various categories of things 'which shall not be regarded as patentable inventions'. These include 'a mathematical method, a scheme, rule and method for performing mental acts, a program for computers and a presentation of information'. However, Art. 52 goes on to provide, in sub-clause (3), that the patentability of such subject-matter is excluded only to the extent that the application for a European patent relates to such subject-matter or activities 'as such'.

As the EPC only came into effect in 1977, and examination in the European Patent Office only began in June 1979, it is still too early for an established practice of treating applications which involve software to have formed. The European Patent Office's Guidelines for Examination do point out the difference between a program as an abstract entity and as a step in a process operating on a computer. The Guidelines suggest that an invention will not be patentable if the sole novelty over the prior art is the particular computer program involved. They also suggest that Art. 52(3) will be applied by carefully examining the substance of the application, rather than its form, but the application will not be rejected if it provides new technical features which are not unpatentable subject-matter.

United Kingdom

The Patents Act 1977 was enacted to bring United Kingdom patent law into line with the provisions of the EPC. Section 1(2) of the 1977 Act provides for the same exclusions from patentability as are provided by art. 52(2) of the Convention.

There have not been any decisions so far on computer-related inventions under the 1977 Act. In a number of decisions under the 1949 Act, the Patents Appeal Tribunal took a liberal view of the patentability of inventions essentially consisting of a computer programmed in a novel way. The leading case is generally considered to be *Burroughs Corporation (Perkins') Application* [1974] RPC 147, DC. That involved the patentability of a claim for a 'method of transmitting data over a communication link between a central processor and designatable ones of a plurality of addressable remote data terminals coupled via said communication link to said central processor'. The practice of the Patent Office at that time was to allow claims to computers programmed in a particular way, in accordance with the decision in *Slee and Harris's Applications* [1966] RPC 194, and to allow claims to programs embodied in some physical form, following *Gevers' Application* [1970] RPC 91. However, a distinction was drawn between claims to a programmed computer, which were patentable subject-matter, and claims to methods of controlling a computer or methods of transmitting information, which were not. The judge, Graham J, rejected this distinction as being inconsistent with case law on non-computer inventions, and held that any claim clearly directed to a method involving the use of apparatus modified as programmed to operate in a new way was patentable, as were computer programs embodied in a physical form which have the effect of controlling a computer. This liberal view was followed in *International Business Machines Corporation's Application* [1980] FSR 564.

While claims to a program, whether or not embodied in physical form, would seem to be clearly excluded under the wording of s. 1(2) of the Patents Act 1977, the Patent Office appears to be following the generally liberal line of the decisions referred to above so far as claims to a programmed computer and method steps using a programmed computer are concerned.

Other European countries

In general, decisions on computer-related inventions in European countries other than the United Kingdom have not been favourable to such inventions.

The Federal Republic of Germany has the best developed case law on the subject. The decisions require control of natural forces for an invention to be patentable, so that rules for computing and for organisation of computations, 'algorithms' in the broad sense of the word, are not patentable. Claims are to be analysed for their content; a claim which is directed to control of natural forces to produce a useful result will be patentable, however worded. If, however, the only novelty in the claim lies in the use of a non-patentable algorithm, in either the narrow or the broad sense of that word, the fact that there is a useful result will not save the claim.

Decisions in Austria, France, Switzerland and the Netherlands have all been similarly unfavourable. In all these countries, claims which were essentially to a programmed computer have been held to be unpatentable, regardless of the result of using such a computer.

Following the European Patent Convention, the new French patent law expressly excludes software from patentability. However, the court in *Schlumberger* v *Director of INPI* (Paris Court of Appeal 15 June 1981) PIBD 1981, 285 iii–175, ruled that this does not exclude from patentability processes, one or more stages of which are effected by the use of computer programs.

United States

Unlike Europe and the United Kingdom, there is already a considerable body of case law in the United States concerning the patentability of inventions which include software or a programmed computer as part of the invention.

To be patentable, an invention must come within at least one of the statutory categories, which are machines, processes, manufactures, compositions of matter and improvements to any of the above, 35 USC s. 101. Therefore, a computer program is not in itself patentable as it is not within these categories; the question of patentability arises in the context of a process or machine which incorporates or uses software. There is no express exclusion of computer programs from patent protection as there is under the EPC and the UK Patents Act 1977.

There is, however, a judicially developed exclusion from patentable subject-matter of the laws of nature, physical phenomena and abstract ideas. Amongst the excluded ideas are mathematical formulae and algorithms, and purely mental steps.

It was this exclusion of 'algorithms' and 'purely mental steps' that caused problems to courts considering the patentability of computer-related inventions. The problems largely arose from the broad use of the term 'algorithm' in the computer field, and from a failure to analyse fully the scope of the 'mental steps' doctrine. The term 'algorithm' can be used to describe any step-by-step procedure for solving a problem or achieving some purpose; a mathematical algorithm is such a procedure for solving a mathematical problem. Similarly, 'purely mental steps' are steps which can *only* be performed in the human mind, and are therefore unpatentable as abstract ideas. Purely physical steps, on the other hand, are steps which can only be carried out by a machine or a physical process, and are clearly patentable. The steps required to program a computer, although mental in origin, are not *purely* mental and therefore fall somewhere between the two extremes.

The first computer-related invention case to come before the US Supreme Court was *Gottschalk* v *Benson* 409 US 63 (1972). This was an appeal from a refusal by the Patent and Trademark Office to allow patent claims directed to a method of converting binary coded decimals to binary code, using a piece of apparatus called a re-entrant shift register, and also claims to the method alone without any reference to apparatus. The first level of appeal from the refusal of the examiner to allow these claims on the ground that they constituted non-statutory matter as being purely mental steps was to the Board of Patent Appeals, which upheld the Examiner. The next higher court of appeal, the Court of Customs and Patent Appeals (commonly referred to as the CCPA) reversed this tribunal. They interpreted the first set of method claims as being essentially directed to the operation of the apparatus, the re-entrant shift register, and therefore patentable subject-matter. As to the second set of method claims, they held they were not directed to *purely* mental steps because in practice the method would only be used with a machine, namely a digital computer.

The Supreme Court reversed the CCPA. They felt that the claims were so broad as to apply to use with any existing or future machine, and were, in effect, an attempt to obtain a patent on the formula for converting binary code to pure binary. This meant that 'the patent would wholly pre-empt the mathematical formula and in practical effect would be a patent on the algorithm itself'.

The next Supreme Court decision on a computer-related invention appeared to restrict even further the patentability of such inventions. *Parker* v *Flook* 437 US 584 (1978) involved claims to a method of updating an alarm limit in a process involving the catalytic chemical conversion of hydrocarbons. The CCPA had held that, although the claims involved an algorithm, they did not pre-empt that algorithm. The Supreme Court disagreed, holding that, as the only novelty in the invention was a mathematical formula, the invention was unpatentable. The court stated that a limited, though useful, category of post-solution applications of the formula did not make the method eligible for patent protection.

There was a dissent by three justices in *Flook*, unlike *Benson* which was a unanimous decision. The dissenters believed that the claims in *Flook* were distinguishable from those in *Benson* because the use of the formula was merely one step in a process, and up until then numerous processes and combinations had been patented despite the fact that they contained an unpatentable step or ingredient.

The point of view of the minority in *Flook* became the majority opinion in *Diamond* v *Diehr* 450 US 175 (1981), the latest and most authoritative Supreme Court decision on this subject. Diehr's invention was a process for curing synthetic rubber in a mould. The formula for calculating the cure time was well known, but had previously been difficult to apply in practice because one variable in the equation is the temperature inside the mould, and this had previously been regarded as an uncontrollable variable. Diehr's process involves a means of continually measuring the temperature inside the mould and feeding these measurements into a suitably programmed computer. The computer repeatedly recalculates the cure-time equation until a calculated time equals the actual time that the press has been closed. When this occurs, the computer sends a signal to machinery which opens the press.

The claims had been rejected by the examiner on the ground that the step of computer calculation was non-statutory matter, and the remaining steps were conventional in the rubber industry. The Board of Appeals agreed, but the CCPA reversed on the ground that the claims were not directed to a mathematical algorithm or a method of calculation, but to a process for curing rubber.

The Supreme Court, by a five-to-four majority, upheld the CCPA decision. The majority held that the process came within the historical definition of a process, which is patentable subject-matter, and that this was not altered by the fact that several steps of the process involved the use of a programmed digital computer. The Court distinguished its previous decisions, *Benson* and *Flook*, as being directed to claimed inventions which were essentially to an algorithm, defined by the court as a 'procedure for solving a given type of mathematical problem', stating (at 187):

> In contrast, the respondents here do not seek to patent a mathematical formula. Instead, they seek patent protection for a process of curing synthetic rubber. Their process admittedly employs a well known mathematical equation, but they do not seek to pre-empt the use of that equation. Rather, they seek only to foreclose from others the use of that equation in conjunction with all of the other steps in their claimed process.

Although this decision considerably clarified the law relating to patents that involve use of a computer as part of the invention claimed, it still left a number of questions outstanding. In particular, the question of whether all 'algorithms' are unpatentable was left open in a footnote to the majority opinion. After referring to the *Benson* definition of 'algorithm' as a procedure for solving a *mathematical* problem, the footnote discusses the much wider definition of the term submitted by the government in its arguments against patentability in the following way:

The term 'algorithm' is subject to a variety of definitions. The Commissioner of Patents and Trademarks defines the term to mean:

1. A fixed step-by-step procedure for accomplishing a given result; usually a simplified procedure for solving a complex problem, also a full statement of a finite number of steps. 2. A defined process or set of rules that leads [sic] and assures development of a desired output from a given input. A sequence of formulas and/or algebraic/logical steps to calculate or determine a given task; processing rules.' . . .

This definition is significantly broader than the definition this Court employed in *Benson* and *Flook*.

One result of the *Diehr* decision was that the Patent and Trademark Office put out new guidelines for examiners dealing with patent applications involving mathematical equations, mathematical algorithms and computer programs. Examiners analysing such claims for patentability under 35 USC s. 101 are to follow the two-step analysis laid down by the CCPA in *Re Freeman* 197 USPQ 464 (1978). The first step is to determine whether a mathematical algorithm is either directly or indirectly recited by the claim being analysed. If there is no direct recitation, the specification must be studied to see if there is an indirect claim to such algorithm or formula. If there is such a direct or indirect recitation, the second step is to determine whether the claim as a *whole* merely recites a mathematical algorithm or method of calculation. If so, then it is to be rejected under 35 USC s. 101 as being unpatentable. If, on the other hand, the mathematical algorithm is implemented in a specific way to define structural relationships in machine claims or to refine or limit steps in process claims, the claim comes within s. 101.

In conclusion, the present situation under US law is that an invention is not excluded from patentability merely because it contains a mathematical algorithm or use of a programmed computer. It is still undecided whether a non-mathematical algorithm is itself unpatentable if claimed separately from its use in a machine or process. Of course, even if the computer-related invention is patentable subject-matter, it must still pass all the other tests of patentability before a patent will be granted.

Canada

In Canada, the Patent Office at first took the view that, under the Canadian Patent Act, computer programs *per se* were not patentable, but claims to a new method of programming a computer and claims to a computer programmed in a novel manner were patentable (*Re Application No. 961,392* (1971) 5 CPR (2d) 162).

This policy was later modified, in view of developments in US jurisprudence on the subject. The Canadian Patent Office relies on US rather than British jurisprudence because the Canadian Patent Act is closer to the US than to the British statute. The modification was the setting out of the following principles in a 1978 Office Notice:

1.   Claims to a computer program, *per se*, are not patentable.
2.   Claims to a new method of programming a computer are not patentable.
3.   Claims to a computer programmed in a novel manner, expressed in any or all modes, where the novelty lies solely in the program or algorithm, are not directed to patentable subject-matter under s. 2 of the Patent Act.
4.   Claims to a computing apparatus programmed in a novel manner, when the patentable advance is in the apparatus itself, are patentable.
5.   Claims to a method or process carried out with a specific novel computing apparatus devised to implement a newly discovered idea are patentable.

These guidelines were based upon the decision of the US Supreme Court in *Gottschalk* v *Benson* 409 US 63 (1972). They have not yet been revised in the light of *Diamond* v *Diehr* 450 US 175 (1981).

The Canadian Federal Court of Appeal appears to have followed the US Supreme Court decisions in *Schlumberger Canada Ltd* v *Commissioner of Patents* (1981) 56 CPR (2d) 204. The claims in issue involved a method of processing well-logging data produced in seismic surveying by using a computer program. The court analysed the invention as consisting of the making of certain calculations, using certain mathematical formulae. This was held to be unpatentable subject-matter. However, the court refused to hold, as they were urged to do on behalf of the Commissioner, that computer programs *per se* and methods of programming were inherently unpatentable. Also, they found that the

Schlumberger invention involved *mathematical* formulae, which are clearly unpatentable under *Diehr*, as well as under *Benson* and *Flook*. Despite this decision, the Patent Office has not altered its guidelines, and probably will not do so without a court decision.

COPYRIGHT

If patent protection is not available, the other possible forms of protection for the content of software are trade secrets and copyright. In the case of widely published software, trade-secret protection is not a practical possibility. The advent of the personal computer has resulted in a vast increase in the amount of this type of software, some of which represents a considerable investment in time and money by its authors and a valuable source of income. The question whether copyright protection is available, and, if it is, what it protects, has therefore become important to the software industry.

As described in Chapter 13, the history of copyright begins with the communications revolution that resulted from the invention of printing. The concept was then gradually adapted to cover other forms of communication as they were developed. This adaptation was sometimes effected by the courts, sometimes, as in the case of gramophone recording in certain countries, a statute was needed. At present the only major country to have a copyright statute which expressly mentions software is the USA, although there are proposals for such statutory provisions in the UK and elsewhere.

Another question, important to software producers and publishers, is the relationship of source code to object code for copyright purposes. This question, which is far from being settled, arises in an acute form when the software is supplied in the form of ROM chips, which can be regarded as a form of hardware. Other problems arise from video games, where the display on the screen results from an interaction of the player and the game software. The considerable popularity of such games, and their resulting commercial value, has resulted in imitation, outright piracy, and plenty of litigation, so that the courts have had to face up to these problems.

Because the software industry is rapidly becoming international, this chapter will deal with developments in most of the major industrial countries in outline, as well giving a more detailed analysis of UK and US law.

United Kingdom

There has not yet been any binding precedential holding in the UK on the copyrightability of software. In *Sega Enterprises* v *Richard* [1983] FSR 73, the court accepted, without argument, for the purposes of granting an interlocutory order, that copyright existed in both the display and the underlying program of a video game. The grant of the order was reversed on appeal, but only on the ground that it was not a proper case for such an order.

The present British copyright statute dates from 1956, a time when computers were in their infancy. It is therefore not surprising that it makes no reference to computer software. The Whitford Committee, formed to consider the law on copyright and designs and named after its chairman, the Honourable Mr Justice Whitford, considered that it was probable that software was already covered under the law of copyright, but recommended that there should be legislation to clarify the matter. Such legislation has been proposed by the government, but there is no indication of when it will actually be brought before Parliament. It is therefore necessary to examine the existing legislation to determine the likely scope of copyright protection in the UK.

Copyright in the UK is governed by the Copyright Act 1956. Protected works fall into several categories which are dealt with by separate provisions: literary, dramatic and musical works form one category, artistic works another, and sound recordings, cinematograph films and television and sound broadcasts are separately provided for. Under the Act, 'literary works' are defined so as to include 'any written compilation or table'. This corresponds to the extensive case law under previous statutes, in which such things are directories, mathematical tables, timetables and telegraph codes have been held to be literary works within the protection of copyright. It seems clear, and commentators generally agree, that at least source code should come within the category of literary works.

In order to qualify for copyright protection, such a work must be 'original'. This has been interpreted to mean merely that the work is the product of some intellectual effort, and has not been totally copied. Further, in order to qualify for protection the work must be fixed in some material form, and for this purpose, writing includes 'any form of notation, whether by hand, or by printing, typewriting or any similar process' (s. 49(4)). This definition would cover listings, and possibly punched tape or cards, but it would seem that the term 'some material form' is wider than writing, and would be apt to cover magnetic media, and even ROM chips. English law never got stuck with the requirement that the affixation must be in some human-decipherable form that came into US law with the *White-Smith* case, discussed in Chapter 13. It should be noted, however, that the requirement of affixation is not specifically spelled out in the statute, as it is in the US Copyright Act, but results from judicial interpretation of references to the work being 'made'. Section 49(4) of the 1956 Act defines references to the making of a work as references to 'the time or period at or during which it was first reduced to writing or some other material form'. It is therefore questionable whether a program which is only recorded in RAM memory is capable of copyright protection before some more permanent record is made, such as a printed listing. While it is arguable that the pattern of magnetisation in which the program resides is a 'material form', in that it is more than just an idea in the author's head, it is not a permanent form because it can be obliterated at any instant by turning off the current to the memory. It is, however, in a form which can be accessed and copied by a third person. The government proposal is that it should be made clear that copyright protection should be extended to works fixed in any form from which they can be reproduced.

The requirement of originality could cause problems when the copyrightability of object code comes to be considered. Object code in most cases is generated by the computer through a compiler, from the input source code. In attempting to find an analogy with established concepts, most commentators regard this as equivalent to translation. Under the Copyright Act 1956, translating a literary work is one of the acts reserved to the owner of the copyright. Therefore, even if the machine translation is not an independent copyright work, reproducing the 'translation', the object code, is an infringement of the underlying copyright in the source code. The British courts have yet to consider the copyrightability of object code and its relationship to the source code from which it is generated by a compiler.

Another question yet to be decided, although the proposed legislation would answer it, is what acts with regard to software are infringements of the copyright in that software. If compiling source code to object code is held to be a 'translation', then the inputting of the source code into the compiler should itself be an infringement if done without licence. The proposed legislation would make the act of loading the program into the computer a 'restricted act'; it is only such an act under the present legislation if loading the program is equivalent to reproducing the work in a material form, or possibly making an adaptation of the work. Transmitting the program, or other copyright material in the computer, through a data link of some kind is probably analogous to broadcasting the work.

While it can be seen that there are a considerable number of important questions that arise under the present Copyright Act with regard to the application of that Act to software, none of which have yet been resolved by the courts, it should be borne in mind that the English judiciary tends at present to be pro-copyright in its decisions. It is likely that a judge faced with one or more of these issues would seek to protect the person who has expended time and effort in the creation of the software against one who was seeking to reap where he did not sow.

United States

As mentioned above, the United States does have statutory provisions which expressly cover computer programs. A long process of consultation and discussion culminated in the revision of US federal copyright law through the passing of the Copyright Act 1976. This Act effected some major changes, including bringing unpublished works within the area of federal copyright protection and abolishing state and common-law copyright, at least to the extent that it had previously covered such works. By the early part of the 1970s, the importance of the computer industry was clear, but it was decided to deal with the copyright problems raised by the new technology separately, rather than further delay the introduction of the new copyright law. The 1976 Act contained a provision designed to maintain the status quo with regard to computer uses of works. It was generally agreed that computer programs had been protectable under the previous copyright statute, and the US Copyright Office had been accepting programs for registration since 1964.

In 1974 Congress passed a law establishing the National Commission on New Technological Uses of Copyrighted Works, known as CONTU. The commission, whose purpose was to study and prepare recommendations on the creation, reproduction and use of copyrighted works involving the use of computers, reported in 1978. As a result of their report, the Copyright Act was amended to add a definition of 'computer program' as 'a set of statements or instructions to be used directly or indirectly in a computer to bring about a certain result' to the definition section, s. 101, and s. 117, the section that had maintained the status quo, was amended. The new s. 117 provides that it is not an infringement of copyright for the lawful owner of a copy of a computer program to input that program into his computer, either directly or in an adapted form, and to make copies for archival purposes. However, such back-up copies can only be disposed of together with the original copy, or they must be destroyed when lawful ownership of the original copy ceases. In *Atari Inc.* v *J S & A Group Inc.*, 6 December 1983, 27 PTCJ 171 (N.D. Ill. 1983), the court held that this provision only permitted archival copying in the case of programs which are subject to 'destruction or damage by mechanical or electrial failure'. The case involved a machine for copying programs on ROMs, and the court held that making copies using such a machine did not come within s. 117 because programs in ROM were not subject to this type of destruction or damage. Accordingly, copies made on such a machine were infringements of the copyright in the original program.

These provisons, together with their legislative history, mean that there can be no dispute that source code, at least, is copyrightable subject-matter under US law. The position of object code is, however, more debatable. While computer programs are defined in the statute, they are not expressly included in the list of copyrightable subject-matter set out in s. 102, but are left to come within the general category of 'literary works'. While the majority report of CONTU thought that object code should be equally protected with source code, a dissenting report by Commissioner Hersey disagreed on the ground that object code which communicates only to machines should not be within the same category as works which communicate to human beings.

The question of the copyrightability of object code under the 1976 Act has come before the US courts on a number of occasions in the early 1980s. All but one of these decisions have held that object code is protectable, and the odd man out, *Apple Computer Inc* v *Franklin Computer Corp.* 545 F Supp 812 (E.D. Pa. 1982), has been reversed on appeal (714 F 2d 1240). The argument that object code is not copyrightable because it communicates only with a machine has been raised in a number of cases, but was firmly rejected by the Third Circuit Court of Appeals in *Williams Electronics Inc.* v *Artic International Inc.* 685 F 2d 870, 215 USPQ 405 (3d Cir. 1982), a video games case. The defendant had put forward the argument that the object code cannot be recognised as a copy of the source code and protectable because for copyright purposes a 'copy' must be intelligible to human beings. The court rejected this argument in the following way (215 USPQ 405 at 410):

The answer to the defendant's contention is in the words of the statute itself. A 'copy' is defined to include a material object in which a work is fixed 'by *any* method now known or later developed, and *from which the work can be perceived*, reproduced or otherwise communicated, either directly or *with the aid of a machine or device*' 17 USC s. 101 (emphasis added). By this broad language, Congress opted for an expansive interpretation of the terms 'fixation' and 'copy' which encompass technological advances such as those represented by the electronic devices in this case. [Footnote omitted.] We reject any contention that this broad language should nonetheless be interpreted in a manner which would severely limit the copyrightability of computer programs which Congress clearly intended to protect. We cannot accept defendant's suggestion that would afford an unlimited loophole by which infringement of a computer program is limited to copying of the computer program text but not to duplication of a computer program fixed on a silicon chip.

The Third Circuit had no hesitation in following its decision in *Williams Electronics* in its decision in the *Apple* v *Franklin* appeal, *Apple Computer Inc.* v *Franklin Computer Corp.* 714 F 2d 1240 (3rd Cir. 1983). The court further held that it made no difference to copyrightability if the work was fixed in a ROM, following the established line of case-law on this topic. They then examined Franklin's claim that operating-system software is *per se* uncopyrightable, because the idea and its expression are coextensive, and therefore uncopyrightable under the principle laid down in *Baker* v *Selden* 101 US 99 (1879). When there is only one way of expressing an idea, to give copyright protection to that expression would, in effect, give a monopoly over the idea. However, such a monopoly can only be given by the grant of a patent. An alternative, but related argument, was that an operating system is uncopyrightable because it is utilitarian. The court had no problem in rejecting the latter argument as being inconsistent with the language used by the Supreme Court in *Mazer* v *Stein* 347 US 201 (1954). The Third Circuit, in considering the argument that the idea had merged with the expression in the case of the Apple operating system, stated that this could not be the case if there were a number of different ways in which the same results could be achieved. The fact that these other ways would not give total compatibility with applications software written for the Apple, which was the true heart of Franklin's argument, was stated by the court to have no relevance to the question of whether the idea and the expression had merged. As the district court had made no findings on this issue, the case was remanded for reconsideration. Subsequently, the parties settled the case before it could be reheard.

As explained in Chapter 13, US law requires that certain formalities be observed if copyright is to be maintained and enforced. The copyright notice is the most important, because its omission can lead to complete loss of copyright in that work if it has been 'published' within the meaning of the Copyright Act. In the case of software, the rules about placement of notices are not as well established as in the case of traditional media. The Copyright Office has published a regulation relating to the placement of copyright notices on 'works reproduced in machine-readable copies'. This provides that:

For works reproduced in machine-readable copies (such as magnetic tape or discs, punched cards, or the like), from which the work cannot ordinarily be visually perceived except with the aid of a machine or device, each of the following constitute examples of acceptable methods of affixation and position of notice:

(1)   A notice embodied in the copies in machine-readable form in such a manner that on visually perceptable print-outs it appears either with or near the title, or at the end of the work;

(2)   A notice that is displayed at the user's terminal at sign-on;

(3)   A notice that is continuously on terminal display; or

(4)   A legible notice reproduced durably, so as to withstand normal use, on a gummed or other label securely affixed to the copies or to a box, reel cartridge, cassette, or other container used as a permanent receptacle for the copies.

As nothing is lost by having duplicate notices, provided they are consistent with each other, the best rule to follow is; if in doubt, put a notice on it. It should be noted that, even though the regulations provide that any one of these forms may be used alone, a court may hold that use to be insufficient to satisfy the statutory requirements. All printed listings of code, both object code and source code, and all physical objects embodying code, such as discs, tape packs and ROMs, should bear a human-readable copyright notice in the proper form. A specimen copyright notice is included with the precedents at the end of this chapter. In addition, a copyright notice should be programmed in so that it appears each time the program is run, on the CRT screen, or on the print-out, or on whatever other method is being used to display the program. Preferably, the notice should appear at the beginning of the run, in prominent form. If use of the software is covered by trade-secret confidentiality, or contractual licensing restrictions, a notice to this effect may also appear at the same time.

The rules relating to registration of software copyrights with the Copyright Office are still in the process of development. The actual registration is straightforward, and is made on Form TX, for literary works, which is obtainable from the United States Copyright Office, Library of Congress, Washington, DC 20559. The form comes with detailed instructions for its completion. One note to those who register copyrights regularly: the office will not accept registrations on photocopies of the form, so a suitable supply of the printed forms must be maintained. The problems arise with the statutory requirements for deposit of copies of the work in order for registration to be obtained. The Copyright Act contains two requirements for deposit. The first of these, s. 407 of the 1976 Act, requires deposit of one copy of the best edition of all published works. This requirement is independent of registration, and its purpose is to maintain a complete collection in the Library of Congress. (The UK law has a similar provision which benefits the British Library and certain university libraries.) However, software is exempt from this deposit requirement by regulation. The other deposit provision, s. 408, provides for mandatory deposit as a condition of registration, and does apply to software. Normally two complete copies are required, but there are special provisions for software. When the work is published only in machine-readable form, which is normally the case with software, only one copy of 'identifying portions' of the program is required. 'Identifying portions' are defined by the regulation as:

either the first and last 25 pages or equivalent units of the program if reproduced on paper, or at least the first and last 25 pages or equivalent units of the program if reproduced in microform, together with the page or equivalent unit containing the copyright notice, if any.

Notice that this regulation insists on either paper or microform; the Copyright Office has consistently refused to accept the deposit of ROM chips containing programs to be registered. The office will accept object-code print-outs, but only upon the applicant's written representation that the work contains original matter, and the registration is effected under the office's 'rule of doubt'. It is at present unknown what the effect of such a registration is, but it may be that a court faced with a copyright-infringement claim brought by the owner of such a registration will refuse to apply the normal rule that registration is prima facie proof of the validity of the copyright and of the facts stated in the certificate, and make the owner adduce evidence of these matters.

This requirement of deposit is the greatest disadvantage attached to registration, because it can potentially reveal the secrets of the program to a competitor, who can then make sufficient adaptations to make the success of a copyright infringement action doubtful. Without access to the listing, it would in many cases be as easy for the competitor to start from scratch than to try to figure out how the program is put together and then make the changes. Various means of overcoming this disadvantage have been suggested. One is to deposit object code, which is difficult to deciper, even for the skilled programmer, rather than source code. This course, however, produces the rule-of-doubt registration discussed above, with its attendant uncertainties. Another suggestion is to ensure that the deposited first and last 25 pages do not contain any important matter. The problem here is that manipulation of this kind may lead to problems in later litigation. The Copyright Office routinely certifies copies of deposited material for use in litigation; absence of any of the matter the subject of the complaint of infringement may mean that the statutory presumptions do not apply. Also, defendants have been known to raise as a defence 'fraud on the Copyright Office', adapted from the established defence of fraud on the Patent Office available in patent infringement actions. This defence has not yet succeeded, but there is as yet no reported case where it has been raised against a listing deliberately padded so as to keep valuable matter out of the deposited copy.

The regulations do provide for special secured deposits in the case of certain tests which are registered before they are taken, and for a discretionary relief from the deposit requirement. Because the Copyright Office has been receiving so many requests for such relief in connection with the registration of software, almost all of which have been refused, they recently published a 'Notice of Inquiry', asking for public comment upon the possibility of providing some type of secured deposit for trade-secret software, and setting out the considerations for and against such a provision.

It has been indicated in one case, *Warrington Associates Inc.* v *Real-Time Engineering Systems Inc.* 522 F Supp 367 (N.D. Ill. 1981), that deposit as required for registration will not destroy the confidentiality required for trade-secret protection 'as a matter of law'. This does not, however, avoid the practical problems of access by competitors described above.

Another method of avoiding the problem is to delay registration until infringement has actually occurred. The disadvantage of this course is that several potentially valuable benefits of early registration are lost. Amongst these are statutory damages and attorneys' fees relating to periods before registration, unless registration was made within three months of publication, and the presumption of validity does not apply unless registration was made within five years of the first publication of the work. Further advantages of registration are the possibility of getting the United States Customs Service to bar the importation of infringing copies of a registered work, and the possibility of curing an inadvertent omission of the copyright notice from published copies of the work if registration is made within five years from the date of first publication and certain remedial steps are taken.

Other Common-Law Countries

Australia
The first reported decision in Australia on copyright in software has gone against the general trend of finding it to be protectable by copyright. This is *Apple Computer Inc.* v *Computer Edge Pty Ltd* (New South Wales District Registry, No. G130 of 1983). The case concerned an Apple][look-alike, marketed under the peculiarly Australian name of the 'Wombat'. Much of the judgment of Beaumont J concerns claims under the Trade Practices Act 1974. However, there was also a claim under the Copyright Act 1968 for infringement of the copyright of a number of Apple programs, including Applesoft and a number of utilities programs. The judge held, without real discussion, that a computer program is not a 'literary work' for copyright purposes, and was therefore not within the statute. It is interesting to note that among the string of cases cited in support of this proposition (but not discussed), are the *Northern Office Micro Computers* case from South Africa, discussed below, which held that software is the subject of copyright, and the *Sega Enterprises* case from the UK, in which, as is mentioned above, the existence of copyright in software was assumed for interlocutory purposes. The case is under appeal. The Australian government has

expressed grave concern about the effect of the decision on the Australian software industry, and has proposed amendment of the Copyright Act 1968 to protect software.

Canada

Copyright in Canada is exclusively governed by federal law. The current copyright statute is the Copyright Act 1924, which is based on the 1911 UK Copyright Act.

Needless to say, the Act does not deal expressly with computer software, and there is no immediate prospect of legislation to provide protection for computer-related works.

Commentators generally believe that source code will be protected as a literary work. This belief is strengthened by a recent decision concerning copyright in business forms, *Bulman Group Ltd* v *'One Write' Accounting Systems Ltd* (1982) 62 CPR (2d) 149. The decision, after a detailed examination of the meaning of the term 'literary work' in both Canadian and British law, followed the view that 'literary' means written or printed matter, not the dictionary meaning of imparting ideas, information or knowledge. Indeed, this view of the meaning of the term 'literary' under the Copyright Act would also include object code in a written form. It may be more difficult to find protection under the 1924 Act for object code in the form of a ROM.

There has not yet been any clear judicial decision on the copyrightability of software. In two cases involving video games, *Nintendo of America Inc.* v *Coinex Video Games Inc.* (1982) 69 CPR (2d) 122 and *Bally Midway Mfg Co.* v *Coinex Video Games Inc.* (1983) 71 CPR (2d) 105, the existence of copyright in the games was presumed for the purposes of interlocutory proceedings. Other cases involving video games are also proceeding through the courts, so there may be some decisions on the subject before too long.

Although Canadian law does not require any formalities for the existence of copyright, there are provisions for the registration of works, registration providing prima facie evidence of the existence of copyright in the registered work. At present the Copyright Office refuses registration of copyright in a video game itself.

Hong Kong

The copyright law of Hong Kong is the same as that of the United Kingdom. The question of the copyrightability of computer software arose recently in two video game cases, *Atari Inc.* v *Video Technology Ltd*

(Civ. App. No. 117 of 1982); *Atari Inc* v *Soundic Electronics Ltd* (Civ. App. No. 118 of 1982) (comment by M. Pendleton, [1983] EIPR 132). These were appeals from the grant of interlocutory injunctions to restrain alleged infringement of copyright in the Pac-Man video game. The trial judge appeared to regard the video game as being a composite of various literary and artistic copyrights, and stated that he had no difficulty in holding that the underlying program could be said to have been reduced to a material form and was capable of supporting copyright. The South African decision, *Northern Office Micro Computers (Pty) Ltd* v *Rosenstein*, discussed below, was referred to in support, as was the latest edition of *Copinger and Skone James on Copyright*.

On appeal, the Court of Appeal felt that there had been no copying of the drawings which appeared on the screen, or of the musical works or the sound recordings of those works which were heard as the game progressed. They also discounted the possibility that what appeared on the screen could be a 'cinematograph film' for copyright purposes as there was no set sequence of images. The only prospect of success appeared to lie with the claim of infringement of copyright in the program embodied in the ROM chip, and the court stated that the question whether there could be copyright in ROMs was an undecided question dependent on public policy. As a result, the plaintiff's case was held to be insufficiently strong to justify the grant of an injunction under the principles stated in *American Cyanamid Co* v *Ethicon Ltd* [1975] AC 396.

As a result of this decision, it seems unlikely that the Hong Kong courts will hold that copyright can subsist in ROM chips unless there is legislation to that effect.

South Africa

It should be immediately stated that South Africa does not strictly come within the category of 'common law' countries in the sense in which that term is used in this book, i.e., English common law. South African law is based upon Roman Dutch common law, but nevertheless the history of the country has resulted in English common-law influences, and it fits most closely into this category.

The copyrightability of computer programs was one question which had to be decided in *Northern Office Micro Computers (Pty) Ltd* v *Rosenstein* 1981 (4) SA 123. The case involved a dispute between a programmer and his employers over the employee's rights to the programs which he had written. The employers claimed that the programs were a trade secret of their business, the respondent claimed that they were his copyright which he was free to dispose of as he pleased.

The court first discussed whether computer programs are capable of being copyright works under the relevant statute, the Copyright Act 1978. Although the 1978 Patents Act specifically provided that a computer program may not be patented, there is no mention of software in the 1978 Copyright Act. In order to obtain copyright protection under the Act, a literary work must be 'written down, recorded or otherwise reduced to material form'. Marais A J stated that:

> it can be said that this suite of programs has been written down, recorded or otherwise reduced to material form. The formulae which were evolved were written by hand on paper. The source code which was used has been recorded upon a computer print-out . . . [T]here can be no doubt that a computer print-out is a reduction to material form of the information which it contains . . . It has long been held that, to qualify for copyright protection, it is not necessary that what is written or recorded should express a meaning in language. That is why copyright protection has been accorded a list of meaningless words used in a telegraph code.

The judge then went on to state that a computer program which does no more than produce multiplication tables or the alphabet would not be the subject of copyright because the amount of skill and effort involved would be too trivial to render the work original. However, that was not the case with the programs in this case, and it was held that the respondent had established copyright in the programs. Under the law in force at the time the programs were created, that copyright belonged to the respondent, but the court held that he was not able to use that copyright in any way which revealed to others the confidential information belonging to his employers embedded in the programs.

There are several other cases proceeding through the courts which could provide further development of the law if they proceed to final judgment. In one of these the South African sole distributor for Atari obtained a temporary injunction against a firm selling an apparatus for copying ROM video game modules, on the basis of contributory infringement. Apple also has a case in the Republic of South Africa regarding copying of its software, in which Apple has been awarded an injunction.

Europe

The countries of Continental Europe are all civil-law countries. Although there are differences in detail between the copyright laws of these countries, they are all based on the same principles, and so can advantageously be considered together.

In civil-law copyright, the main emphasis is on protecting rights in property which arise from the creativity and intellectual effort of the author. There is a basic philosophical or jurisprudential difference between the approaches of the civil and the common laws to intellectual property, which is revealed most clearly in the realm of copyright. Civil law regards this property as a natural right, due to the author because of his or her intellectual effort and creativity, which should be protected against the world. Common law regards these rights as being given by the state as exception to the general rule that all ideas should be free for general use and that there should be free competition, under specified circumstances in which the common good is better served by giving this protection than by denying it. Therefore, civil-law systems tend to go further than common-law systems in protecting the underlying idea, at least when it is clearly original and shows a high degree of creativity. There is no requirement of fixation for copyright to exist, and no formalities are required.

Most commentators regard copyright as applying only to expressions which are perceptible to the human senses and mind. However, the courts in civil-law systems have for a long time protected works which require a mechanical intermediary before they are perceptible by humans, such as cinematograph films and sound recordings on gramophone records or magnetic tape. Therefore, it is unlikely that a court would deny computer programs copyright protection because they are directions to a machine, generally with results that are perceptible by humans.

The rights of the author in civil-law systems are generally divided into two groups, the 'patrimonial' and the 'moral' rights. The patrimonial rights generally correspond to the rights under common-law systems, such as the rights to reproduce, to adapt, to translate and to display or perform the work in public. Civil-law courts, like the courts of most common-law systems, have yet to grapple with the problems which arise when the application of these rights to computer technology is considered. For example, when the computer owner inputs a program from a disc which he has bought from the copyright owner into the memory of his computer, is that a use, analogous to reading a book, which is permitted, or is it a reproduction of the work, which is the author's exclusive right? One patrimonial right which does not generally exist in common-law systems is the '*droit de suite*', the right for the author and the author's heirs to benefit when the ownership of the copyright is transferred, even after the author has parted with it by assignment.

It is the author's 'moral' rights, which have no counterpart in common-law systems, which could cause the most problems in the context of computer programs. These basically allow the author to prevent things being done to his work which damage the artistic integrity of the work, or which could damage his reputation positively (by altering the work in a derogatory way) or negatively (by failing to credit him with authorship). It is hard to see how this could be applied to software, but it does raise the spectre of a programmer who has assigned a program to someone later objecting to adaptations made to that program, perhaps as a way of getting more money for the program, or because he has fallen out with the owner.

France

An important decision in this field was recently handed down by the Paris Court of Appeal in *Pachot* v *Babolat-Maillot-Witt* (comment by C. Le Stanc, in [1983] EIPR 222). The case involved a dispute between a former employee, an accountant, and his employer over the ownership of some computer programs written by the employee. The court held that the programs were covered by copyright, that they were owned by the employee because they did not come within the circumstances under French law in which employees' works are deemed to be owned by the employer, and that the principles of '*droit d'auteur*' applied.

In an earlier decision, a lower court, the Tribunal de Grande Instance de Paris, held that a video game is a copyrightable work, *Atari Ireland* v *Intermeals* (8 December 1982). However, the discussion concerns the visual display, rather than the underlying computer program.

Germany

The Munich district court has given copyright protection to the Visicalc software, in *Visicorp* v *Basis Software GmbH* (No. 7.0.2490/82, 21 December 1982). The court stated that it was following the general view of the legal literature on the subject, that computer programs are copyrightable under certain conditions. These are that the program must meet the requirement of s. 2(2) of the Copyright Act that it be a personal, intellectual creation. This condition will generally be fulfilled if there are several ways to achieve the result sought, and the author of the program must make choices and use various ideas, according to the court. Anyone with any knowledge at all of programming knows that, in all but the most trivially simple program, there are almost as many ways of writing the program as there are programmers. Therefore, most computer programs likely to come before a court in Germany should be held to be copyrightable. The infringement in this case was the exact copying of the discs, but there was no discussion of the difference between source code and object code, and the issue does not appear to have been raised by the parties. The defendants had also translated the manual and the reference card into German, which was held to be an infringement of the copyright in those works.

Italy

In *Atari Inc. & Srl Bertolini* v *Sidam Srl* (Tribunal of Turin, 17 October 1983) (comment by M. Introvigne, [1983] EIPR 347) the court held that video games are fully protectable by copyright law. While the decision does not deal with other types of computer programs and specifically found that video games came within the classification of 'cinematographic works', it does contain language broad enough to suggest that other software should also come within copyright.

Other European countries

There have not as yet been any decisions in other European countries on the copyrightability of computer programs, so far as the author is aware. The general opinion is that there is no copyright protection under Swiss law, and there may not be protection in Belgium or Luxembourg.

Japan

The Japanese law of copyright is contained in the Copyright Act of 1970. It is closer to the civil law than the common law, in particular it lays stress on the creativity of the author, and provides 'moral' rights similar to those of civil-law systems.

Copyright protection is given in Japan to computer software. Although the Copyright Law of 1970 does not specifically refer to software, at least two decisions have given wide protection. These are *Taito Co* v *ING Enterprises Co.* 25 PTCJ 139 (12 December 1982) and

Taito Inc. v *Makoto Electronics Industries Inc.* [1983] EIPR D-138
(30 March 1983). Both involved the 'Space Invaders' game, and copies
of the ROM containing the game software. In the ING case, the court
held that the source-code program was the expression of intellectual
ideas, its creation involving choice and intellectual effort, and therefore
came within the requirements for copyrightability. The object code,
created mechanically by a computer from the source code, was held by
the court to be a copy of the source code, so that copying the ROM was
an infringement of the copyright in the source code.

International copyright conventions and computer programs

Both the Berne Copyright Convention and the Universal Copyright
Convention (UCC) define works covered by them so widely that they
are generally agreed to cover computer programs. They would appear
to apply to software in both source and object code, as well as to manuals
and other documentation. The protection extends to unpublished as
well as published works, although it is possible that, under the UCC but
not under the Berne Convention, publication will only occur if a
human-readable copy is published.

   In addition, the World Intellectual Property Organisation (WIPO)
has produced a draft treaty for the protection of computer software by
contracting states on the lines of the Model Provisions on the Protection
of Software produced by an advisory group in 1977. These provide for a
copyright-like protection for computer programs, defined as 'a set of
instructions capable, when incorporated in a machine-readable
medium of causing a machine having information-processing
capabilities to indicate, perform or achieve a particular function, task or
result'. These rights are to last at the most 25 years from the date of
creation. WIPO is also studying the question of protection for integrated
circuits.

Advantages and disadvantages of copyright for protection of software

Probably the main advantage of copyright is that it is cheap and easy to
obtain and maintain. In countries which do not require formalities, the
costs are zero, and even in countries with formalities, they cost very
little. Registration of copyright in the United States costs $10, and you
do not need to have a lawyer acting for you. Other advantages are that it
lasts for a long time, it is specifically designed for widely distributed

works, and in most countries it is relatively easy to obtain interlocutory injunctions against infringers.

The main disadvantage is probably the difficulty of policing widely distributed matter. It is almost impossible to stop individuals copying the protected works at home, as owners of copyrights in sound recordings and video tapes already know. There is also the problem of determining just how much of a change from the original is needed to take a work outside the copyright of the original. At present, there is also the disadvantage of the uncertainty in many countries whether software in certain forms is copyrightable at all, and what acts would infringe such copyright.

TRADE SECRETS

A recent survey showed that, at least until recently, trade-secret law was the form of protection most frequently relied upon by the producers of software. This is becoming less true as the growth of the personal computer industry is resulting in the mass marketing of software for such computers. Because the essence of trade-secret protection is that the information to be protected is and remains secret, mass marketing is in almost every case incompatible with such protection.

How can you keep your software a secret?

As explained in Chapter 13, in order to have trade-secret protection you must do two things — keep it secret yourself, and make anyone to whom you reveal the secret promise that they will keep it secret.

In the case of the individual who has written a piece of software on his own, the main problems with maintaining secrecy arise when he wants to show it to someone else, either for independent testing or (more likely) try to persuade a publisher to publish it. If you give a copy to a friend to test it is difficult to ask him to sign a formal secrecy agreement, but you must at least try to impress on him or her the importance of not showing the program to others or giving away copies of it. The main problem you will find with publishers is that many of them are reluctant to sign any sort of secrecy agreement in respect of software that is being submitted to them. One of the main reasons for this is that they may see many submitted programs which all essentially do the same thing, and if they choose to publish one they do not want any trouble from the authors of the others. When the ideas behind the programs are very similar, it may be extremely difficult for the publisher to convince a disappointed author that the similarity is not caused by theft of his ideas. However, you should at least try to obtain a signed agreement that the publisher will not do anything with your program except to review it for possible publication, that he will only show it to those of his employees who need to see it, and that he will not show it to any third party without your prior consent.

In the case of a business which produces software, precautions must be taken that all employees who have access to the software keep it secret. The employer should require all employees to sign a suitable secrecy agreement before they commence their employment. Employee agreements are discussed more fully in Chapter 12 of this book. This should be followed up by routine reminders to all staff, and particularly to the programmers, of the importance to the firm of its secrets. When an employee leaves, he should be interviewed before his departure, and reminded that he has a continuing obligation to maintain this information secret. This interview should also be the time when a check is made to ensure that he has returned all documents belonging to the firm which contain any proprietary information, and that he does not have any code in his possession. This is particularly important in the case of programmers who have worked at home through a remote terminal.

Because trade secrecy can only be maintained once the software has been distributed to third parties if those third parties agree to maintain the secrecy and if those agreements are monitored by the trade-secret owner, it is clear that the owner of rights in mass-marketed software would be most ill advised to rely only upon trade secrets. The more copies that are out in the world, the more likely it is that the secret will get out, either through a deliberate act or by inadvertence. While there is no hard and fast rule about when trade-secret protection becomes impracticable, probably if more than 100 copies of the software are to be distributed some other form of protection, in most cases copyright, should be used. On the other hand, if the material is distributed in such a way that it is possible to police secrecy agreements, trade-secret protection has advantages over copyright. The main advantage is that the underlying idea can be protected by trade-secret law, whereas copyright protects only the expression of the idea, and leaves others free to take your idea and use it in some different way.

In order for the trade-secret owner to retain some control over the third-party user of his software, it is preferable that the transfer is structured as a licence rather than an outright sale. This permits continuing control of what the licensee does with the software, and allows you to get the software back in the event of a breach by the licensee of a term of the licence. A form of software trade-secret licence will be found at the end of this chapter. This licence agreement should preferably be signed before a copy of the software is handed over. While this is not always possible, you should be aware that there are dangers in relying on the procedure used by many publishers of mass-marketed software. This is to provide the software in a sealed package which bears a message that opening the package is deemed to be acceptance of the terms of an associated licence. While this may be valid, particularly if the licence is separately supplied so that the purchaser can review its terms before deciding whether to open the package, there has not yet been any judicial decision on the subject. It is also probable that a licence imposed in this way is much less likely to impress on the licensee the importance of maintaining secrecy, and the consequences of his failure to do so, than a licence which he has signed.

In addition to the secrecy agreement, the software should be marked with a notice that it contains trade secrets and is to be kept confidential. This provides notice to any outsider who may obtain a copy that he is under an obligation of confidence, which is implied by law, and that he is not free to do as he pleases with the software. A suitable form of notice is set out at the end of this chapter. This notice should appear whenever the software is run, and should also be on the disc or tape containing the program, and in any accompanying documentation.

It is not enough to get secrecy agreements, they must also be enforced. If the licensor does not take any action against a licensee who breaches the agreement, it is likely that he will be held to have condoned the breach, and will then have lost the secrecy and with it his trade-secret protection. One way of ensuring that leaks can be traced so that action can be taken against the defaulting licensee is to code each copy of the software with a control number. If this is done in such a way that it would involve considerable time and effort for a third party to find and remove the code, it is likely that any pirate copies which may come to the licensor's attention will still have their control number in the coding. This will make it possible to identify the licensee who has the copy from which the pirate copy was made.

So far this discussion has been about software in general. There is, however, the possibility of retaining trade-secret protection for widely distributed software. This can be done in many cases by distributing only the object code, and keeping the source code secret. Because considerable effort is required in most cases to decipher object code, the underlying ideas and source code remain effectively concealed even though the object code is freely available. The disadvantage to the software user of this procedure is that it makes it impossible for him to maintain the program himself, and forces him to rely on the supplier for maintenance. This is of minor importance in the case of standard, well tested and debugged software. However, in the case of custom or highly specialised software, the user should be very reluctant to agree to such a position, because if the vendor becomes unable to supply such maintenance, the software may become unusable. With the high rate of business failure which has so far been common in the software industry, this is a real problem, which has been discussed in detail in Chapter 8.

Advantages and disadvantages

The main advantage of trade-secret protection is its breadth. Unlike copyright, it can protect the underlying idea as well as the expression of the idea. As has been discussed above, patent protection for the idea is in general not available for software. Trade-secret protection has an advantage over patent protection in that an interlocutory injunction (in the USA called a preliminary injunction) against misuse of a trade secret can usually be obtained. By contrast, in the United States (although not in the UK since the *American Cyanamid Co.* v *Ethicon Ltd* decision of the House of Lords [1975] AC 396) it is almost impossible to get an interlocutory injunction in a patent case. No formalities are required to secure trade-secret protection, and it lasts as long as the secret.

The disadvantages are the ever-present danger of loss of protection through loss of secrecy, and its unsuitability for use when the software is widely disseminated. Unlike a patent, trade-secret law does not protect against independent development of the same idea. It does require a continuous effort on the part of the trade-secret owner to maintain secrecy and monitor any third-party breaches of confidence.

There is a further possible disadvantage which applies to the United States. Under the federal system of the US Constitution, if there is a conflict between a federal law governing a matter which is the concern of the federal government and a state law, the federal law prevails. This is called pre-emption. Copyright is now governed exclusively by federal law, whereas trade-secret law is exclusively state law. The 1976 Copyright Act contains an express pre-emption provision, s. 301(a), which provides:

On and after 1 January, 1978, all legal or equitable rights that are equivalent to any of the exclusive rights within the general scope of copyright . . . in works . . . whether created before or after that date and whether published or unpublished, are governed exclusively by this title. Thereafter, no person is entitled to any such right or equivalent right in any such work under the common law or statutes of any state.

The question whether this provision pre-empts trade-secret rights has been considered in a number of cases. In *Avco Corporation* v *Precision Air Parts Inc.*, 210 USPQ 894 (M.D. Ala. 1980) there was a claim for trade-secret misappropriation regarding use by the defendant of the plaintiff's drawings for parts for aircraft engines. The court held that these drawings, which were not copyrightable because they were for useful articles, could not be protected by state trade-secret law because that law had been pre-empted. In other cases, misappropriation claims have been held to be pre-empted, in one case the claim being for misappropriation of computer input formats (*Synercom Technology Inc.* v *University Computing Co.*, 474 F Supp 37 (N.D. Tex. 1979). Against these cases can be set a number of cases in which there was held to be no pre-emption. One of these involved computer software, *Warrington Associates Inc.* v *Real-Time Engineering Systems Inc.*, 522 F Supp 367 (N.D. Ill. 1981). There is also a division of opinion amongst commentators on the issue, although it seems to be generally agreed that Congress probably did not intend to pre-empt trade-secret protection, at least where it is not exactly coextensive with copyright. However, those proposing to rely on trade-secret protection in the United States should be aware that there is at present a danger that uncopyrighted software may be held to be unprotectable by trade-secret law.

A further problem awaits those who decide that, for software distributed in the United States, they will hedge their bets and go for both trade secret and copyright protection. As explained in Chapter 13, certain formalities are required under US law for copyright protection, in particular the placing of a copyright notice on all published copies. A number of commentators have raised the question whether the presence of the notice is equivalent to a declaration that the work has been published, i.e., released to the public, and therefore cannot be a trade *secret*. This question has so far come before the courts in one case, *Technicon Medical Information Systems Corp.* v *Green Bay Packaging Inc.*, 211 USPQ 343 (E.D. Wis. 1980). The case involved an allegation of trade-secret misappropriation involving a computer-system reference manual. The manual had been marked with both a copyright notice and a trade-secret notice. The court held that the presence of the copyright notice did not, in itself, prevent the owner from asserting a trade-secret claim.

Criminal remedies

The criminal law may also provide protection against trade-secret misappropriation. If a tangible object incorporating the trade secret is taken, then this is covered by the general law of theft. However, most jurisdictions, including the UK, do not include the taking of intangible information within their definition of theft. A number of states in the USA have remedied this deficiency of the common law by providing expressly for criminal penalties for the theft or misappropriation of trade secrets. Under the California provision, there has even been a conviction for wrongfully obtaining secret information by accessing the victim's computer through a telephone line. An advantage of using criminal, rather than civil proceedings, is that it may be possible to recover stolen documents, etc., from the defendant through police action. On the other hand, it does have the disadvantage of taking the control of the litigation away from the trade-secret owner, who may later find his secrets being revealed in open court.

TRADE MARKS

Up to this point, this chapter has been examining means of protecting the content of software. A trade mark cannot provide this type of protection, nevertheless, trade-mark protection may be valuable in certain circumstances.

The software industry is still a very young industry, and is in the process of rapid growth and evolution, largely caused by the rapid growth of the personal and micro-computer industry. In this process of growth and evolution, certain software producers are starting to stand out from the general field as being bigger, more successful and better known. Often this pre-eminence has been achieved through the marketing of a very successful product, such as Digital Research through the CP/M family of operating systems, Microsoft through the MS-DOS operating systems and Visicorp through Visicalc. These three product names, CP/M, MS-DOS and Visicalc, have become valuable trade marks, and their owners appreciate this. A computer owner who has decided to buy Visicalc because he has heard of its reputation will not buy a differently named spread-sheet program, even if it contains the same ideas and performs in the same ways.

In a similar way, the trade name of the software producer may become valuable property. A particular software producer may gain a reputation for producing reliable, well executed software. That reputation may influence a purchaser to choose that producer's software for a particular purpose when faced with a number of software packages which all fulfil essentially the same function.

Trade marks for computer software may be registered under the registration provisions of the relevant country or countries in which the mark is used, as explained in Chapter 13. Similarly, in jurisdictions permitting registration of service marks, service marks used by those providing computer services such as time-sharing, service bureaux and custom programming may be registered. When registering a trade mark or service mark the correct class must be selected. The United States Patent and Trademark Office has identified the following computer-related goods and services as falling within the following International Classifications:

Item	International class
Magnetic tapes for recording	9
Computer programs recorded on tapes, discs or cards	16
Computer programs (paper tape and cards for the recordal of)	16
Computer program manuals	16
Computer programming services	42
Computer hiring, including time-sharing	42
Computer software (designing)	42

The application for trade-mark registration need not state the application for which the program is designed, and the goods may be identified simply as 'pre-recorded computer programs'. The US Patent and Trademark Office regards the names of the computer programming languages as generic, so that a registration will only be granted for a mark containing the name of such a language, e.g. 'BETTER BASIC', if all rights to the language name (i.e., in the example given above,

'BASIC') are disclaimed. Problems with registration may also be encountered if the trade mark is an acronym widely used in the industry. Registration will probably also be refused if the trade-mark is descriptive of the goods, for instances 'LEDGER' for a bookkeeping program.

EXTRA-LEGAL METHODS OF PROTECTION

In addition to, or even in substitution for, the means of software protection provided by the law described above, various extra-legal methods have been devised to protect against piracy, or, at least, to discourage it. These methods can be broadly divided into two categories, technological and commercial.

A number of technological means for preventing or discouraging copying can be used. One of the most common is 'copy protection', in which the program contains coding which makes direct disc-to-disc or tape-to-tape copying impossible. The use of this type of protection has a major disadvantage as far as the purchaser of such software is concerned, because it means that he cannot make back-up copies as protection against damage to the original. While the publisher of copy-protected software usually will provide a replacement for a damaged disc at nominal cost, this process usually requires an exchange by post and therefore takes time. A delay does not matter in the case of a game or other recreational software, but could be very damaging to the user if the software is necessary for the running of his business. The tendency, therefore, is for these latter kinds of software to be unprotected, as the consumer is reluctant to buy copy-protected business software. Further, copy protection is not infallible; a knowledgeable and determined programmer can 'unlock' the copy-protection code key, and it is also possible to purchase commercially available software which allows copying of software protected by currently used types of copy protection.

A different approach recently adopted by at least one software publisher is to include code which allows the purchaser to create one back-up copy of the original disc, and to transfer that copy of the program from one disc to another. However, when the copy is transferred, the program automatically compares the two copies for accuracy, and, if the new copy is correct, deletes the first copy. Needless to say, it will only be a matter of time before a programmer discovers how to defeat this protection, too.

A number of means are used to discourage copying by making would-be copiers at least think about the legality and morality of what they are doing. A novel approach taken by a newly issued program is that a notice that the copy being used is unlicensed by the copyright owner appears on the monitor during the whole time that the copy is being used, and on every page of print-out produced using the illegal copy. More conventional is the appearance of a notice on the monitor setting out the fact that the program is proprietary and that copying is unlawful every time that the program is booted.

Commercial means for discouraging copying are based on giving the licensed owner advantages or services not available to the owner of a pirated copy. For example, updates, or patches to fix bugs, are supplied only to licensed owners, or a telephone assistance service may be made available only to owners who have registered their purchase and signed a licence agreement.

Despite all precautions, unlawful copying will almost certainly occur. The prudent software author should take steps to make it easier to prove that copying has occurred. One method of doing this is to 'salt' the code by adding some non-operative lines of coding at various points throughout the program. If the pirate copies verbatim, the same non-operative coding will appear in his program, strong evidence that his program was not independently created. It would take so many hours of skilled work to detect and remove these non-operative portions of the coding that doing so would make copying unattractive financially to the commercial pirate, and the home copyist is unlikely to worry about the presence of such coding. Another method is to code into each copy a unique identification code, and to keep records correlating the name of the purchaser with the code of the copy he purchased. Then, if an extra copy bearing that particular code is discovered in the possession of an unauthorised user, it is made much easier to trace the source of that copy and to find the pirate who made it.

As software becomes bigger and bigger business, further technological ingenuity will doubtless be put to work by software authors and publishers to protect their works, in most cases to be met by equal technological ingenuity by those determined to make unlawful copies for their own use or for commercial gain. The impossibility of absolute protection from unlawful copying should not, however, deter those in the software business from doing all they can to prevent such copying.

PARTICULAR PROBLEMS: VIDEO GAMES

While devoted players have been battling aliens with advanced weapons or gobbling dots with greedy, haunted masticators in arcades and on their home computer or television screen, the producers of these games have been battling the pirates who have been gobbling their profits in the courts. The phenomenal commercial success of video games in the last few years, and the ease with which they can be copied, has produced a considerable amount of litigation. While most of this has been in the United States, the courts of several other nations have also had to face the problems of the new technology such games represent.

The steps in the production of a video game are as follows: first, the idea for a game is worked out into a detailed scenario, and sketches of the images that are to appear on the screen may be made. Then a computer program is written, usually in source code, to produce the sequence of images and to allow for the interaction of the player planned in the scenario. This program is then compiled or otherwise translated into object code. In the case of arcade games, the object code is recorded and reproduced in the form of ROM chips, in the case of games for the home computer it is recorded on magnetic discs or tapes. Operation of the game causes images to appear on the screen, some of which are in a fixed sequence, some of which are movable by the player by some means. In the case of arcade games, there are usually two parts to the display; an attract sequence, which is a fixed sequence which gives a sample of how the game appears and which is designed to attract customers, and the play mode, which comes into operation when a coin is inserted in the machine. Only in the play mode can the images be manipulated.

There are, therefore, several 'works' which could possibly be protected by the law. These are the scenario for the game, the source-code program, the object-code program and the display on the screen. Because of the wide, unfettered distribution of these games, the most useful form of protection is copyright.

It is well established law that the idea for a game, and the method of playing it, are not capable of copyright protection. However, the board or other equipment for playing the game, if novel, is protectable, as is a particular expression of the rules. This law has been similarly applied to video games. In *Atari Inc.* v *North American Philips Consumer Electronics Corp.*, 672 F 2d 607 (7th Cir. 1982), certiorari denied 103 S Ct 176 (1982), the Seventh Circuit stated (at 617):

Plaintiffs' audiovisual work is primarily an unprotectible game, but
. . . to at least a limited extent the particular form in which it is
expressed (shapes, sizes, colours, sequences, arrangements, and
sounds) provides something 'new or additional over the idea'. *See*
Goodson-Todman Enterprises Ltd v *Kellogg Co.*, 513 F 2d 913 (9th Cir
1975).

The court then went on to describe the basic idea of the game
involved, 'Pac-Man', and to distinguish the particular form of
expression from the idea. They then found that the defendants' game
had infringed the plaintiffs' copyright, because of the similarities
between the characters in the two games, which were part of the form of
expression.

The copyrightability of source code, object code and ROM firmware
is discussed elsewhere in this chapter. It should be noted that many of the
cases referred to in those discussions deal with video games. In addition,
video games have their own peculiar problems arising from the nature of
the visual display which is an integral part of the game. The most
important of these problems are as follows:

(a)   What category of copyrightable works, if any, does the display
come within?

(b)   Is the visual display sufficiently fixed to qualify for copyright?

(c)   Does the visual display have a separate copyright from the
underlying computer program?

(d)   What is the effect on copyright, if any, of the fact that the display
in play mode is a result of the interaction of the program and the player's
manipulation of the images on the screen?

(e)   Is the copyright in the audiovisual display protected if the ROM
chip containing the underlying program does not bear a copyright
notice (in countries requiring a copyright notice)?

(f)   Is the copyright in the audiovisual display actionable if the
copyright in the underlying computer program has not been registered
prior to the commencement of the infringement suit (in countries
requiring such registration)?

These questions have all been raised and answered in the United
States. Elsewhere, they remain largely unanswered. The following
paragraphs will first look at the American answers, and then discuss the
possible answers under UK law.

(a)   What category of copyrightable works, if any, does the display come within?

United States
The 1976 Copyright Act provides for the copyrightability of a class of works termed 'audiovisual works'. These are defined in s. 101 as:

> works that consist of a series of related images which are intrinsically intended to be shown by the use of machines, or devices such as projectors, viewers, or electronic equipment, together with accompanying sounds, if any, regardless of the nature of the material objects, such as films or tapes, in which the works are embodied.

This definition, especially when viewed in the light of its legislative history, seems clearly to cover the display of a video game. The courts agree. The Second Circuit, in *Stern Electronics Inc.* v *Kaufman*, 669 F 2d 852 (2d Cir. 1982) expressly held that 'the [audiovisual] display satisfies the statutory definition as an original "audiovisual work".' All other courts which have considered the subject have agreed, see *Atari Inc.* v *Amusement World Inc.*, (Civ. No. Y-81-803) 558 PTCJ A-6 (D. Maryland 1981); *Midway Mfg. Co.* v *Dirkschneider*, 543 F Supp 466 (D. Nebraska 1981); *Midway Mfg. Co.* v *Artic International Inc.*, 218 USPQ 791 (7th Cir. 1983).

United Kingdom
The Copyright Act 1956 does not, as might be expected, contain any definition equivalent to that of the recent US copyright statute. Video technology was as much in its infancy in 1956 as computer technology was. The nearest technology which was expressly provided for was the cinema. A 'cinematograph film' is defined in s. 13(10) as:

> any sequence of visual images recorded on material of any description (whether translucent or not) so as to be capable, by the use of that material, —
>
> (a)   of being shown as a moving picture, or
> (b)   of being recorded on other material (whether translucent or not), by the use of which it can be so shown.

The difficulty with this definition is that, in the case of video games, what is recorded is not a 'sequence of visual images', but rather a sequence of magnetic bits which are translated into the sequence of visual images by the computer and the CRT. It is questionable whether an English court, applying the restrictive English rules of statutory interpretation, would stretch the definition to include computer-generated video displays. Perhaps video games could sneak in under para. (b), as it would be possible to film the video display. However, this would be somewhat fictional as the displays are not, in ordinary circumstances, filmed, and the sequences of images can be shown without such a film. It would obviously be desirable for the issue to be expressly dealt with by any new legislation designed to cover the protection of computer-related property. At present, the copyright-ability of the video display associated with computer games must remain in doubt.

(b)   Is the visual display sufficiently fixed to qualify for copyright?

United States
It is a requirement for the existence of copyright protection under the present US copyright statute that the works are fixed in 'any tangible medium of expression, now known or later developed, from which they can be perceived, reproduced, or otherwise communicated, either directly or with the aid of a machine or device' (Copyright Act 1976, s. 102(a)).

The issue of fixation was argued in the case of *Williams Electronics Inc.* v *Artic International Inc.* 685 F 2d 870 (3d Cir. 1982). The defendant's argument was that there was a lack of 'fixation' because the video game generates or creates 'new' images each time the attract mode or the play mode is displayed. The court rejected this argument on the basis that the features of the game repeat themselves over and over, albeit in differing combinations. The issue was also argued in the District Court in *Midway Mfg. Co.* v *Artic International Inc.* 211 USPQ 1152 (N.D. Ill. 1981), but rejected on the rather weak ground that the fact that a video tape of the display had been deposited with the Copyright Office was sufficient evidence of fixation. Sounder reasoning for rejecting the same argument was given by the Maryland District Court in *Atari Inc.* v *Amusement World Inc.* 558 PTCJ A-6 (1981). The court pointed out that it is necessary to distinguish between the 'work' itself, and the tangible medium in which it is fixed. The 'work' in this case is the visual presentation of the game, the tangible medium of expression in which it is fixed is the ROM circuitry, from which the work can be perceived by use of a machine.

Although various reasons have been given for the decision, every court which has had to decide the issue of fixation of the visual display of a video game has decided that the statutory requirement of fixation has been met.

United Kingdom

Unlike the US, the UK statute does not have an express requirement of fixation for copyrightability. This requirement can, however, be found indirectly in the Copyright Act 1956, and has always been recognised in the case law.

Assuming that video games, if they are copyrightable, come within the category of 'cinematograph films', then the requirement of fixation comes from the definition of a 'cinematograph film' given in (a) above. As in US law, a distinction must be made between the film, the 'work', and the medium in which it is recorded. It will be interesting to see whether a court would be prepared to treat a ROM as 'material of any description', by use of which the work can be shown as a moving picture. In broad terms, it would seem to come within the statutory language.

(c)   Does the visual display have a separate copyright from the underlying computer program?

United States

This question has been raised in a number of cases. It is particularly important in a country, such as the USA, which requires registration formalities. A number of defendants in video games cases have tried to raise the defence that the plaintiff's failure to register the copyright of the underlying software, even though the visual display was properly registered with the Copyright Office, prevented suit on either. In every case, this defence has been rejected.

In *Stern Electronics Inc.* v *Kaufman* 669 F 2d 852 (1982), the argument was made in the form that the audiovisual display was not an 'original' work, because the only original work of authorship which could attract copyright protection was the underlying computer program, which had not been registered. The argument was rejected on the grounds that the video display is an audiovisual work, which is a separate statutory class of copyright subject-matter from a literary work, the class that computer programs fall under. The court also pointed out that the commercial value of the game arose from the creativity of the design of the visual display, not from the program. Similar rejections are to be found in

Midway Mfg Co. v *Dirkschneider* 543 F Supp 466 and *Atari Inc.* v *Amusement World Inc.* 558 PTCJ A-6 (1981). A possibly more compelling argument is to be found in *Midway Mfg. Co.* v *Strohon*, 564 F Supp 741 (N.D. Ill. 1983), where the court pointed out that it is quite possible to design a game that would infringe the audiovisual copyright in another game, but which was based on a substantially different computer program.

United Kingdom

This fact, that it is possible to produce substantially similar audiovisual displays from different computer programs, would seem to present just as strong an argument for separate copyrights in the display and the program under UK law as it does in the USA. The Copyright Act 1956 also treats literary works, into which computer programs clearly fall, and cinematograph films, into which the displays less clearly fall (see the discussion above) as separate categories of copyright. The question of separate copyrights is less likely to arise in the UK where there are no registration formalities, but if it did it seems likely that the British courts would reach the same conclusions as their American counterparts.

(d)   What is the effect on copyright, if any, of the fact that the display in play mode is the result of the interaction of the program and the player's manipulation of the images on the screen?

United States

The whole purpose of a video game is that the player is able to manipulate some of the images on the screen, so that they interact in certain ways with other images which are not under the player's control. For example, in Pac-Man, the only image controlled by the player is the yellow gobbler. The maze remains completely fixed, the dots are in fixed positions but are 'consumable' by placing the image of the gobbler over the image of the dot, while the ghosts move around the maze in pursuit of the gobbler in a manner controlled by the program. This manipulation of some of the images means, of course, that the visual display is never exactly alike for any two games.

This fact has led to two copyright challenges: the first is that this variability means that the display is not 'fixed' and so is not eligible for copyright protection. This challenge has been discussed under (b) above. The second challenge is based on the argument that the player is in some way an 'author' of the display.

Both these challenges seem to have been first raised, but not answered, by the US International Trade Commission in *In re Certain Coin-Operated Audio-Visual Games and Components Thereof* (No. 337-TA-87) 537 PTCJ A-5 (1981). The authorship point was, however, raised and answered by the Third Circuit Court of Appeals in *Williams Electronics Inc.* v *Artic International Inc. supra.* The court rejected the argument, stating (at 408):

> Although there is player interaction with the machine during the play mode which causes the audiovisual presentation to change in some respects from one game to the next in response to the player's varying participation, there is always a repetitive sequence of a substantial portion of the sights and sounds of the game, and many aspects of the display remain constant from game to game, regardless of how the player operates the controls.

The court seems to be implying that, because of this substantial repetition, the player is not making a sufficiently substantial change to the underlying work as to create what amounts to a derivative work. The absence of creativeness in the copyright sense on the part of the player was discussed in more dramatic language by the Seventh Circuit in *Midway Mfg Co.* v *Artic International Inc.* 218 USPQ 791 (1983) at 793:

> . . . the particular sequence of images that appears on the screen video game machine when the game is played is not the same work as the set of images stored in the machine's circuit boards. The person playing the game can vary the order in which the stored images appear on the screen by moving the machine's control lever. That makes playing a video game a little like arranging words in a dictionary into sentences or paints on a palette into a painting. The question is whether the creative effort in playing a video game is enough like writing or painting to make each performance of a video game the work of the player and not the game's inventor.
>
> We think it is not. Television viewers may vary the order of images transmitted on the same signal but broadcast on different channels by pressing a button that changes the channel on their television. In the WGN case [693 F 2d 622] we held that the creative effort required to do that did not make the sequence of images appearing on a viewer's television screen the work of the viewer and not of the television station that transmitted the images. Playing a video game is more like changing channels on a television than it is like writing a novel or painting a picture. The player of a video game does not have control

over the sequence of images that appears on the video game screen. He cannot create any sequence he wants out of the images stored on the game's circuit boards. The most he can do is choose one of the limited number of sequences the game allows him to choose. He is unlike a writer or a painter because the video game in effect writes the sentences and paints the painting for him; he merely chooses one of the sentences stored in its memory, one of the paintings stored in its collection.

If the player is to be an author, he must either be a joint author with the programmer, or what he produces must be a derivative work. The cases cited above really address the 'derivative work' concept, and show that there is an insufficient creative addition to the original work to bring a derivative work into existence. The argument against the 'joint author' approach is that joint authorship requires an intent to make a joint creative effort at the time the work is created (Copyright Act s. 101). As the player only comes on the scene after the work has been created and published, this intent is missing.

United Kingdom
The factual arguments about the insufficient creativity which prevailed in the USA should also prevail in the UK, as the tests for originality needed for a derivative work are almost the same in the two countries. Similarly, the player is not a joint author under UK law.

(e)   Is the copyright in the audiovisual display protected if the ROM chip containing the underlying program does not bear a copyright notice?

(f)   Is the copyright in the audiovisual display actionable if the copyright in the underlying computer program has not been registered prior to the commencement of the infringement suit?

United States
Both these questions have been answered by the discussion of question (c). As the audiovisual display has a separate copyright, it is protected and actionable, even if the underlying program is not so protected or actionable.

United Kingdom
As the UK does not require formalities for protection or actionability of

copyright, these questions do not arise in the context of the protection in the UK.

PARTICULAR PROBLEMS: FIRMWARE

What is Firmware?

A computer is operated by a program through a pattern of electronic pulses. This pattern is stored for input into the computer in various ways. At one time punched cards or paper tape were used, now magnetic discs or tape are the most common means of storage. This pattern is fed, as needed, into the internal, changeable memory of the computer, the RAM. This type of memory is volatile, in that it is erased when the power supply is turned off.

There is another type of memory which is non-volatile and which can therefore permanently store programs. This permanent memory can be supplied by three types of silicon chips, ROMs, PROMs and EPROMs, which were described in Chapter 2. Certain types of program are continually needed for the operation of a computer, such as input/output routines, arithmetical functions and compilers. In general it is more convenient to have these programs permanently stored in memory, and this is done by installing suitably programmed ROM chips. The program, the 'pattern', is fixed in the chip through the integrated-circuit equivalent of hard wiring.

It will be readily appreciated that these programmed chips are hybrids. The chip is a piece of *hardware*, a machine, which provides instructions, *software*, for the functioning of the computer. The name 'firmware' was devised to convey this hybrid nature. This hybridity gives rise to legal problems when the question of how firmware is to be protected is considered.

Patent

If the hardware aspects of the firmware chip are patentably novel, then the chip should be patentable as hardware under the principles discussed in Chapters 13 and 14. If, on the other hand, the novelty lies only in the stored program, the software aspect, then the rules relating to patentability of software, discussed above, apply. A case involving a patent application for a piece of firmware, *Diamond* v *Bradley*, 450 US 381 (1981), went on appeal to the US Supreme Court at the same time as

Diamond v *Diehr*, discussed above in the section of this chapter dealing with patents. The court affirmed without opinion the decision of the CCPA that the application should be granted, but only because the court was evenly divided, one of the nine justices having withdrawn from sitting on the case because of a possible conflict of interest.

One possible problem that could arise if a piece of firmware is patented on the basis of what it does rather than how it does it is whether such a patent could be infringed by use of functionally equivalent software, even though expressed differently and in a different medium, e.g., on a disc.

Copyright

The copyrightability of the hardware element, the integrated circuit, has been discussed in Chapter 14.

The question whether the software stored in the ROM is copyrightable involves two issues. First, as the program is in the equivalent of object code, whether object code itself is copyrightable. This issue has been discussed above. Second, whether the fact that the software is permanently programmed into a piece of hardware deprives it of copyright protection.

The only case law considering the second question of which the author is aware is all in the United States, not surprisingly in view of the country's leading position in this technology. The decisions are, unfortunately, divided, although the majority of the decisions favour the existence of copyright for software embodied in ROMs.

The first case to consider the question, *Data Cash Systems Inc.* v *J S & A Group Inc.*, 480 F Supp 1063 (N.D. Ill. 1979), affirmed on other grounds 628 F 2d 1038 (7th Cir. 1980), produced a decision at first instance against copyright for ROM-based software. However, this decision was based on a Supreme Court decision which has clearly been abrogated by the 1976 Copyright Act, to the effect that a work could only be the subject of copyright if it was readable by the human eye. Further, a good argument can be made that the appellate court's decision in that case impliedly overruled the district court's holding on this point.

The only decision on the subject under the new Copyright Act which goes against copyrightability is *Apple Computer Inc.* v *Franklin Computer Corp.* 545 F Supp 812 (E.D. Pa. 1982). The judge refused to grant an application by Apple for a preliminary (interlocutory) injunction restraining the defendant, which manufactures an 'Apple-compatible' computer, from using certain programs, both in ROM and on disc, in which Apple claimed copyright. The basis of this refusal was the judge's doubt that Apple would succeed in its claim of copyright at trial. However, this decision has now been reversed on appeal to the Third Circuit Court of Appeals (714 F 2d 1240), which held that the Apple operating system and programs were entitled to copyright protection, in whatever form they were fixed. This decision reaffirmed the decision of the same court in *Williams Electronics Inc.* v *Artic International Inc.* 685 F 2d 870, 215 USPQ 405 (3rd Cir 1982). In *Williams*, the defendant had argued that ROMs could not be protected by copyright because they are utilitarian objects, equivalent to machine parts. The court dismissed this argument as follows: (215 USPQ 405 at 408-9):

> Defendant's argument in this regard is misdirected. The issue in this case is not whether the plaintiff, if it sought, could protect the ROM itself under the copyright laws. Rather, before us is only the plaintiff's effort to protect its artistic expression in original works which have met the statutory fixation requirement through their embodiment in the ROM devices.

The court then went on to approve the rejection of a similar argument by the district court in *Midway Mfg Co.* v *Artic International Inc.* 211 USPQ 1152 (ND Ill 1981).

These decisions, together with the other decisions in which the copyrightability of firmware was considered, *Tandy Corp.* v *Personal Micro Computers Inc.* 524 F Supp 171 (N.D. Cal. 1981), *GCA Corporation* v *Chance*, 217 USPQ 718 (N.D. Cal. 1982), *Apple Computer Inc.* v *Formula International Inc.*, 562 F Supp 775 (C.D. Cal. 1983) and *Midway Mfg Co.* v *Strohon*, 564 F Supp 741 (N.D. Ill. 1983), all hold that software is copyrightable, regardless of the form in which it is stored. This is consistent with existing principles of copyright law; a novel is the subject of copyright whether it is printed in a book, stored on microfiche or a reading of that novel is recorded on a record or tape. Software should be similarly protected, whether it is permanently recorded on paper, in a magnetic medium, or in permanent integrated circuits.

PRECEDENTS

Copyright notice

The first word in a copyright notice should be 'Copyright', 'Copyr.'

or ©. This should be followed by the date of first publication, and then the name of the copyright owner. Certain South American countries also require the words 'All rights reserved'. For example, the notice on this book should read: 'Copyright 1984, Hilary E. Pearson. All rights reserved.'

There is a potential problem with use of the '©' abbreviation; technically, this should be a 'c' completely surrounded by a circle, and most computers cannot produce this symbol. While many people are using '(c)' instead this may be insufficient. Better to use the full word, or the abbreviation 'Copyr.'

Trade-secret notice

The following notice includes a statement concerning copyright. This is primarily intended for use in the United States. Possible problems with the use of such a combined notice are discussed in this chapter at page 270.

> This program is an unpublished work which is protected by copyright. It is proprietary to [owner] and may be used only as authorised by persons who have signed a licence agreement controlling such use. Any unauthorised copying, use or disclosure of this proprietary information is strictly prohibited.

In cases, where there is doubt about whether the work could be held to be published, despite attempts to retain it as a trade secret, in order to avoid the potential problem of loss of copyright because of publication without notice, a formal copyright notice should be inserted. For this notice to be valid, it must include a date. Under present US law, the notice is not invalidated if this date, inserted in good faith, is incorrect. To avoid the potential holding that this use of the notice is an admission of publication, discussed above at page 270, the date used should be the date that the software was first licensed, and the notice should read as follows:

> © 1984, Software Company. This program has not been published by the copyright owner, and has been disclosed to third parties only under licence prohibiting unauthorised disclosure, copying or use. Any unauthorised copying, use or disclosure is strictly prohibited.

Non-disclosure agreement

In the case where you are submitting a new piece of software for evaluation only, either by a potential publisher or by a potential customer, the non-disclosure agreement can appropriately be in a relatively informal letter form.

To [Name and address of disclosee]

Dear Sir,

I have indicated to you that I have developed a new computer program for [purpose of program], and you have indicated that you are interested in evaluating this program for the purpose of [purpose of evaluation by disclosee].

The contents of this program are secret and proprietary to me. I therefore request that you sign the duplicate of this letter to indicate that you agree to take the following steps to preserve the secrecy and my proprietary rights:

(a) You will hold in confidence and secrecy the contents of the program and all information received from me relating to the program for at least three years from the date on which you sign the duplicate of this letter.

(b) You will not reproduce the whole or any part of the program in either source-code or object-code form without my prior written consent.

(c) You will only disclose the program and all information received from me relating to the program to those of your employees who need such disclosure for the purpose of your evaluation, and you will ensure that those persons are aware of the contents of this letter.

(d) You will use the program only for the purpose of evaluation.

(e) Upon completion of the evaluation, unless we enter into a further agreement, you will return to me all copies of the program in your possession, and all documents containing confidential information regarding the program which I have disclosed to you.

These obligations do not, of course, apply to any confidential information disclosed to you:

(a) Which is now available to the public.

(b)   Which subsequently becomes available to the public through means other than disclosure by you or any person to whom you have disclosed the information.

(c)   Which was already in your possession before I disclosed it to you, and you have documentary evidence of that possession.

(d)   Which is received from a third party who was not under an obligation of confidence regarding the information.

signed . . . .

ACCEPTED AND AGREED TO THIS _____ DAY OF _____ 198____

signed . . . .

Index